TABYEEN

THE NEGLECTED OBLIGATION

AYATOLLAH KHAMENEI

*In the name of God, the Merciful,
the Compassionate*

Collected from the speeches of
Ayatollah Sayyid Ali Khamenei

First Published in 2023 by
Ahlulbayt Islamic Mission (AIM)

ISBN: 978-0-9957589-6-4

© AIM Foundation 2023

All rights reserved. No part of this publication may be reproduced, stored in a retrieval system, or transmitted in any form or by any means, digital, electronic, mechanical, photocopying, recording, or otherwise, or conveyed via the internet or a website without prior written permission of the publisher, except in the case of brief quotations embodied in critical articles and reviews.

Ayatollah Sayyid Ali Khamenei

Contents

Preface 11
In the Words of Imam Khomeini 15
General Discussion 21
    Introduction 23
    The Struggle 25
    Tabyeen: Clarification 33
    The Benefits and Effect of Clarification...................... 62
    The Harm of Not Carrying Out Clarification 73
    Historical Examples of Clarification 74
    Exemplars of Clarification 82
The Requirements 99
    Align with the Revolution 101
    Reliance Upon Allah and the Divine Traditions 108
    Strengthening Faith and Spirituality 109
    Maintaining Ethics 111
    Observing the Laws 120
    Importance of Researching 123
    Clarification vs the Illusion of Clarification.............124
    Combination of Clarification with Action 133
    Being Timely...135
    Steadfastness and Insight 140
    Keep Repeating..143
    Practical Strategy and Compassionate Guiding........145
    Mannerism..146
    Special Attention Towards the Online Space............149

Courage 150
Lack of Expediency 154
Far From Agitation and Commotion 156
Far From Creating Sedition and Honesty 156
Avoiding the Creation of Negativity 157
Innovation 159
Being Skilful 161
Making Use of Emotions... 162
Embracing the Islamic Revolutionary Thinkers 165

Methods and Types 175
Considering the Audience 178
Using Indirect Methods... 180
Formation of Gatherings 181
Formation of Intellectual Committees..................... 183
Knowledge-Based Circles 184
Using Media and Online Platforms 185

Subjects in Need of Clarifications 189
Fundamental Beliefs... 192
Values and the Constitution 214
Governance of Religion 216
The Islamic Republic 232
Imam Khomeini and His Path................................ 236
The Concept of Resistance 241
Negotiating and Combating Arrogant Powers......... 242
Identity 245
The Economy of Resistance................................. 247
The Objective and Aspirations of the Revolution..... 248
The Achievements of the Revolution..................... 260
The Middle Path of Being a Revolutionary 263

The Country, Region and the Dominating System ...264
Progress 275
The Rights of Women 279
Family and Increasing Offspring...............................280
Hijab..282
Unity and Avoiding Division 283
Obstacles to Progress 285
The Enemy and Their Schemes 296
Infiltration...302
The Stage We Are In 308
Prayer 311
The Days of Allah...315
The Lives of the Martyrs 317
The Value of Work and the Worker 327
Work and Societal Discipline 329
The Value of a Teacher...331
Modern History and Constitutional Revolution 333
Internal Capabilities For Resolving Problems 334
The Dangers of Distortions and Innovations............336
Incidents of Events 337

Other Important Passages 339

Those in Place of Responsibility – The Officials.......341
Friday Prayers - Headquarters for Clarification 346
The Heavy Responsibility of Prayer Leaders 350
Scholars and Preachers 351
Students and Youth 362
Artists and Poets 364
Eulogists..371

Preface

This significant text serves as a profound compilation of Ayatollah Khamenei's teachings centred on the critical theme of Jihad Al-Tabyeen, known as the Struggle for Clarification. Its significance transcends mere documentation, offering a compass for navigating our current era, steeped in rampant misinformation.

Jihad Al-Tabyeen refers to the Islamic concept of actively striving to clarify and articulate the truth, particularly in times of confusion, misinformation, or misunderstanding. It involves the effort to elucidate and present the true principles and values, aiming to dispel misconceptions and promote clarity and understanding. This concept underscores the importance of communication, education, and actively disseminating accurate information to counter falsehoods or misconceptions.

The Almighty has emphasised this concept when He says: "Invite to the way of your Lord with wisdom and good instruction, and argue with them in a way that is best. Indeed, your Lord is most knowing of who has strayed from His way, and He is most knowing of who is [rightly] guided."[1]

---
1. Surah An-Nahl - Verse 125

This verse highlights the importance of using wisdom and positive communication when conveying the message of Islam, which aligns with the principles of Jihad al-Tabyeen. It underscores the need for patience, understanding, and respect in this discourse.

In light of this Quranic injunction, Ayatollah Khamenei's focus on Tabyeen, resonates as a crucial but often overlooked obligation in contemporary discourse. He has notably highlighted the urgency of this duty, urging for its renewed attention and prioritization. His insistence on elevating Tabyeen reflects a call to action, urging individuals and communities to rekindle their commitment to this neglected obligation.

Ayatollah Khamenei's guidance within these pages doesn't just outline the importance of clarity; it provides tangible strategies and approaches for individuals navigating this turbulent sea of misinformation. In essence, this text doesn't merely document words; it empowers action. It equips individuals with the tools and wisdom necessary to engage actively in the battle against misinformation, fostering a society grounded in truth and clarity.

Originally scripted in Farsi, the book has now found its voice in English through this meticulous translation. The team at AIM are deeply honoured to have worked on this text and facilitated its journey to the English language.

Numerous individuals have been instrumental in bringing this book to life, and we extend our heartfelt gratitude to each one. We are profoundly grateful for the tireless dedication of the anonymous translator, whose motivation and countless hours made this book a reality. Our appreciation also extends to the meticulous editors and publishing team, all pivotal in shaping and realising this work. A special acknowledgment is also reserved to the donors whose financial support was essential to making this book available to you, our dear reader.

We ask the Almighty to reward everyone who contributed with their support and efforts and pray that this book remains a timeless contribution to the Islamic library.

Finally, we thank the Almighty God who blessed us with this opportunity to serve and ask that He accepts this little that we offer in His way.

Wasalaamu Alaikum

Sayyid Samir Al-Haidari
Ahlulbayt Islamic Mission (AIM)
15th December 2023

In the Words of Imam Khomeini

We must strive to support the front lines. The masses are helping the front lines. However, the articulate scholar, the great orator, and the honourable preacher must also strive; their jihad is the jihad of propagation. Their jihad is to explain the value of this victory, the reason you rose up, and the reason for which you carried out the revolution. They must explain to this nation and other nations how big of a victory this was and how it needs to be protected. Just as the presence of the masses in the various arenas and battlegrounds helped attain victory, protecting this lofty divine blessing also requires their presence. Our youth need to be ready so that they can go and defend Islam whenever they are required.

Islam is a duty for which the Prophets (s), the Holy Messenger (s), the children and loyal companions of the Holy Messenger (s) put in a tremendous amount of effort and sacrifices. Islam is something that has come from God and must be protected. God forbid, if this victory you have attained after this revolution turns into a defeat due to our lethargy, weak propagation and lack of participation by the masses, know that Islam will not be able to raise its head again for centuries to come. This is a heavy responsibility, and everyone must accept this heavy responsibility.

The last issue concerns martyrdom, reaching the station of meeting Allah, and being in the presence of the Master of Martyrs (a) and his likes. This is the destination of those who love Allah. At the front lines, we see and also hear from the narrators the spiritual state of these youth during the nights; the remembrance, thoughts, supplications and prayers they have. We hear about the blissfulness with which they go to the front lines. The Almighty bestows this blessing upon this nation, and this blessing must be protected.[2]

We have a responsibility right now to help our brothers who are drowning in their own blood. The help those of you in Europe or any other country can provide is assisting in propagation. The crimes this evil front chain has committed, especially this individual, the Shah, need to be revealed to the people. Tell your European friends in your universities, workplaces and wherever else they may be about this issue. This individual has committed treason, and the people have risen and want freedom. They scream out for freedom and scream out for independence. These people are not wild; they are cultured and wish for freedom and independence.[3]

---

[2] 17/10/1982 – Speech of Imam Khomeini to a gathering of scholars from Qum, Tehran and Azerbaijan. Saheefa-e-Imam, V 17, P 57.

[3] 19/11/1979 – Speech of Imam Khomeini to a gathering of Iranian living abroad. Saheefa-e-Imam, V 5, P 42 and P 43.

Wake the people up! Make the people understand and explain the issue.[4]

I advise you, inform this country and the countries around it too, in the face of the enemie's actions which pull a lot of your youth towards them, you need to create religious institutions. In societies that wish to drag you towards the centres of corruption, create institutions for propagation, invite people towards religion, speak to them of what is good and expose society's ills in this day and age. We are responsible for this, meaning this must be done. They will cut your youth from your hands if this is not done. Create institutions for youth where they can be preached, issues can be discussed, and the ills in this country can be addressed.[5]

God forbid, if you ignore this responsibility, a dangerous reckoning awaits you in front of the people and the nations of this world. More than anything, you will be held responsible in front of Allah. Therefore, these newspapers must guide the people. This is an act of worship greater than a deed one may carry out in one corner of their house. This [guidance] is greater than the guidance carried out in previous times, which, at most, reached thousands of people within a particular gathering. This is guidance for a nation that consists of millions of individuals. If the pen you hold in your hand can guide, it can potentially drive a whole nation

---

[4]. 27/12/79 – Speech of Imam Khomeini to a gathering of those working in the oil industry. Saheefa-e-Imam, V 11, P 443.

[5]. 09/09/1964 – Speech of Imam Khomeini to a gathering of the people of Qum. Saheefa-e-Imam, V 1, P 394.

towards the correct path and save them from deviance. Today we find that the deviated pens stand in opposition to the pens of guidance, and the deviated voices stand in opposition to the guiding ones.[6]

From the beginning, I have repeatedly said that you must show the people the work you are carrying out. If you do something in Sistan, the other side of the nation will not hear about it. If something is done there, the other part of the country will not know. You must continuously make the people aware of the services you have carried out, and I know there have been many. Do not act sanctimoniously, saying, God forbid, what if something happens? This world has armed itself against you, your government and Islam. They wish to find and prop up anything and say whatever they want. One issue they would like to propagate is that the government has done no work for the people. We have already seen that some people have said this government does not work for the people. Sure, they have bad intentions; however, the people need to know their government works for them. This rule was there that the government would present to the people everything they have done for them, all of the significant duties they have fulfilled, from the beginning. As a greater opportunity has become available because it is "The week of the Government", this issue must be pursued more fervently. Two or three individuals should

---

[6]. 02/06/1981 – Speech of Imam Khomeini to the workers of the Keyhan Newspaper. Saheefa-e-Imam, V 14, P 397 and 298.

be responsible for their respective ministries to present their achievements to the people. The people can then understand what those ministries and the Islamic Republic have done for them in the past few years, despite their difficulties. I had to discuss this issue as we have fallen short and must make up lost ground.[7]

Another issue concerns the sermons of Friday prayer. The people must be instructed towards God-consciousness. Commanding God-consciousness is obligatory in the first sermon and, according to precaution, mandatory in the second sermon. Speak about ethical issues with the people and attract them towards having Islamic ethics. Speak to the people on topical matters and about the incidents that have occurred in the country that week.

Keep the people present in the arena as it is their presence in the arena that has protected the revolution and Iran. In this regards, you will not find a better people than the people of Iran in the whole world. Today the people support the Islamic Revolution and Government. They support the government because it is Islamic, and they know the government's support is supporting Islam. This is the only reason they support the government; this support must be protected. The Friday prayer leaders hold the biggest congregations throughout the country. You must use these

---

7. 26/08/1984 – Speech of Imam Khomeini to the Cabinet of the Government. Saheefa-e-Imam, V 19, P 33 and 34.

congregations and remind the people of the religious and political direction. You must equip them in the face of Satan.[8]

It is necessary; in fact, it is obligatory upon you, the Friday and congregational prayer leaders, to wake the people up. Make the people understand that this deviation planted in the Islamic countries - that scholars must not get involved with politics - is nothing but a scheme of the superpowers. They are the planters of this thought inside these countries. Do not listen to their words. Tell them and let them hear; they wish to separate the scholars from politics, tell them about what has happened to us. We must be aware, and we must be mindful of what this means. The generation to come must also be attentive to what this means, and they must not lose this path; the path found by the Muslims now should not be lost.[9]

---

[8]. 25/05/1983 – Speech of Imam Khomeini to the members of Supreme Council of Friday Prayer Leaders. Saheefa-e-Imam, V 17, P 453

[9]. 24/12/1980 – Speech of Imam Khomeini to a gathering of Friday Prayer leaders from around the country. Saheefa-e-Imam, V 13, P 434

Chapter 1

General Discussion

Introduction

All Islamic nations and the Ummah have a duty in the struggle to provide clarification. This is the number one priority. Religious scholars, thinkers, the educated, and those with a pulpit or platform to speak have a responsibility to present the realities of the Islamic world to the people. This clarification is a jihad. Jihad does not just mean holding a sword and fighting on the battlefield. Jihad includes intellectual jihad, practical jihad, the jihad to elucidate, the jihad of propagation and the jihad of wealth. Some have been misguided today as we have not carried out the jihad of clarification.[10]

You, dear youth and university students, who are, in reality, the fruits of this nation and the hope of the future of this country, need to give importance to the issue of clarification. Many realities need to be elucidated. A movement of misguidance hurtles towards the nation of Iran from a hundred different directions that is effective in influencing public opinion and is one of the greater objectives of the enemies of Iran, Islam and the Islamic revolution. This movement keeps people in a state of doubt and detaches the

---
10. 18/05/16 – In a visit to the reciters and memorisers that participate in international Quran competitions.

intellect, especially in our youth. The movement to elucidate is the pacifier of these conspiracies and actions of the enemy.

As a matter of duty, each one of you, like a lantern, should light up your surroundings. Luckily today, the arena is open for the spread of different thoughts. This public space, alongside the problems which may exist, also comes with tremendous blessings. You can use it to spread correct views and answer criticisms and doubts that may be created. This is an arena where you can carry out jihad in the true sense of the word. That being said, a definite principle in this arena that must be adhered to is the use of ethical means. Some confront public opinion on social media, the press, in articles with insults, slander, deception and lies; this must be avoided at all costs. Realities should be presented with solid logic and eloquent speech, underpinned by intellectual rigor. This presentation should be further enhanced by human care and affection by making use of ethics. Today, we can all act in this arena, each one of us in a certain manner on a certain level.

I hope, by the will of Allah, God Almighty makes you all successful. Our youth today, praise be to Allah, are armed. They are armed intellectually and logically and with plenty of information to work hard in this field. Get yourself ready, increase these capacities within you and in the real sense of the word, arm yourselves and enter into this arena, the battlefield of clarification and exposition, the same path taken by Zainab al-Kubra (s).

I address the youth from different strata of this country and the different families belonging to the various classes of society. My dear ones, the heavy burden of protecting this divine trust, which is the trust of the Prophets (s), rests upon your shoulders. The Islamic Republic is the historical trust of the great divine Prophets (s). It is the wish of Musa (a), Isa (a), the Awliyyah and Aa'ima (a) that has been actualized, although incomplete. It will be complete if Allah wills, during the greater governance and lofty authority of the 12th Imam (a.j), may our souls be sacrificed for the dust under his feet. This is a hefty and valuable burden. You must protect this.[11]

The Struggle

Living means jihad in the way of your objective

The Islamic Republic is a new system, from the lens of it being a system established on new values and a special direction going towards lofty objectives. What does bringing about a revolution mean if not bringing about something new? It must have new values, and it is upon these values that its objectives are established. It is by these objectives the journey is specified. Life is the effort that is placed to traverse this journey. This is what is meant by the phrase: life is only beliefs and jihad.

---

11. 05/01/1991 – In a meeting with the Commanders of the IRGC on the occasion of "The Day of the Pasdar".

Jihad does not only mean fighting with the sword or guns; all your efforts can be a form of jihad. Jihad means putting in effort. Living means establishing our objectives, specifying the values dear to us and then putting in all our efforts to achieve them. Life has no meaning apart from this. If a person does not have values, regardless of what they are, then they are reduced to becoming a stagnant mass or left in a vegetative state. At most, they may have an animalistic life. They would take, then grow, and then put in more effort to take more, and then they grow again, and they do this repeatedly and grow physically and materially. This has no value; this is not life, at least not a human life.

This matter that I am discussing is not something specific to us either. It is not like someone can claim that this solely applies to an exact geographic location or doctrine. For any wise person, anywhere around the world, life has no meaning aside from this. They think, establish an objective and, for the love of that objective, continuously strive. The more challenging the task and the more sweat they have to shed to achieve it, the happier they are once they have completed it. If one day, you take part in a heavy workout, you feel more content at the end of it. Aside from the natural physical effect of exercise on your body, there is another effect on you: a feeling of contentment as you feel you have done more work. If one day you make a good plan, execute it well and do something new, you will feel happier. If you can work an extra hour of your own free will, not something forced upon you, you feel satisfied with yourself and your work. Therefore we understand a general principle: The greater the effort and the more difficult the task, at its completion, leads to greater contentment and happiness. This principle is not specific to Iran, this region, the East, or the West; it is the same wherever you go.

However, we live here, in this system, at this moment. This system has been created in the pursuit of values that are themselves in the pursuit of objectives. This system is not our property that we can give to each other or take away from each other as we like. Or, for example, we make changes to it as we please because of who we may be. We have no right to gift others from the pouch of the caliphate, nor does anyone have a right to give us anything from this pouch. These are accepted principles related to the revolution and the system of the Islamic Republic.[12]

Definition of Jihad

Jihad is a broad concept. A general, beneficial and encompassing act that has no end and can be realised in various forms. At the beginning of the jurisprudential books of jihad, we have stated that the yardstick defining jihad is not the sword or the battlefield. The yardstick defining jihad is best understood in the Persian word used today for the term, to struggle. This person struggles; this person

---

12. 18/02/1992 – In a meeting with the members of the social group – The Voice of the Islamic Republic of Iran.

does not struggle. You can have a writer or a scholar who takes on the struggle or those who do not. You can have a university student or a seminarian who takes on the struggle or those who do not. You can have a society that takes on the struggle or a society that does not. Jihad means to take on the struggle.[13]

This revolution wished to show everyone in every corner of the Islamic world that this ideal is realistic, possible and here is the example. This wish was always one of the objectives of the revolution. This objective was there from the beginning, remains today, and will remain in the future. This matter was the first level of our discussion. The second level of our discussion looked at the reality of the Islamic Revolution's context. Did the realities around us in which we live help this objective, or were they harmful to us in pursuing it?

Of course, if the obstacles I will list did not exist, we would not have needed much time to reach the objectives. In 5 to 10 years, a robust structured group could have achieved our goals; however, obstacles exist in the path man wishes to take. Fundamentally it is these very obstacles that give meaning and spiritual reality to the efforts of a person. This is what we call jihad. If barriers did not exist, jihad would have

---

13. 11/09/1994 – At the start of Dars al-Khaarij.

no meaning. Jihad means to struggle and strive alongside difficulties, trials and obstacles.[14]

What is jihad? Not every action is classified as jihad. Actions alongside specific attributes are known as jihad. One attribute that makes an act classified as jihad is knowing it is carried out in the face of opposition. It is knowing that this act is being carried out in the face of an agenda motivated by animosity.

The second type of attributes in the term jihad consists of continuity, smartness and sincerity. It is such actions that are considered to be jihad. Therefore the economic jihad is the continuous, all-around and purposeful effort of the Iranian nation to pacify the hostile scheming enemy.[15]

Jihad does not just take place on the battlefield. In the arena of knowledge, like other arenas in a person's life, jihad is necessary. Jihad means restless effort, accepting its difficulties to the extent that it is wise, and advancing and being hopeful towards the future.[16]

The Pillars That Establish Jihad

Two things are necessary in jihad. Firstly, there needs to be effort and action involved. A person can not fight lying on their bed or in the corner of their house! So firstly, work and

---

14. 03/05/2008 – In a meeting with teachers and students from the Universities in Shiraz.
15. 17/08/2011 – In a meeting with activists in Iran Economics sector.
16. 24/09/2008 – In a meeting with a group of outstanding performers in academia and university professors.

effort must be included in jihad, and secondly, there must be an enemy in opposition.

Jihad in an arena that has no enemy has no meaning. Jihad comprises these two pillars, one, there is effort involved, and two, its in opposition to an enemy. If someone puts in an effort against their friends, this is not jihad; this would be sedition. If someone stands against the rightful government or the rightful system, this would be sedition and waging unlawful war. These efforts may take varying forms such as written, spoken, book-form, newspapers, spreading rumours, destructive criticism, and creating negativity. All of these would be considered sedition, and in some cases, they would be regarded as waging unlawful war. If these were used to confront the enemies of God, they would be considered jihad in the way of Allah. This is the type of jihad the Holy Messenger (s) invites you to. Therefore, what is required of the Islamic Ummah is not laziness, sitting down, idleness or apathy; instead, it is continuous jihad.[17]

The Different Arenas of Jihad

Jihad means striving to attain a lofty and divine objective. This effort can take place in various arenas. One of those arenas is the military battlefields currently active around the world. There are also the political, educational and spiritual arenas. For it to be classified as jihad, it must be an action that is purposeful and faces obstacles, the removal

---

[17]. 11/09/1994 – At the start od Dars al-Khaarij.

of which requires an increased effort; this is called jihad. Jihad is taking on such a struggle, and when its purpose and direction are divine, it would also be considered holy. Your pursuit of knowledge is a jihad, as you have a stubborn enemy who does not want this research and knowledge-based movement to succeed. Therefore I do not believe the jihad in universities is limited to an institutional nature; instead, it is a culture, purposeful, and a movement. The more we spread this culture within the society and establish and strengthen it, the more we will have taken the country further towards true honour, dignity and independence.[18]

Branches of Jihad

The Commander of the Faithful (a) has explained various terms such as steadfastness, certainty, justice and jihad. For example, he states that jihad has four branches; enjoining the good, forbidding the evil, speaking the truth and being honest in your stances. This means a person is sincere in their political and social stances. Being honest in your stance is also a form of jihad. "*Among the faithful are men who fulfill what they have pledged to Allah…*"[19]

Another branch of jihad is *shina'aan al-faasiqeen*. This term means separating from the movements of decadence and disbelief. I say this, especially to you; pay attention to this. Your account must be clear and separate from such

---
18. 21/06/2004 – In a meeting with the academic board and experts from The Jihad of Universities organisation.
19. Surah al-Ahzab: 23

movements. You know me, and we have been with you for the last eight years, with some of you much longer. I do not believe we should cut our relations with the disbelievers. However, the border between you and the disbelievers, the decadent, and those against the Islamic Republic must be known. There are places when someone must cooperate with someone opposed to the Islamic Republic; however, it is known that they are them, and you are you. Do not get confused. I was constantly upset by some in this system and our institution as they would erase these boundaries. The danger of not having boundaries is many go from this side to the other side, and those on the other side come to this side. They regularly traverse over these boundaries meaning they do not know the limits. If a nation does not have defined borders, its social identity and unity can not exist. Allow the borders to be known, so it is known where you stand and where they stand. *"...and whoever detests the vicious and becomes angry for the sake of Allah, then Allah will be angry in favour of him and will keep him pleased on the Day of Judgement..."*[20] Be angry for the sake of Allah; Allah will also be angry for your sake.[21]

Jihad and effort have the same root meaning. There is an element of effort; however, jihad is not just that. Jihad means to struggle in the language used today. This jihad can be of many types. There is the educational, press, political,

---

20. Nahj al-Balagha – Saying No.31
21. 10/11/2004 – In a meeting with members of the cabinet.

economic and military jihad. Jihad can also be apparent or hidden. However, the common factor in these variances is a struggle against an opposition or an enemy. Jihad against your friend has no meaning; jihad occurs against your enemy.

For example, during the sufficating period of the Shah's rule, someone may read five books a week. This act required much effort; however, this was not necessarily jihad. If they wanted this to be jihad, the books they read should have been those that impacted their stand against the oppressive and suffocating regime. This act would have been jihad; this is what jihad constitutes.

The areana's of your jihad are knowledge and skills. You do not require swords, spears, and guns over here. You must use your brain and other intellectual tools through your thoughts, pens and eyes.[22]

Tabyeen: Clarification

One of the jihads is the intellectual jihad. The enemy could surprise us, deviate our thoughts and create distortions and misunderstandings. Any person putting in the effort to raise awareness among the people, protecting them from distortions and becoming an obstacle in the path of misconceptions in the face of the enemy, would be carrying

---

22. 16/07/2007 – During a visit to the Ruyaan Academy

out jihad. That too is a form of jihad which is considered to be important today.[23]

In addition to the enemies intense military wars, We believe the enemy is pursuing two objectives in the soft war. The soft war is more challenging and more dangerous than military warfare. In this soft war, the enemy is carrying out two manoeuvres: severing the ties to truth and steadfastness, and misrepresenting facts by portraying them in a completely reversed manner. They utilize extensive propaganda to distort global realities, presenting falsehoods as truths.

These deceptions are delivered with such conviction that listeners are swayed into believing them. The enemy confidently and calmly presents the truth turned on its head. For example, six years have passed since the Americans, hand in hand with the Arabs, have been bombing the oppressed people of Yemen in their houses, on their roads, hospitals, and schools. For the past six years, they have enforced an economic blockade and prevented food, medicine, and fuel from reaching them. These acts have been carried out by the hardened, blackened heart and oppressive Arab governments in Yemen, all with the green light from America. This is the reality of the situation. The Yemeni's are capable and resourceful people; through different phenomena, they have assembled defensive tools for themselves, either securing them from other sources or producing them. Through this,

---

23. 09/06/1996 – In ameeting with the Commanders of the 27th Muhammad Rasullullah (s) Battalion.

they can respond to the six-year-long bombing campaign; however, as soon as the Yemeni carry out a single operation, the shouts of the enemy's propaganda rise, and they start screaming, 'there has been an attack!' or, 'this is terrorism!'. Even the United Nations says this, showing the ugliness of their work which, in this case, is worse than America. America is an arrogant, oppressive government, but why would the United Nations do this? It does not condemn a government for six years of bombardment; however, when they [the Yemeni] defend themselves, they condemn it, and then everyone follows and joins the attack. This is one example of their falsification.

Another example is that America has the world's most extensive nuclear weapons arsenal. They have maybe a thousand atomic bombs in their storage, and they have used them too. The American government is the only government that has ever used nuclear weapons. The Americans killed 220 thousand people in one hour, in one day and then they raised the slogan of being against the spread of atomic weapons! They claim to be against weapons of mass destruction! They lie as they have the biggest and most dangerous weapons of mass destruction, they have used them.

America supports a criminal that cuts their opponents to pieces using a saw and then claims to support human rights. The world knows the Saudis trapped one of its opponents and cut him to pieces with a saw. They distort the truth to such an extent in such a manner. The Americans established

ISIS, which is what the Americans now say themselves; we are not the ones saying this. They said they created it, and then when they wanted to attack it, they said they were their opponents. They all accepted and stated that America created ISIS, and then, using the excuse of the presence of ISIS, they established military bases in Iraq and Syria, claiming to be against them! They give them modern media capabilities, money, and permission to steal Syrian oil and use its profits; at the same time, they say we are fighting against ISIS. This is what they do, create a façade utterly opposite to the truth.

With hate, they speak about the presence of Iran in the region, meaning, why are Iran in Syria, Iraq and some other places even though our presence was not military, and even when it was military, it was on an advisory level. In certain areas, there is no trace of a military presence; it is purely political; however, even with this, they look at it with hostility and see it as a huge problem and a source of unrest. This is despite the fact that this is our region, and anywhere we have entered, it has been to support the legitimate governments of those countries, whether Iraq or Syria. Our objective was to support the legitimate governments on their requests and with their permission. Americans amplify this when they have intervened and occupied unjustly and without the consent of Syria a whole area of Syria in which they have established a military base.

Another example is Iraq, where they have established several military bases. Distorting reality is what they do, and they do this in every field. That said, they must leave Iraq, which is what the Iraqis desire and as per their law, this goes for Syria, too; the quicker, the better.[24]

Clarification of Lies

We have external impediments too, as some plant hopelessness, a feeling of being incapable etc., among the people. They continuously inject these feelings of despair and incapacity. Terms like 'it's not possible', 'there is no point' or 'we can't' are repeatedly being pumped in.

Clarification of lies looks to clarify those issues that have been presented opposite to reality. Distorting historical facts is not something new, but in the last few years there has been a movement to purify the image of the unjust regime, the Pahlavi regime. If only it was something that could be purified! Those that have written about their personalities, even after trying their utmost to clean up around them, have had no choice but to confess certain things. Is a corrupt, weak, controlled, deviant, elitist regime with individuals who only cared about personal profits defensible? Is Huweida[25] defendable? Is Muhammad Raza defendable? For those people who had not seen that era, they have started a movement which will lead them to say, 'These people weren't so bad!', 'the conditions weren't too bad!', or ask, 'why did you carry

---

24. 11/03/2021 – In a televised speech on the occasion of Eid al-Mabath.
25. Amir Abbas Huweida was one of the Prime Ministers during the Pahlvi Regime.

out a revolution?'. Everything goes back to placing doubts in the revolution, and this is happening from the outside.[26]

Another issue is the image that the enemy is creating. There is currently an intense propaganda and media war against us, just like the Imposed War. We did not even possess an RPG at the beginning of the Imposed War! In front of us, large mechanised divisions stood in formation. I was in Ahwaz, and we saw how continuous mechanised divisions entered one after the other. We needed anti-tank weaponry to respond. The RPG was an ordinary and easy-to-use anti-tank device, even that we did not have. The enemy had access to different types and forms of weapons. The same situation is before us now. The media and propagation capabilities we have in the face of the enemy now are just like the lack of capabilities we had in the face of the enemy then. We were able to attain victory over the enemy in those days, and we will also be able to achieve success today. Without a doubt, we will be victorious; however, this is the current situation we find ourselves in. The enemy wishes to portray a false image of this country using their vast capabilities. They create this false image not just for the rest of the world but also for those living inside this country. They speak in a manner that even the person who lives and breathes in this environment will start accepting that which is not per the reality around them. So, this battle exists, and if we cannot

---

26. 28/05/2018 – In a meeting with university students.

play our part in this war, if the elites cannot play their part, then we have not carried out our duty.[27]

Striving to clarify is a responsibility upon all the Islamic nations and all the Islamic Ummah. This is on the first level. The scholars, thinkers, the educated, and those occupying a pulpit or podium are responsible for clarifying and presenting the realities of the Islamic world to those who do not know. This clarification is jihad. Jihad is not just holding a sword and a shield and fighting on the battlefield. Jihad is inclusive of intellectual jihad, practical jihad, jihad of propagation and monetary jihad. As today we have not been able to carry out the obligatory duty of clarification, some have been misguided and whilst thinking they are working for Islam, they are working against Islam. The terrorist groups in our region have stolen security from Muslims and Islamic nations, fighting Muslims instead of the enemy. These takfiri outfits close to the Wahabis have taken it upon themselves to carry out the role the enemy wanted to play among the Muslims. They have created a division between the Muslims. When Muslims are busy fighting each other, the issue of Palestine is forgotten by them, just as the issue of Palestine is being forgotten currently. We must clarify, explain and work! You, those who have come from various countries, must make your nations aware and propagate. Guide them towards the teachings of the Quran, the jihad of the Quran, and the clarifications the Quran asks you to make. "*You shall*

---

27. 27/10/2018 - In a meeting with outstanding performers in academia.

explain it for the people, and you shall not conceal it,"[28]. Present and explain these to them.

God willing, Allah will create the foundations for the movement of the Islamic Ummah. If we strive, move and purify our intentions, God Almighty will help us. If we are lazy or do not carry out our responsibility, we should naturally not await divine help. God Almighty helps those people and those nations who put in effort and move. Put in the effort and move, and God Almighty will help us.

We have no doubt victory belongs to Islam. The front of faithlessness, despite its vastness, lightning and thunder, weapons and ammunitions, at the end of the day, will be forced to retreat in the face of the Islamic Ummah and the Islamic fighting front. *"If the faithless fight you, they will turn their backs [to flee]. Then they will not find any protector or helper..."*[29] This is the divine tradition, and there is no doubt about it. The only condition it has is that we must work. We must move, be on our way and work, for if we work, the divine tradition dictates the enemy must and will retreat.[30]

The most dangerous incident that can occur is sedition. Sedition creates a foggy situation confusing a person about who is a friend or foe, who has entered the arena with an agenda and who has provoked them. Sedition must be quelled by clarification. Whenever clarification occurs, the hands of

---

28. Surah Aal al-Imran – Verse 187
29. Surah al-Fath – Verse 22
30. 18/05/16 - In a meeting with those reciters and memorisers of the Holy Quran that participated in international Quran competitions.

the sedition-makers are reduced. Wherever aimless words are spoken, aimless shots fired, and aimless slander exists, the sedition-makers are happier as this helps blur the lines further.[31]

The Importance of the Jihad of Clarification

An important aspect relating to a leader's attention towards the people is the concept of the neccessity of continually raising the people's awareness. Despite his old age, Imam Khomeini used every opportunity to present the realities to the people. Distortions and misguidance play a hazardous role in propaganda institutions around the world. Imam Khomeini was aware of this danger. The untrustworthy tools of communication connected to the enemies of this nation forced Imam Khomeini to always be in a position clarifying, explaining and guiding the people alongside continually advising others to propagate the realities to the masses in the face of the enemies that are trying to keep them in the dark. For this reason, we continually ask the people of the pen, those who speak and hold podiums, to present the correct clarifications of the realities.

Currently, the enemy is working in direct opposition to this very fundamental issue in Islam. From the beginning of the revolution, one of the essential objectives of the enemy was to distort realities and history. If you saw a pen connected to the enemy write a distortion of the war, the revolution

---

31. 30/07/1999 - Friday Prayers Sermon

or Islam, you would see the calls of encouragement from different parts of the world. The same is the case today. Today, if someone in the country says or writes distortions about Islam, the history of the revolution or the face of the revolution for the sake of acceptance and happiness of the enemies of Islam or this nation, observe how institutions of propagation around the world belonging to the arrogant powers start congratulating and encouraging them! Clarification is a critical issue. People are obedient to what they see and observe. If someone can distort the realities in the eyes of the people, they can misguide their acts and intentions. Today, if someone equips their pens against Islam, the sanctities and efforts of this nation, expresses an opinion against the best children of this nation, the martyrs and the fighters on the path of Allah, or speaks or writes against the Basij, jihad or martyrdom, the foreign radio stations, politicians and writers will encourage them. Today, every person has a responsibility, regardless of whether they belong to vast institutions or those who belong to smaller institutions where they have an influential voice, such as classes, schools or workplaces. If they see that the realities and the established facts of Islam and the revolution are being distorted, they have a responsibility to clarify, and they cannot remain silent. Imam Khomeini emphasised this point repeatedly. This is one of the secrets to the system's strengthening and continuation.[32]

Clarifying the truth and informing the people's thinking is also essential and must not be forgotten. The people must not be left in a state of ambiguity. In the Holy Messenger's (s) story, God Almighty informed the people through this verse.[33] He showed them the reality of the situation and made them understand how this dangerous step[34], which would attract many ill intentions, was for breaking a wrong custom that had gripped society. *"There is no blame on the Prophet in respect of that which Allah has made lawful for him."*[35]. God Almighty made it obligatory upon him to carry out this act as an incorrect custom had taken hold and created issues within that society. It needed to be removed from among the people. To carry this out, God used the Messenger as a sacrifice for the truth and brought him to the midst of the battleground; that being said, he did defend his Prophet (s). He made the people aware. Therefore, you are supposed to act but also make the reality known to the people. Without

---

32. 04/06/2001 - In the 12th commemoration ceremony for the passing of the Late Imam Khomeini.
33. Surah al-Ahzab – Verse 37: *When you said to him whom Allah had blessed, and whom you [too] had blessed, 'Retain your wife for yourself, and be wary of Allah,' and you had hidden in your heart what Allah was to divulge, and you feared the people though Allah is worthier that you should fear Him, so when Zayd had got through with her, We wedded her to you, so that there may be no blame on the faithful in respect of the wives of their adopted sons, when the latter have got through with them, and Allah's command is bound to be fulfilled.*
34. The order to the Prophet (s) of marrying the divorced wife of Zayd.
35. Surah al-Ahzab – Verse 38

explaining the truth, the people's thinking will remain in darkness and a murky environment, and the enemy will look to use such an environment.[36]

Clarification; the Foundation of our Work

Clarification is the foundation of our work. We are facing minds and hearts, and we must persuade the hearts. If the hearts are not convinced, the bodies will not act. This is the difference between Islamic thought and Non-Islamic thought. I was sitting with a friend, years before the revolution, at their house in Tehran. Whilst we were there, a youth entered all of a sudden. I knew him and his father; they were from Mashad. He was a part of MKO's guerrilla force that had gone up to the mountains, where they held their positions and carried out operations. As we knew each other, he sat down, and it appeared he had come to get a bit of financial aid from the house owner. I asked him what they were up to, and he told me a few things. I told him that they must speak to the people and explain themselves if they wished to be successful. The people should know why you have gathered in the North, why you are carrying out an armed struggle and why you are carrying out various acts in the city. The people should know, and you should clarify this for them. He gave me a look and shuffled a bit. He was a man, at least ten years younger than me, but he gave me a contemptuous look. He said, 'Yes, this is in your Islamic

---

36. 28/06/2003 - In a meeting with the officials from the Judiciary.

thought process; this is not how we think.'. What he meant to say was providing clarification is not necessary. This way of thinking belongs to the Dialectic Marxist doctrine that is slowly returning to our universities. They say the natural result of the Dialectic is a war between labour and those who provide the work; there is no need to clarify anything. This is how they explain it. The incorrectness of this has now been tested and proven. The government founded upon this has wholly eradicated because it was understood to be problematic from the core after 60-70 years. Yes, this is the method of Islam! The method of Islam is to clarify, which has led to the Islamic Revolution being successful over many of these historical movements and incorrect teachings. However, certain habits Islam has not conquered yet, such as extravagance and wasteful spending. These have been attained as an inheritance from the past. Unfortunately, we have kept this custom.

Now again, you see some people betting on a losing horse. They are betting on Marxism again! That is not us; according to that man who died later on, we have clarification in the Islamic school of thought. "...your duty is only to communicate"[37]. Allah says to the Messenger that he must deliver the message. You must clarify through your words the critical issues facing the nation, issues relating to the economy of resistance, matters related to the advanced sciences and the problem of relations with

---

37. Surah al-Ra'ad – Verse 40

America, you must clarify. These issues are not apparent to a lot of people. If these issues are not clear for you, the student body, then go and clarify these issues for yourself. If these issues are clear, explain them to the broader student body in the university. Why do I persist in not building relations with America, even not negotiating apart from particular issues for a benefit? What is the reason? This has a reason, and this reason has even been accepted by those politicians who support America. I have mentioned that I have had repeated discussions on this issue with one of the Presidents in various settings. They then went to the Supreme National Security Council and stated that so and so has reasons I cannot refute. He was right. I had reasons for rejecting establishing relations with the Americans, for which he had no response. The reasons we have are strong reasons. It is not easy to reject these reasons. If you also can understand these reasons, then go and explain them. You are university students, young and positive; the words you have spoken made me completely hopeful. This is not just from the perspective of the content, which was good too; however, more so from the perspective that I felt your minds are working intellectually. This is important for me. Your minds are working, and you are using solid discourses; this has a lot of value. So now, sit down with this mind, develop the needed arguments, and progress this.

The issue of living a simple Islamic lifestyle that we had presented is being studied and has to be explained. You have to do this practically and also by offering clarification. Cultural issues are one of the most critical issues; you should clarify them. So this responsibility of clarification is a duty within the environment of the universities and outside it. Just like I have stated, the Friday congregational prayer and such platforms create the narrative; they build the thoughts and opinions of the public, which is very valuable. They take the country towards one specific direction. However, continuation, steadfastness, clarifications and repetitions are necessary and may take a lot of time too. [38]

Clarification; the Islam Method

I want to mention the significance of clarification in parenthesis to you, the youth who feel a sense of responsibility. In all forms of Islamic struggle, in every state, clarification and explanation of the realities, getting the truth across, and propagation is essential, and this must not be left.[39]

If someone states something incorrectly, should another answer them or not? Yes, of course, they should. Responding to an incorrect utterance has its methods. There is a time when someone says something wrong, and we go and spread their false words in a hundred different places and let everyone know that so and so said something incorrect. This method is a mistake and is erroneous. I do not oppose the

---
38. 02/07/2016 - In a meeting with university students.
39. 03/05/2008 - In a meeting with professors and students from the universities in Shiraz.

movement to clarify issues from anyone or any institution; in fact, I strongly believe in the issue of clarification. The matter of clarification has been a part of our essential processes from the beginning. Clarification is necessary; however, this does not mean we create internal division. Be careful. Everyone must be cautious of this.

It is inappropriate to cause inflammation in various political, intellectual and methodological movements. Praise be to Allah; all of you have insight, you are aware, and you are aware of the current trends. This situation exists in the country where you can see; unfortunately, one person is against another. Foreign organisations are celebratory towards this. They analyse such a situation and say differences have erupted between them, and they will be finished. They repeatedly express their desire. This is a weakness that exists within us. Do not allow this weakness to continue and grow. This issue must be taken care of. The movement needs to be meticulous, logical and well-founded. If someone has a different opinion, they should present it with reasoning. I have stated I believe in clarification.

During the fight for the revolution, we differed from the leftists and the Marxists, who were also fighting. We would say you must clarify to the people, but they did not believe in the need to clarify; they had another way of looking at things. From the beginning, the revolution's role was based upon the foundation of clarification, explanation, logical presentations and far from emotional noise. If emotional noise got involved, it would ruin the logical arguments too. It is possible four people are attracted by this method; however, you would have repelled four more intellectual people. This is what we are saying; this is what we believe.[40]

The Growing Importance of Clarification Today

The enemy has given up hope in having the ability to cause fundamental harm to the Islamic Republic because they know that internally, there is sufficient motivation, faith, sincerity and readiness. However, they still have not lost hope in having the ability to infiltrate, and there are plenty of infiltration tools these days.

The enemies are training the Iranian youth so that they end up becoming what they want. Suppose an Iranian youth is brought up in a manner that they are pro-American or supportive of the arrogant powers. In that case, the Americans do not need to spend too much more to implement their plans for Iran. This youth will work as a voluntary servant for them. This is how they wish for the Iranian youth to turn out. A few years ago, four individuals lacking self-worth spoke and acted in a manner leading an American visitor to go back to America and report that there were people in Iran with weapons in their hands waiting for our orders to start firing! They saw four people with no self-worth and were deceived. The biggest problem America has is that they do not understand our country or our people and lack the

---

40. 04/07/2011 - In a meeting with the Commnders of the IRGC.

ability to do so. The issue of the arrogant powers is they rely primarily on what they can observe in the apparent; however, they cannot see the hidden. Even their strength is limited to apparent physical force, and they can not hold power over the hearts as they would like. They made a mistake. However, they have not lost hope in the ability to infiltrate; they wish to infiltrate and win over the hearts and change people's minds. Defending against this is a huge responsibility upon those sympathetic towards the nation of Iran, the responsibility of clarification; a burden upon all of our shoulders. I stress the jihad of clarification so much because today, the great jihad relies upon it. Today, this clarification, explanation and illumination is necessary. We must think at a deeper level to understand the deeper issues and realities.[41]

These steps need to occur in the second stage of the revolution. Firstly, we need to understand and give importance to what we possess. This includes our merits, capacities, the merits of this country and its capacities. We must understand these and take them seriously and make use of them. The country has a vast capacity. Secondly, we need to understand the harms, corruptions and penetrating ways of the enemy, and we also need to be serious in being steadfast against them. This is the second stage of the revolution. Understanding our capacities and merits, making use of them, and understanding the corruptions, what lacks and challenges, and then fighting to resolve them. Be attentive to

---
41. 23/05/2016 - At the Imam Hussain (a) Military University.

the fact that the West and America have concluded that if Iran wants something, they will achieve it. They have concluded that you can not fight against the national determination of the Iranian nation. If the Iranian nation makes a decision, they understand there is no use in putting obstacles in its path. So what do they do? They have concluded that they must do something that does not allow the Iranian nation to reach a decision and that their willpower needs to be weakened; this is what they are looking to achieve. Today around the world, billions are being spent so that our youth's political and religious belief systems can be penetrated and their will to move and make a stand is destroyed. They wish to obliterate your determination and take away your ability to decide. Their efforts are so that the Iranian nation does not decide to progress, be an opposition, or establish an Islamic society or civilisation. They know that if this is decided, then without a doubt, it will be actualised.[42]

The enemies are upset that the environment is clear. They do not wish for a clear environment; they wish for it to be murky. It is in a murky environment that they can get closer to their objectives and cause a blow to the movement of the Iranian nation. The murky environment is sedition. Sedition is when a group of people enter the arena looking like friends but actually being the enemy. They muddy the waters. In this murky environment, the enemy can quickly hide their

---

42. 21/03/2019 - In the gathering of the visitors to the Shrine of Imam al-Ridha (a) in Mashhad.

faces, enter the arena, and strike. The Commander of the Faithful (a) said: *"The basis of the occurrence of evils are those desires which are acted upon and the orders that are innovated. They are against the Book of Allah. People co-operate with each other about them even though it is against the Religion of Allah. If wrong had been pure and unmixed it would not be hidden from those who are in search of it."*.[43] If falsehood came obviously and in the apparent towards one searching for the truth, it would not be difficult for them; they would understand clearly that this is falsehood. *"And if right had been pure without admixture of wrong those who bear hatred towards it would have been silenced."*.[44] The same is for the truth; if it comes clearly and in the apparent, the antagonist can not slander the truth with falsehood. Then he says: *"What is, however, done is that something is taken from here and something from there and the two are mixed!"*.[45] A person who causes sedition takes a part of the truth and a part of falsehood, mixing them up and placing them together. Then, it becomes difficult for those searching for the truth. This is what sedition is.

What is the treatment in the face of such a phenomenon? Using sound intellect alongside divine sources presents the following definitive treatment. The treatment is to be forthright in clarifying and explaining the truth. When you see a movement has begun under the guise of the elections,

---

43. Nahj al-Balagha – Sermon 50.
44. Same as above.
45. Same as above.

an element of the enemy has entered this murky arena, and you can hear their slogans and their words enter the battlefield manifesting their lack of conscience, it is here that you must make the boundaries clear. Every person has a duty to do this. More than anyone else, this responsibility falls on the elites; among them, it is more of an obligation to those with a larger audience. The duty is to specify the boundaries and make clear who is saying what. It should not become such that falsehood can hide in the arena amidst the layers of smoke, strike, and the front of truth does not even realise the source of the hit. This is where talking about neutrality from the side of the elite is not desired. The elite need to state and explain these issues clearly. This duty is not specific to a particular political leaning either. In the Islamic system, groups belonging to all political leanings need to specify whether or not they believe the support from the arrogant powers is acceptable. When the heads of the arrogant powers, oppressors, the occupiers of Islamic lands, the murderers of the innocent people of Palestine, Iraq, Afghanistan and many other places, enter the battle and speak and take up a position, it must be known what position this person, who is in the system of the Islamic Republic, has concerning them. Are they willing to disassociate with them and say we are your enemy, and we are opposed to you?

In times of sedition, when someone comes and rejects Islam, the slogans of the system of the Islamic Republic and creates doubts about the Republic and the elections; when this phenomenon becomes apparent in the society, the expectation from the elites is that they make the boundaries clear and state their position. Speaking ambiguously helps in confusing the environment further; it does not help in eliminating the sedition or in clarifying the issues. Clarifying is the enemy of the enemy; it is an obstacle for the enemy. Creating confusion is helping the enemy. This in itself is a topic; who helps in clarifying and who helps in creating confusion. Everyone should consider this and use this as a yardstick.[46]

Political analysis carried out correctly in a manner that inculcates the mind is something vital. The mind must be trained.

A difficult period for any revolution is when truth and falsehood compound—the Commander of the Faithful cries out, *"What is, however, done is that something is taken from here and something from there and the two are mixed! At this stage Satan overpowers his friends and they alone escape for whom 'virtue has been apportioned by Allah from before"*.[47] This was not the case at the time of the Messenger (s). At the time of the Messenger (s), there were rows and rows of illumination and clarity. On the other side, you had the polytheists and the people of Mekkah. The Muhajirun had stories about each one of them. They knew, 'he was the one that hit me on this

---

46. 19/01/2010- In a meeting with members of the Council of Coordinating Islamic Propagation.
47. Nahj al-Balagha – Sermon 50.

date!', 'He imprisoned me!' and, 'he was the one who stole my possessions!'. As a result, there was no confusion. The Jewish tribes were conspirators but the people of Medina, Muhajir and Ansar, were aware of their conspiracies. The war with Banu Quraidha ended, and the Messenger (s) gave the order for a large number to be executed. There were no signs of hesitation on anyone's face, and no one questioned it because there was clarity in the arena. In such a situation, war and protecting your faith is easy. However, during the time of the Commander of the Faithful (a), who opposed Imam Ali (a)? Do you think this was a joke? Do you think it was easy that Abdullah ibn Mas'oud, a companion with great stature, according to some narrations, did not remain upon the wilayah of the Commander of the Faithful (a) and became one of those who deviated? Rabee' ibn Khatheem and some others who had come to the Battle of Siffeen expressed they were upset at his killing and wished for permission to go to the border frontiers and not to enter the battle. This is where the challenge becomes difficult. As the environment becomes more polluted, you reach the time of Imam Hasan (a), and you can see what happened during that time. At the time of the Commander of the Faithful (a), the murkiness in the air was lighter as great exponents existed, like Ammar ibn Yassir. Whenever an issue would arise, Ammar ibn Yasir, this great companion of the Prophet (s), would go, speak and explain and at the very least, the air would become clearer for some. However, during the time of Imam Hasan (a), even this did not exist. In times of doubt and indirect war with disbelievers who can take your slogans and use them to further their objectives, the situation becomes complicated. You must remain vigilant. That being said, praise be to God; we are not yet in such a situation. Until now, the boundaries are intact, and many principles and truths are apparent. However, we should not feel content that this is how the situation will always remain. You must stay aware, have insight and check whether your hands are working for Allah. This requires insight, do not take it lightly.

Once I researched the almost five years of governance of the Commander of the Faithful (a) and whatever occurred in it. The summary of everything I had understood came down to the issue of weakness in political analysis. Secondarily, other factors existed too; however, this was the most critical issue. If this were not the case, many would have been recognised as being among the faithful now. Instead, they faithfully fought for the Mother of the Believers in opposition to Imam Ali (a)! Their analysis was incorrect.[48]

Many times, a set of issues require propagation, and this need would remain for five or ten years; however, it is possible that five years after, that need is no longer there. This propagation needs to be planned. We have always advised the propagators, the seminarians and the virtuous to understand what is required. Then they should speak in accordance with the audience and their level of understanding. However,

---

48. In a meeting with a gathering of the Commanders of the IRGC.

this is not the work of one person. Some individuals may make mistakes in their understanding and analysis. This is the work of a focused collective and requires planning. God willing, this must be done.

The most critical times and places where propagation is essential are where sedition exists. The most effort spent at the beginning of Islam and the time of the Messenger (S) were the efforts spent dealing with the hypocrites. After the Messenger (s), during the time of the Commander of the Faithful (a), the energies of the Islamic government were spent fighting and contesting individuals claiming to uphold Islam. The same happens after this, and the same happens during the time of the Aa'ima (a), a period of an unclear environment. At the time of the Battle of Badr, carrying out your responsibility was not difficult. Being present on the battlefield against an obvious enemy, when what they say is clear, is not difficult. It becomes problematic when the Commander of the Faithful (a) needs to stand in opposition to those who are claimants of Islam and believe in Islam. It was not such that they were not practising Islam or that they had returned from Islam, but they had taken the wrong way, and their lowly desires directed their path. This brings about the most difficult circumstances that lead to a person being thrown into a state of doubt. To this extent, a companion like Abdallah ibn Mas'oud comes in the presence of the Commander of the Faithful (a) and says, "We have doubt regarding this fight!.".⁴⁹ Why should they doubt? This doubt among the elites eats up the legs of the correct movement of the Islamic society like a termite. When the elites begin doubting the evident truths, this makes work more difficult. This was the difficulty of the work of the Commander of the Faithful (a). Today, the same applies. Today, if you look across the world, the same applies, and if you look internally within our society, the same applies. Clarification is necessary.

On the international level today, the enemy is using every tool to taint the minds of every individual, whether it be the elites or the general public, wherever they are able.⁵⁰

Whatever they have said and what we have said regarding the revolution and Imam Khomeini, needs to be readdressed and repeated. If reality is not repeatedly recalled, including its specifics and details, the possibility of its distortion increases over time. Most of you know about the motivation to distort the character of Imam Khomeini and the revolution, the revolution being his most significant achievement. We must repeat the realities we have stated about Imam Khomeini and the Revolution. We must repeat it so we can take away the opportunity to distort them from those who wish to misrepresent them. The Divine sources, the historical realities, and many religious understandings command us to carry out actions repeatedly. For example, we are asked to continuously recite the Holy Quran so that the Quranic

---

49. Waqi'at al-Siffeen – P 115
50. 13/12/2009 - In a meeting with a gathering of seminarians and clergy.

realities are not forgotten. The same goes for the repetition of historical realities; they must be repeated. Suppose our nation would not have persisted in the presentation of Ashura over these centuries. In that case, it may have been possible that this crucial event would have been forgotten, or it would have been a lot weaker than the reality we see manifested today.

My address today is mainly directed to you, the dear youth. Firstly, this is because the youth have not experienced and did not see the era of epic sagas. The youth have only heard about the period of the revolution's victory, the Holy Defence and the great mobilisation and struggle against the separatists. These events are all a part of history for our youth. That is why it is even more necessary for us to explain and clarify for them. Secondly, the minds of our youth are the target of distortions from the distortionists. Today, they wish to work more upon the minds of our youth and do not wish the younger generation becomes aware of the realities. Therefore, my address today is to the youth.[51]

Distorting Realities Alongside Sanctions Movement

In parallel with the sanctions, there is also a movement to distort; pay attention to this. Distorting truths and presenting realities contrary to what they are regarding our country or those realities linked to our country are

---
51. 04/06/2014 - In the 28th annual commemoration of the passing away of Imam Khomeini.

among the things they do. They are trying to achieve two objectives through these distortions. Firstly, it is to attack the spirit of the people, I will explain how they are trying to do this, and secondly, it is to pressure the people in the wrong direction to find a solution to the sanctions. This distortion occurs in these two areas to achieve these two objectives. They are even spending a lot of money to distort the truth's presentation. You can witness how these heads of state, their ministers, presidents and others are travelling from one place to another to speak against Iran. They conduct interviews and try somehow to mention the name of Iran in every issue. They are going to great lengths to carry this out; this is the movement of distortions.

However, that first issue, weakening the public spirit and the people's happiness, hope and motivation, has happened since the revolution began. This has been the established path the enemy took from the beginning of the revolution. They would address the people of Iran using television and radio, which used to be much more limited. This has dramatically expanded, and this communication can occur in various ways. They try to make the people feel hopeless, and their work no longer has value, no one will be able to help them, their situation is terrible, etc. They were a bit confused at the beginning of the revolution, but they came to their senses and began a propaganda campaign against the country. One of their objectives was to make the Iranian people believe that severing the links between Iran and the colonial powers during the time of the Pahlavi government would lead to immense difficulty for the country. They pursued this from the beginning and seek the same objective today. They present the situation as dire using a hundred different ways. If a positive point exists in the country, they deny it entirely or say nothing about it. Positive achievements are being attained in this country, but not one of them can be seen reflected in the foreign media of the enemy.

If a weakness exists, they magnify it by ten and sometimes by a hundred, for what? This weakens the people's spirit and hope, especially the youth's hope. If the youth are hopeful, they are motivated, and the motivation of the youth is exceptional. The youth are speedy and active. If hope is taken away, they stop, like a car that loses fuel.

Their objective is to make our youth hopeless and take away their happiness and motivation. They do not wish for the youth to have motivation, take the lead or initiative. This is what they pursue, and at times, it works. There are some internally who start repeating their words too. For example, you read and hear the opinions of certain people who belong to specific political organisations. Two days later, you see those views reflected upon social media or certain newspapers in the country. Unfortunately, such actions take place internally.

Regarding the second objective, pressuring people towards wrong solutions, they say, 'If you wish the sanctions to be lifted, you have to compromise in front of America'.

In summary, they say that you must compromise in front of America and that you must not stand against them. I will speak about this in a lot more detail later on. This is also a part of the movement to distort. This affects some, and they repeat their narratives, exaggerating our problems, understating the points of strength and advancements of the country and pointing in the wrong direction. However, this affects some people, but this does not affect most of the people of Iran. The majority of people have understood America and the enemy. They know that they lie and speak with an agenda; therefore, even the movement of distortion has not given them the desired result. I declare that if the movement of distortion is defeated, the sanctions campaign will also be defeated. This is because this arena is an arena of the battle of wills. When the movement to distort loses, the determination of the Iranian nation will get stronger and remain steadfast. It will certainly be victorious over the enemies' resolve and come out victorious.[52]

The Benefits and Effect of Clarification

Fostering Public Discourse and Accountability

This content we have presented is not just expressing frustrations and advice between us that you come and speak, and I listen, and then I speak, and then you listen. Instead, it must come out in the shape of a discourse. Discourse means

---

52. 31/07/2020 - In a televised speech on the occasion of Eid al-Adha.

it should be something the people believe, something which they accept and are attentive towards. This is achieved by speaking out, presenting logical, scholarly clarifications and being free from various types of exaggerations. It must be transferred through the use of correct language, a language that is logical and well-mannered.[53]

No matter how much we speak about the future, in reality, it is looking at, talking about and pointing towards a period that concerns you. Your true presence in that period will be the determining factor and making work happen. The issue about your future is regarding the slogan of progress and justice. This is for those in the fourth decade [of the revolution], which has already begun. We have announced that this decade is the decade of progress and justice. It must be noted that just by announcing this, progress will not be achieved nor justice. However, progress and justice can be attained by clarification, repetition, wills, and firm determinations. We wish to convert the issues of progress and justice into a national discourse. We must all want it; unless we want it, planning and execution will not occur, and we will not reach the objective. We must clarify. I wish to speak a bit more about the issue of progress. The point of justice is another long and vast topic; as I mentioned, these are not attained just by words. We must be focused, pursuant, and we must research them. The intellectuals in the universities should sit down and conduct studies on this. An academic

---
53. 06/03/2014 - In a meeting with members of the Assembly of Experts.

clarification must be presented, and theoretical models must be created so that it can be turned into a program and then thrown into the field of implementation so that by the end of ten years, the nation feels that real progress has been made.[54]

Protecting the Chain of Truthful Advice

Two elements are necessary when it comes to dealing with the enemies. This is what I have always advised, and I will continue to advise. Two characteristics need to exist in every individual. The first is insight, and the second is steadfastness. If these two characteristics exist, the enemy cannot do anything. They will not be able to cause any harm or find any opportunity in their opposition to the Islamic system. The Commander of the Faithful (a) stated, *"And this banner will be borne only by him who is a man of sight, of endurance and of knowledge of the position of rightfulness."*[55]

So if these two exist, the enemy can not be victorious. One way to protect these two virtues in society is by advising one another, just like it appears in the Chapter of Al-Asr: *"and enjoin one another to [follow] the truth, and enjoin one another to patience."*[56] The people should advise one another. They should advise each other towards the truth, emphasising the truth, and they should enjoin each other to steadfastness. This protects everything. If this advising of one another towards steadfastness and insight exists within a society,

---
54. 17/05/2009 - In a meeting with teachers and students from Kurdistan.
55. Nahj al-Balagha – Sermon 173.
56. Surah al-Asr – Verse 3.

the enemy will not be able to trigger that society easily; however, if this culture of advising is cut off, which serves as the chain of protection for the faithful, then harm will undoubtedly be dealt. *"except those who have faith and do righteous deeds, and enjoin one another to [follow] the truth, and enjoin one another to patience."*[57]. If this advising does not exist, a loss will undoubtedly be incurred. The enemy is targeting this essential element.

The cutting of the chains of the faithful advising each other is very dangerous. They work to stop the faithful from advising one another, protecting one another and giving hope to one another. If the culture of advising one another is halted in society, it is perilous. This will lead to people feeling alone and hopeless, weakening their resolve, their aspirations will reduce, and they will lose the tenacity to act. If advising one another does not exist, then these problems will arise. Naturally, if there is less hope, less resolve, and the wills have been weakened, this will lead to loftier objectives gradually getting beyond reach. Eventually, they will appear impossible to achieve and then be forgotten. Our officers of the soft war are responsible for ensuring this does not happen. We must understand we have a duty concerning this trust, the Islamic Republic, which has opened the path of success in front of this nation, placed on our shoulders, on the shoulders of the nation of Iran. A part of that responsibility is enjoining towards the truth and steadfastness. That is understanding

---

57. Same as above.

the enemy and remaining firm in the face of the enemy, not capitulating in front of them and not trusting this betraying enemy.[58]

Operational

One need concerning all Islamic communities, all Islamic countries and especially our nation, which is governed by the Islamic system, is the need to transfer Islamic concepts into the realm of implementation and the arena of action. The system of Islamic knowledge and values is a collective of concepts; bringing these concepts to the people and raising them to the level of implementation is a critical task. In whichever arena we have been able to achieve this, an overview of which I will present later, it has been a source of pride and honour for this nation and country, and it has been valuable for the honour of Islam and the Islamic Republic. Wherever we have been negligent towards this, we have lost out. In truth, I am stating that the Islamic cognitive concepts have a practical dimension, and they need to find their practical manifestation and acting upon them needs to become possible and widespread. This will not happen by itself and requires effort. Let me present two or three examples concerning this.

For example, let us take the recent issue of the Coronavirus. The concept of being charitable is a key concept within the collective of concepts in the Islamic value system. With a

---

58. 11/03/2021 – In a televised speech on the occasion of Eid al-Mab'ath.

bit of clarification in society, a movement was created in those days. A campaign to help the faithful, and this was a considerable act. The people could take the concept of being charitable from an authentic concept and an Islamic value to the implementation stage. You observed throughout the country how much work was done and how much value these youth, the people, various groups, governmental bodies and revolutionary institutions created. A movement was established, groups were made, and work was done. This is the attraction the concept of being charitable held, and it was able to affect society in such a manner.

Other important notions that Imam Khomeini made use of were the concepts of reliance upon Allah (Tawakkul), duty (Takleef), sacrifice (Eethaar), martyrdom (Shahadah) and Jihad. These were presented through Imam Khomeini by his presence, motivation, clarification and wishes, which were in sync with the divine will, and they entered the people's practical lives. As a result, for example, we were able to come out victorious in an 8-year war against our opposition. This great movement of the people on the battlefield was born out of our concepts. Imam Khomeini made these concepts prevalent among the masses and brought these concepts from the realm of theories into the practical arena. We had heard and spoken about these concepts in the Quran and the narrations; however, we had not seen them in the practical arena.

Another example, which in my opinion, is more critical than the examples mentioned, is the verse from the noble Quran: *"We did not send any messenger but to be obeyed by Allah's permission"*[59]. The sending of the Messengers (s) was so that they are obeyed. This obedience is unconditional, meaning it applies to every aspect of one's life. What is understood from this verse is that every individual's life, whether it is personal or societal affairs, has to be governed by religion. Some may restrict this to personal matters, for example, praying, fasting and other such acts; however, this is not the case. Firstly, this is understood due to the unconditional nature of this verse. Secondly, this is concluded from other verses, such as: *"How many a prophet there has been with whom a multitude of godly men fought."*[60] This killing with *rabbiyyun* is not an individual act but a societal and public act and an act of governance. This is one conclusion understood by this verse, and it is this meaning Imam Khomeini brought forward in the arena of action. He used the verse: *"Say, 'I give you just a single advice: that you rise up for Allah's sake, in pairs or on your own..."*[61] to understand this meaning. Not that this verse means to go and pray, but rather, it is to go and establish a government and an Islamic system. Imam Khomeini used this verse and created a movement in the year 1963. The thinkers, supporters, and students of Imam Khomeini and at the head,

---

59. Surah al-Nisa – Verse 64.
60. Surah Aal al-Imran – Verse 146.
61. Surah al-Saba – Verse 46.

Imam Khomeini himself, transfused this thought to the point that a revolution was created and became victorious. Then a system was formed from this revolution.

As you can see, Quranic and Islamic concepts can affect life in such a manner when they are brought into the realm of action. This is just one example of such a movement's miraculous effect and workings. How this movement takes place is a separate discussion in itself.[62]

What responsibility does a person have in this arena? This includes both men and women. In my opinion, the burden is heavy; it is a big responsibility. The most important duty is to propagate and clarify, *such as "deliver the messages of Allah and fear Him, and fear no one except Allah."*[63] This is one yardstick. Once you have understood the truth, it must be presented. No one expects you to speak against that which you have understood. The expectation is that you talk about what you have understood. Hard work must be put in to ensure what is understood is correct. This is because, at times of sedition, it is difficult to understand the arena and the different sides of the story. It is difficult to differentiate between the aggressor and the defender, the oppressed and the oppressor, and the enemy and the friend.

If the situation is such that a poet too can be deceived, lacking insight, this is beneath the status of an artistic and cultural individual. Therefore the truth must be understood,

---

62. 22/02/2021 – In a meeting with members of the Guardian Council.
63. Surah Al-Ahzab – Verse 39.

and then that truth must be propagated. You can not use political methods and the ways of politicians to travel in the world of culture; this goes against the status of culture.

In the world of culture, we must resolve issues, open up realities and untie the knots in our minds. This necessitates clarification; this was the duty the Prophets (a) carried out. Eloquence and articulation are also necessary for these explanations.

Eloquence in technical books has a meaning in accordance with the science of eloquence. However, this is just one definition of eloquence, not the primary and apparent meaning. When we say this poetry of Haafiz is eloquent, what are we saying this eloquence is? What we mean to say is that it is comprehensible. Eloquence means it is understandable, clear, and coherent. However, only say that which you understand. There is no expectation or right for someone to speak against what they understand. Effort must also be made to make sure whatever has been understood is accurate.[64]

Protecting the People

Do not see the schemes of the enemy as being far. Our negligence creates opportunities for our enemies. Imam Ali (a) taught us: "*If he sleeps, the enemy does not sleep.*"[65]. Our experience in the Islamic Republic in this arena has been full

---

64. 05/09/2009 – In a meeting with a gathering of poets.
65. Nahj al-Balagha – Letter 62.

of lessons. With the victory of the Islamic Revolution, the arrogant Western powers and America suddenly realised their negligence. Their governmental organisations, intelligence agencies, and command rooms started working to atone for this devastating defeat. Before the revolution, these were the same powers that had held the secular Iranian rulers by the throat for many years and dictated our country's political, economic, and cultural future. They were negligent towards the strength of the Islamic faith within society, and they remained uninformed about the capabilities of the Basij and the guidance of Islam and the Quran.

We have seen numerous conspiracies and schemes from them over 35 years. Two factors have reduced their plans to nothing, firstly, remaining steadfast upon the principles of Islam and secondly, the people being present in the arena. The first factor is ensured by sincere faith in the divine promises, and sincere efforts and truthful clarification ensure the second factor. These two factors are the key to victory everywhere.

A nation that believes in the honesty of its leaders will fill the arena with its blessed presence. Wherever a nation enters the arena with a strong will, no power could inflict a defeat upon them. This successful experience is possible for all nations with which, through their presence, they have attained the Islamic Awakening.[66]

---

66. 29/04/2013 - In the International Scholars and Islmic Awakening conference.

Another critical issue is the protection of the support of the people. They should not be cut off from the people. The people have expectations, and they have needs. The real power also belongs to the people. Wherever the people united, their hearts became one, and they were able to synchronise their direction with the country's leaders. In such a situation, America and those much more significant than America can not make any mistake against us. The people need to be protected and preserved. This is among your responsibilities—the responsibility of the thinkers, writers, poets and religious scholars. The scholars of religion are more effective than anyone else and therefore have a heavier responsibility upon their shoulders. They have to clarify for the people, make apparent what it is they desire, and where they are on this journey. They must clarify the obstacles and who the enemy is and preserve people with insight and awareness. It is in such a situation that no harm will be felt.[67]

Resolving Issues

Foreign hands have been active in enforcing difficulties, trials and tribulations upon the Muslims and increasing the intensity of their calamities. However, suppose the collective of thinkers, scholars and those working in culture and arts, with the hearts and minds of the Muslims, show courage,

---

67. 11/12/2012 - In a meeting with the participants of the Internanionl Professors of the Islamic World and the Islmic Awakening conference.

understanding of the time and work correctly on the skill of clarification. In that case, whilst relying upon the will and capabilities of the people, they can alleviate the difficulties and problems faced.[68]

The Harm of Not Carrying Out Clarification

Two factors affect the minds of the youth more than any other. The first is the various types of propaganda of the enemy. Propaganda that makes the youth apathetic and lethargic concerning the sacred realities of Islam, the realities which are understood to be established in the revolution and the understood fundamental foundations and pillars of belief.

The second factor is the lack of clarification and proper defence of these realities and principles. I estimate that the effect of this second factor is not less than the first factor. This is because, in the Islamic Republic, there is less open and apparent propagation against Islam; the Islamic principles, the Islamic sources, and the Islamic sciences and the grounds for this are not readily available. Therefore the propagation of the enemy only has a superficial effect. However, regarding the second factor, there is no restriction or limit.

If we do not propagate, present the realities, and provide a robust defence and clarification of Islamic understandings, the effect of this lack of defence, clarification, and correct explanation is not limited and can affect everyone. [These

---

68. 11/12/1997 - In a meeting with figures of the cultural, religious and academic fields of the Islamic world.

include the knowledge of] Tawhid, divine governance, the necessity of servitude to God, and submitting to divine law.[69]

Historical Examples of Clarification

The Effect of Clarification Carried Out by Imam Khomeini

God Almighty blessed this nation with a divine gift in the shape of the leadership of Imam Khomeini. The Honourable Imam Khomeini created awareness in the nation, gave them insight, and took on tribulations, imprisonment and exile, yet, he did not give up. Gradually this awareness and insight took over to the point that in 78'/79', it became a popular movement among the Iranian nation. The objective of this movement was not just targeting the apparatus of the monarchy system; it was also America. The nation understood and knew that the hand behind the atrocities inflicted on them in their country was America. In 1963, Imam Khomeini, at the beginning of the Islamic movement, stated, "The President of America is the most hated individual currently in Iran."[70]. He made the people realise and clarified for them that whatever exists, exists because of America. America is behind all of the mischief.

Wherever a nation moves, makes a stand, remains steadfast and shows resistance, victory will be guaranteed. This is the case everywhere. The problem in resistance work that leads

---

69. 16/01/1991 - In a meeting with Friday prayer leaders from across the country.
70. Sahifa -e- Imam – Vol.1, P 42.

to defeat can either be because a nation does not have the resolve to remain standing or they do not have leaders who can manage them correctly. In these recent years, we have seen places in which nations have moved, shown will and determination and have reached specific results. However, they did not have leaders that could correctly manage them, specify objectives, or present a path to their destination. Therefore they suffered a defeat. You have experienced this in the last few years; I do not wish to name any country.

The nation of Iran walked on this path correctly, and they carried out their movement properly. They had a powerful, aware and determined leader who relied upon God and divine promises such as: *"If you help Allah, He will help you"*[71] This led to this nation attaining victory. The enforced government connected to the CIA; the Pahlavi family, and the humiliating monarchy were destroyed and left Iran. The system of monarchy is a source of humiliation for any country, according to logical humanitarian calculations. The people became in charge of their own will.[72]

The Jihad of Clarification Undertaken by the Seminarians and Scholars Against the Pahlavi Regime

We are grateful for the fight carried out by the university students. We appreciate the value they brought accompanying the revolution. However, as I stated, if we take out the struggle fought by the scholars from the diary

---
71. Surah Muhammad – Verse 7
72. 03/11/2015 - In a meeting with teachers and university students.

and evaluation of the revolution, the revolution would have been limited to specific universities throughout the country. There would have been a battle, then there would have been a response, and then it would have finished. However, the seminary was not like this.

The Jihad on the seminary was all-encompassing. Almost all of the seminarians, at least most of them, engaged in the struggle carried out by the scholars, when the seminary of Qum entered the arena, everyone joined the battle. This was one feature.

The second feature was the effect of the seminary of Qum. The seminary of Qum consists of a collective, and this collective has the potential to affect society. A part of this collective is the *Marjaiyyah*; for example, a grand jurist such as Imam Khomeini or one or two others recognised as the most knowledgeable at the beginning of the revolution. However, afterwards, Imam Khomeini alone bore this responsibility upon his shoulders. It was these grand jurists that, through the propagation of the religion, issuing religious edicts and, as a sacred duty, had their words spread to the people; this was the role of the *marjaiyyah*. Alongside them were the seminarians. The movement would not have been as widespread if the seminarians did not exist. The seminarians gather from various places, cities and areas around the country, then, some during holidays and some during term-time, scatter and through the medium of pulpits, presentations, weekly sessions, and religious gatherings disseminate ideas to the level of the people. This is very important. When a seminarian goes to a village, town or city and decides to propagate, explain and clarify a specific thought, there is a massive difference between them and a university student doing the same. During the first phase, the seminarians were able to spread the message of the grand jurists and then, later, the statements of Imam Khomeini, both from Qum and Najaf. The seminarians could permeate these ideas into the hearts of the people in different parts of the country.

In the first year of the revolution, in the first few months after its victory, it was the death anniversary of the Late Agha Mustafa, the son of our dear honourable Imam Khomeini. A remembrance was held in Qum, and they asked me if I could speak. I went there, and Imam Khomeini was also inside Al A'dham Mosque. I gave a talk there and mentioned this verse: "And your Lord inspired the bee [saying]: *"Make your home in the mountains and on the trees and the trellises that they erect. Then eat from every [kind of] fruit and follow meekly the ways of your Lord."*[73]. I addressed Imam Khomeini and stated, 'These honey bees are the seminary students who sat down, tasted the honey, meaning your words, then dispersed all over the country and poured this honey into the cups of the people. Wherever it was necessary, they also used their stingers; they stung, too!'. The seminarians and the Seminary of Qum did this. Suppose the seminary of Qum did not exist. For example,

---
73. Surah al-Nahl – Verse 68 and 69.

if the noble Imam Khomeini had been in Tehran or started his movement in a place which did not have a seminary, we can not be sure the movement would have been successful. Because this movement was in Qum, it could reach such success and turn into a revolution.

I do not remember whether I heard this or someone else told me that Imam Khomeini mentioned this in one of his speeches. Imam Khomeini said, "When we were in Paris, they came and said that in a certain village, one of the villages of Khomein, the people carried out a demonstration. In that demonstration, the village scholar, an elderly man, walked at the front of the procession, and the people chanted their slogans. These were the same slogans that were being given in Tehran.". Imam Khomeini continued, "When I heard this, I said, this revolution is going to be successful.".[74]

A revolution that could permeate to the extent that it could reach this particular village, a village Imam Khomeini knew about, and move even the people from there, meant this was a movement bound to be victorious. This meant the whole nation and every individual was entering the arena. This led to defeat, submission and taking out an experienced regime that relied upon the powers on the top stage in the world. We did not use guns or cannons here. The revolution in Iran did not progress through cannons, guns, coup d'etats or military forces. It progressed through the presence of the people. Winning hearts over is good and effective;

---

74. Sahifa -e- Imam – Vol. 9 P 408.

however, if those hearts only beat in the houses and do not come out, they will have no real effect. When these hearts can create movement in the body and bring it out into the streets, you get the demonstrations that turn into a great movement. Here, a monarchist regime with such a history, with the support of America and others, which also included the Communist countries who were their competition in supporting Shah, can be defeated by the people.

Who brought the people out onto the street? You brought them; it was the seminarians. Imam Khomeini was the leader; this phenomenon would not have happened if he did not exist. However, what was the tool used by Imam Khomeini? The Islamic seminaries were the means that realised, implemented and executed the thoughts, wishes and intentions of Imam Khomeini. This is the relationship between the Islamic seminaries and the revolution. It is correct when we say that all segments of society were involved in the revolution, and this is true. For example, concerning those groups at the forefront, we say it was the university students. There is no doubt about this. However, another connecting group was needed for the students to enter the arena and be at the forefront. This connecting chain was the Islamic seminary in Qum and other Islamic seminaries.

You should be attentive that this great revolution, this astonishing phenomenon and this event that shook the world, goes back to this connecting chain; the Islamic seminary of Qum. This is the relationship of the seminary of Qum to the revolution.[75]

Whatever flows onto the plain of the hearts and minds of the people from this spiritual source grows and develops. We have seen examples of this throughout our lives, and one of the examples of this is the revolution. The most important pillar and factor leading to this great revolution was propagation, regardless of what propaganda the materialistic analyst spread. What we saw and experienced was this, and this is what can ensure any lofty objective.[76]

Before the revolution, some scholars interacted with university students, including this humble servant. This relation was not organisational, institutional, or regarding issues of the struggle. This relationship was intellectual and for clarification. This meant heaving gatherings in which the students participated, or at times, we would participate in meetings organised by the students. In those days, I had a sitting in Mashad that would take place between Maghrib and Isha. I would stand in front of a board and give a presentation that would last twenty to thirty minutes. The youth would make up ninety per cent of the audience. Most of those youth were either in university or High School. One night, Shaheed Bahonar was in Mashad and came with me to our mosque. When he saw the life in the mosque, he was taken

---

75. 15/04/2015 - In a meeting with representatives from the Islamic Seminary of Qum.
76. 24/12/1997 - In a meeting with a gathering of scholars.

aback. Agha Bahonar had relations with youth and university organisations in Tehran. He said in his whole life he had not seen so many youth and university students present in one mosque. How many youths do you suppose were in our mosque? At most, there would have been three hundred and forty or fifty attendees. Just the presence of this number of students shocked and amazed the likes of Agha Bahonar, who had been through university himself and knew of the environment that existed at universities. He would say in his amazement, "Two hundred university students gather in one place, and one scholar speaks to them?!".[77]

Sermons in Friday prayers in the 1980s

I will never forget the middle of the year 1981, when the enemies of the anti-revolutionary movements and the arrogant powers, committed the heinous crime of martyring 72 individuals, including the Prime Minister and the President, whilst I was in the hospital. I think the Friday prayer sermon in Tehran during those days bore the heaviest responsibility for the revolution. Light would spread throughout the country every week from this Friday prayer institution. Realities were explained to the people; they understood what took place in this country and what the enemy was doing. This is what free pulpits are like.[78]

---

77. 11/07/2010 - In a meeting with members of the Leaders representative bodies in universities.
78. In a meeting with representatives from the 4th Revolutionary Council Assembly.

Exemplars of Clarification

The Holy Prophets (s)

The Commander of the Faithful (a) speaks about the proclamation of the Messengers (s) in Nahj al-Balagha[79] in a manner that requires us to contemplate. He states: *"Then Allah sent His Messengers and series of His Prophets towards them to get them to fulfil the pledges."* The Messengers (s) compel mankind to uphold the innate oath set inside humanity. God Almighty wishes for mankind to be free, live a just life, a good life and not to worship other than Allah. [Nahj al-Balagha continued:]*"to recall to them His bounties."* They remind mankind of the blessings they have forgotten. We are negligent towards the blessings of existence, health, intelligence and creativity that Allah has set inside of mankind. The Prophets (s) remind mankind of these blessings. [Nahj al-Balagha continued: *"to exhort them by preaching."* The Prophets (s) complete the divine argument upon mankind, get the truth to their ears and make apparent the realities for them. Clarification and explanation are among the essential duties of the Messengers (s). The enemies of the Prophets (s) make use of ignorance, covering things up and hypocrisy. [Nahj al-Balagha continued:] *"to unveil before them the hidden virtues of wisdom."*

The Prophets (s) open up the treasures of intellect for mankind. They came to compel mankind to contemplate,

---
79. Nahj al-Balagha – Sermon 1

think and ponder. Understand how lofty these objectives are. These are the objectives of the proclamation of the Prophets (s). Today, look how needy mankind is. When the disclosure of the treasures of the intellect within people occurs, [Nahj al-Balagha continued:] *"and show them the signs of His Omnipotence"*, the intellect guides humanity towards Tawheed and the divine signs. The signs of the power of Allah are placed in front of their eyes. An intellect that has not been guided and not received the guidance of the Messengers (s) can not perceive realities the way they are. The Messengers (s) guides mankind to go on this challenging journey with the ability that Allah has placed within them. The realities of this world are made apparent to them. The power of the intellect and being intellectual is essential; however, this has to be accompanied by divine guidance and holding firm to Allah.[80]

The Holy Messenger (s)

An essential duty of the Messenger of God (a) was inviting people to the truth and then to strive in the path of this invitation. In the face of the dark times the Holy Messenger (s) found himself in, he was not phased. He was not phased, whether when he found himself alone in Makkah or when he stood against the arrogant heads of the Arabs, the leaders of the Quraysh tribe with their evil ethics and strong hands.

---

80. 03/05/2016 - In a meeting with the Officials and Ambassadors of Islamic Countries.

The Holy Messenger (s) was not phased, and he was not afraid when the general populous did not take heed of his knowledge. He spoke the truth, repeated it, clarified it and made it apparent. He remained steadfast in the face of insults and took on the trials and difficulties of the world upon himself until a sizeable number became Muslim. He was never afraid when he had become the head of this government and power was in his hands. Even then, various oppositions and enemies stood against him. On one side were the armed Arab tribes, savage groups of people scattered around the desserts of Arabia and Yamamah that should have been reformed by accepting the invitation of Islam but resisted. On the other side stood the two great kingdoms of the world, the two superpowers of that time, the Empires of Persia and Rome. The Prophet (s) wrote them letters, held dialogue, mobilised armies against them, took on difficulties, and fell into economic encirclements to the extent that the people of Medina sometimes could not find bread to eat for two or three days.

Threats had surrounded the Prophet (s) from all sides. Some people would get worried, some would shake, some would disparage him, and some would encourage the Prophet (s) to compromise and cooperate. However, even for a moment, the Prophet (s) did not become lethargic; with strength, he carried the Islamic society forward until they reached the peak of honour and power. It was this same system and society, through the blessings of the steadfastness of the Prophet (s) in the field of propagation and war, transformed into the world's strongest society.[81]

The Commander of the Faithful (a)

The Commander of the Faithful (a) has three categories of virtues. Spiritual virtues that under no circumstance can be compared to anything else. Another category of virtues would be the superior human characteristics he held. These virtues attract Muslims, non-Muslims, Christians, non-Christians, religious and the irreligious alike. The third category of virtues pertains to his governing characteristics that lead to the Imamate issue. The virtues of his governance include justice, fairness, impartiality, clarification etc. He presented the realities for the people. Observe the sermons of Nahjul Balagha; many are clarifications for the people, of realities that occurred in those societies. Whether it be his sermons or letters, his letters were mainly written for those with whom he had an issue. Some letters were for his enemies, such as Muawiyah and his likes. Some, for his appointees, with whom he had a problem. Some of them were advice, instructions and commands, for example, the letter for Maalik al-Ashtar. In all of these letters, the Imam (a) would clarify and present the realities for the people. This was one of the branches of the work of the Commander of the Faithful (a).[82]

---

81. 27/09/1991 - Friday prayers sermon.
82. 20/09/2016 - In a meeting with the people on the occasion of Eid al-Ghadir.

The Infallible Imams (a)

These and hundreds of other meaningful, thought-provoking, and apparently, not connected and even contradicting incidents in the life of Imam Musa ibn Jafar (a) begin to make sense when we see their link to the overall continuous movement of this great individual. A movement which starts from his Imamate and ends with his martyrdom. This campaign is the same path of Jihad the Imams (a) carried out throughout their 250 years in various ways. Their objective, firstly, was the clarification of pure Islam, the correct explanation of the Quran and the presentation of a clear picture of Islamic understanding. Secondly, it was to clarify the issue of Imamate and political governance in an Islamic society. Thirdly, their objective was to put in the effort required to establish and actualise a society pursued by the Holy Messenger (s) and all of the Prophets (s). This was the establishment of justice, and fairness, removing other than Allah from the arena of governance and handing over the governing of affairs to the representatives of Allah and His pious servants.[83]

The Messengers of Karbala

Suppose individuals remaining after Ashura and the martyrdom of Imam Husain ibn Ali (a), did not work to protect the remembrance and effect of that martyrdom. In that case, the later generations would not be able to benefit

---

83. Message to the 3rd Imam al-Ridha (a) International Conference.

much from the sacrifices that were made. It is true that Allah keeps the martyrs alive in this world and that the martyrs remain in history and the remembrance of the people; however, this is carried out through the natural tools Allah has placed in our hands, and it is through our will. It is us that can keep alive the remembrance of the martyrs, the stories of martyrdom, and the philosophy of martyrdom by making the correct decisions. Suppose Lady Zainab (s) and Imam Sajjad (a) had not struggled, not spoken, and not clarified the reality of what had happened. Suppose they had not explained the true philosophy of Ashura and the objective of Imam Hussain ibn Ali (a) throughout their lives, from the afternoon of Ashura in Karbala to Kufa, then Damascus, and then when they reached Medina. In that case, the incident of Ashura would not have remained alive and ablaze till today.

Why is it that Imam Jafar al-Sadiq (a) has stated, according to one narration, "Whoever recites one line of poetry regarding the incident of Ashura, and someone cries as a result of the one line, Allah has made heaven obligatory upon them"[84] Why? Because all propaganda institutions were equipped to keep Ashura and the matters regarding the Ahl al-Bayt (a) in the dark. They did not want to allow the people to understand what had happened and what the issue was. This is what propaganda is like. In those days, just like today, the oppressive and unjust powers made maximum use of false, provocative wicked propaganda. In such a situation,

---

84. Amali al-Saduq – P 141

how can an event in one corner of the Islamic world, in the desert, remain today with such greatness and life? Indeed, it should have been forgotten. What kept this alive were those who remained from the camp of Imam Hussain ibn Ali (a). The true owners and flag bearers of the incident. The difficulty of the struggle of Lady Zainab (s) and Imam Sajjad (a) was on par with the struggle of Imam Hussain (a) with all of the obstacles he had to face. The arena was not the military arena but the cultural battlefield and the theatre of propagation. We must be attentive to these points. The lesson that Arbaeen gives us is this: The remembrance of the truth and martyrdom must be kept alive in the face of the propaganda storm whipped up by the enemy.[85]

These forty days between Ashura and Arbaeen are one of the most critical passages in Islamic history. The day of Ashura is at the peak of importance, and these forty days between Ashura and Arbaeen, hold the same weight as the day of Ashura. Suppose the day of Ashura represents the peak of combat alongside sacrifice, the sacrifice of life, kinfolk, children and friends; these forty days are the peak of striving alongside clarification, revelations and explanations. If these forty days did not exist, if the great movement of Lady Zainab al-Kubra (s), Umm al-Kulthum or Imam Sajjad (a) did not exist, then it is possible that the message would reach us today? It was the outstanding steadfastness of the family of the Messenger (s) with the leadership of Lady Zainab (s)

---

85. 20/09/1989 - In a meeting with the people.

and Imam Sajjad (a) that allowed the incident of Karbala to remain alive. This movement was the complete clarification of that sacrifice.[86]

Ammar ibn Yassir

In the Battle of Siffin, the Commander of the Faithful (a) did not stand in the face of disbelievers. The front opposing the Commander of the Faithful (a) in Siffin were those who prayed, and recited the Quran, and their appearance was good. This made it very difficult. Who must clarify the position in such a scenario and present the truth to the people? Some will suffer in doubt in such a situation. When a person reads the history of the Battle of Siffin, the heart begins to shake. In this significant mobilisation carried out by the Commander of Faithful (a) against Muawiyah, some doubted. This happened repeatedly, and these issues carried on for months. You would receive news that a person has doubts on a particular front. They had started to ask, 'Why are we fighting, and what benefit does it have?'. This is where the companions of the Commander of the Faithful (a), his genuine, pure and sincere companions that had been with him since the beginning of Islam and never separated from him, would come forward. One example is Ammar ibn Yassir, who would take care of the essential duties. There is an example of when in one of the instances, Ammar presented his reasoning. These are reasons which every person should

---

86. 27/09/2021 - At the end of the commemoration of Arba'een.

have at hand to be able to offer when needed. He saw that a group were beginning to doubt, so he went where they were and gave a speech.

He stated in his speech, "This flag you see flying in the ranks of the opposing front is the same flag I saw flying in opposition to the Messenger of God (s) in the Battle of Uhud and Badr. It is the flag of Bani Umayyah, and the same people stand underneath it today that stood underneath it then; Muawiyyah and Amr ibn al-Aas. I saw this with my own eyes. On this side is the Commander of the Faithful (a), and the same flag he has today was there in the Battle of Badr and Uhud, the flag of Bani Hashim, and the same people stand underneath it today. Ali ibn Abi Talib and his friend stood underneath this flag those days, too.".

Is there a better sign than this? Look how clear the sign is. The flag is the same as the Battle of Uhud; the people are the same, opposing each other on one battlefield. The difference is that in those days, they would accept and be proud of being among the disbelievers, and today they are under the same flags claiming to be Muslims, supporting the Quran and the Holy Messenger (a). It is the same people and the same flags. This is insight. When we repeatedly stress the need for insight, this is what we mean.[87]

In this, the greatness of Ammar ibn Yassir's likes can be seen. The greatness of the genuine companions of the

---

[87] 09/01/2010 - In a meeting with the people of Qum on the anniversary of the stand of 19th Dey.

Commander of the Faithful (a) lies in the fact that they did not make a mistake, no matter the situation they were in. They did not get lost in the battle. I observed this greatness repeatedly in the Battle of Siffin; however, it is not limited to the Battle of Siffin. In many places, when the faithful began to doubt and begin to think incorrectly, Ammar ibn Yassir was the one who would go and remove the doubt from their minds. A person sees the existence of this incredible and effective voice in different instances concerning the Commander of the Faithful (a).

The battle of Siffin lasted for months. It was a strange battle. The people saw those in the opposing ranks praying, worshipping and reciting the Quran. They even lifted the Quran at the end of their spears. It takes a lot of courage to unsheathe your sword against such people who pray. Imam Jafar al-Sadiq (a) states in a narration that if the Commander of the Faithful (a) had not fought the People of the Qibla, we would not have understood our responsibility towards the People of the Qibla who were evil and unjust.[88] It was Imam Ali ibn Abi Talib (a) that opened these doors for us and showed everyone what their responsibility is. When our soldiers entered some of the aggressors' trenches, they would find *Muhr* and prayer beads! This was like those who fought against the Commander of the Faithful (a) and prayed. As a result, this would create doubt in some people. The one who would go to deal with these doubts would be

---

88. Tahdheeb al-Ahkam – Vol.6 P 145.

Ammar ibn Yassir. This is intelligence and sharpness, and having someone like Ammar is necessary. If a person does not understand the spirit of his actions and worship, which is attentiveness towards God, and if a person does not try to bring themselves closer to the worship of God in all of their obligations, then his efforts remain superficial. Superficial actions and faith are constantly under threat, which we have seen throughout Islamic history.[89]

Necessity of Scholars Defending Religious Governance

What are the rules of our Islamic system based upon currently? Are they not on the foundations of religion? So what is the duty of the Guardian Council? The judiciary's rules and the country's laws are based upon Sharia. You have such governance come into existence, and now you gather your robe, leave and say you have nothing to do with these issues? How have you got nothing to do with this? This is the same as those holier-than-thou individuals at the time of the Commander of the Faithful (a) that stated their doubts about the battle. Imam Ali (a) asked, "Doubts? What doubts?".

They said, " They are our Muslim brothers, send us to the frontiers, so we defend there".

Imam Ali (a) responded, "Go; we do not need you here.".

The Commander of the Faithful (a) indeed had no use for such individuals; for example, they say this was Rabee' ibn

---

89. 26/04/1990 – In a meeting with the people on the 30th of the Holy Month of Ramadhan.

Khatheem. Abdullah ibn Mas'ud's companions split away from the Commander of the Faithful (a) due to their misguided views. Today, you and I do not like them. Why do you send greetings to Ammar, however, not to another companion who was Ammar's friend in Mekkah and, alongside him, beaten up there too? This is because Ammar did not make a mistake at a sensitive time, and he understood; however, his friend made a mistake. Understand that the path of Ammar is known as the straight path. In my opinion, Ammar has still not been recognised. Even we do not understand Ammar properly. Ammar was a decisive divine argument. When I observed the life of the Commander of the Faithful (a), I could see that there was no one like Ammar ibn Yassir. From the companions of the Messenger of Allah (s), no one played a role like that of Ammar. Many were no long alive but Ammar's blessed life continued. Whenever a problem arose for the Commander of the Faithful (a) concerning doubts in people's minds, this man's tongue acted like a sharp sword and resolved the issue. This was the case at the beginning of the Imam's caliphate, during the Battles of Jamal and Siffin, and it remained the case until his martyrdom in Siffin.

One must be intelligent like Ammar and understand their duty. It can not be said, 'It has nothing to do with me!'. Today, every scholar, everyone with a turban on their head, by the token of wearing this clothing, has a responsibility to defend the Islamic government and the governance of the Quran. Every person must do this in any way they can. One may grab their sword and head to the battlefield, have an eloquent tongue and sit on the pulpit, or take up a role in the judiciary and carry out their duties. One may not be able to take on any of these roles, which is fine, but one can carry out the responsibility in the mosque or as a prayer leader. Everyone must know that this scholar sees themselves as a servant of this revolution. This is a source of honour. Serving this revolution is a source of pride. We could not have even dreamt that such an opportunity would arise for us and we would be able to serve the religion in such a way.[90]

Imam Khomeini

This is the difference between our Imam Khomeini and other reformers in Islamic History. Imam Khomeini entered the arena into the midst of the battlefield; he was with the people, spoke to the people, clarified his principles for them, and brought them towards an optimistic and enlightened faith, just like his own faith. Then he got the faith and motivation of the people, alongside Islam's teachings, and ended the battle in the interest of the front of truth. Others could not traverse this difficult path; however, Imam Khomeini was able. The nation of Iran started to believe in these principles; they became faithful and carried out their struggle in the path of that faith. This resulted in the Islamic system attaining victory and gaining strength day-by-day, despite all the

---

90. 21/08/1991 – In a meeting with a group of scholars from the province of Lorestan.

animosities and hostilities. Secondly, it did not restrict the vision of actualising the revival of Islam and the rescue of the Islamic nation from the clutches of the arrogant powers within the boundaries of this country.[91]

Ayatullah Shaheed Madani

The Late Shaheed Madani is an exemplary example of an active scholar who possessed various dimensions. He was indeed a clear example of a complete scholar. Firstly, he was a heavyweight intellectual, a scholar, a jurist, etc. Secondly, he was an eloquent scholar. We have in one of our narrations: "... an eloquent scholar who acts upon his knowledge..."[92]. He was known as a person of eloquence and articulation among different groups in society. If his audience were the youth, he could make a complete connection with them. I went to Tabriz in the middle of his leadership of the Friday prayers. I saw the warmth between himself and the twenty year olds. It was as if they were speaking to their father or older brother. His weighty academic aura was not tangible in his relationship with the youth. He had a real connection with them; this is how he was with the youth.

He was like this with different groups of society and among the general public too. We went to Susangard in the days it had been freed. This is before it had been captured again and then freed again. I was wearing my military uniform

---
91. 04/06/2003 – In the commemoration for the 14th anniversary of the passing away of Imam Khomeini.
92. Al Amaali – P 344.

in Ahwaz and wished to go to Susangard. In those days, I realized Agha Madani was in Ahwaz. He had come from Tehran and then came to meet us. He asked, "Where are you going?".

"We are going to Susangard." I replied.

"I wish to come with you, too." He requested.

We took him with us and went to Susangard, prayed noon prayers and then I spoke to the people for a while. Naturally, I spoke in Persian, and I could not be eloquent in articulating Arabic, especially not in the local dialect and accent of the people. He stated that he would also speak to the people. He did not wait as the people in the mosque began to leave after I spoke. He went amid the people, and suddenly, we saw that he had gathered a large group of men and women around him, and he was speaking to them in Arabic in their dialect. The words of Agha Madani created this much engagement, excitement and passion in people.

This was the case in his relationship with the scholarly segment of society too. In Qum, we organized the first seminar for all Friday prayer leaders across the country. All the great scholars, including those that would become martyred, were present, whether Shia or Sunni. A few scholars from among them gave speeches. Agha Madani stood up in the corner and started giving a talk. His tears were rolling down his blessed beard as he spoke. We have in our narrations that when the Messenger (s) would supplicate, tears would drip down like water trickling out of a water spout. I saw this on the face of

Agha Madani. He had two streams of tears flowing down his face. I will never forget this scene. That day he had changed the state of the whole gathering; this is what he was like.

When he would sit with the intellectuals, he would attract them. When he would sit with the layman, he would attract them. When he would sit with the seminarians, he would attract them. He was an eloquent and illuminating scholar. He could effortlessly transfer the treasures inside him, his spirit and his pure and enlightened heart that was bright with the light of understanding, to his audience. This was another virtue that existed inside him.[93]

The Martyrs Muttaheri and Beheshti

At every age, a contribution is required from the faithful and the sincere. All of it is striving in the way of Allah. The threat of losing your interests or even your life exists for all. At times this sacrifice may be at war. Or, it could be in the Islamic seminar; it could be the First Martyr or the Second Martyr. It could be in the political arena, in the arena of social advancement, in a great revolution like this divine revolution, and at times it could be due to the danger that exists in presenting religious truths, which happened to the likes of Shaheed Muttaheri and Shaheed Beheshti. Every age has its own need for sacrifice. [94]

---

93. 03/09/2001 – In a meeting with the members of the council for the commemoration of Martyr Ayatullah Madani.
94. 12/04/1991 – In a meeting with a group of scholars.

Chapter 2
The Requirements

- *Compiler's notes*
Policies and principles need to be enacted to fulfil the mission of the jihad of clarification. This will aid in attaining the objective and destination of this struggle in the best of manners. The cases mentioned in this chapter have been gathered from the statements of the Supreme Leader of the Revolution. However, some of these cases may change in priority at certain times. It is also possible that other requirements may be necessary for different instances; however, the researcher of this book was unable to extrapolate them.

Align with the Revolution

A point to consider in any social operation is that a faithful mujahid has to act upon the orders of the Supreme Leader of the Revolution in a manner that aids the completion of the overall plan of the revolutionary movement. Therefore, in the jihad of clarification, a connection must be made with the Leader's statements in any work that looks to understand the matters of importance of the time.

It needs to be a popular, logical and disciplined movement. When we say disciplined, it means the movement can not be turbulent, chaotic etc. Sometimes popular movements are like this but they have no value. A movement requires a few things to be correct, organised, and logical.

Firstly, there should be unity of understanding regarding the arena. Those carrying out this movement, those that are the axis of the movement or, at the very least, those who are motivating it, must understand the arena accurately. They must understand the participating group in this combat. Today you wish to carry out a movement in your nation, the Islamic Republic. You must understand what position the Islamic Republic finds itself in today, who stands in its opposition, what opportunities it has, what the threats are, who the enemies are and who the friends are. This must be recognised and known.

Another necessary element for this movement is that it must have a specified trajectory. A logical and acceptable trajectory that we can advise and explain to the people's movement of the Iranian nation. This trajectory is working towards an Islamic society or an Islamic civilisation. We wish to move towards the establishment of an Islamic society. This popular movement must get us to this point and, ultimately, towards an advanced Islamic civilisation. This is the second element.

The third element this movement requires is that it needs to have a hopeful component to it. A silver lining needs to exist. If this optimistic and bright component does not exist in any movement, that movement will not progress. Fortunately, this component is very tangible for our nation, society and people. This hopeful component is the national capacity we have recognised that exists here. Today, even you, the youth, have understood the national capacity. The nation of Iran has proven that it can carry out huge tasks well and carry out heavy responsibilities. The nation of Iran was able to start a revolution and establish an Islamic Republic; these are like miracles. Establishing the Islamic Republic in a capitalist and communist bipolar world is like a miracle. Indeed it is a miracle like Bani Israel traversing the river or the staff of Musa (a). The nation of Iran managed to carry this out; this is a sign of the existence of a vital capacity. Thereafter, it has been able to preserve it [the Revolution].

There are many other hopeful points. Another optimistic point is the exhaustion of the opposing camp. I say this with certainty. However, some instantly try to explain, deny and justify otherwise; however, I say this with absolute confidence, and I can prove it too, but now is not the right time. Currently, Western civilisation is in a state of degeneration, meaning it is in a state of decline. *"on the brink of a collapsing bank which collapses with him into the fire of hell?"*[95]. It is on the brink of destruction; this is how it is. That being said, societal events and changes happen gradually; they are not immediately felt. Even Western thinkers have felt the same and stated it. This is another point of hope for us. The Western and materialistic civilisation stands against us and is heading towards collapse.

---

95. Surah al-Tawbah – Verse 109.

Alongside this, we have the unbreakable promise of Allah: *"If you help Allah, He will help you."*[96]. *"and who is truer in speech than Allah?"*[97] Who is more truthful in speech than Allah? Who has a promise more certain than a promise of Allah? If you help Allah, meaning if you head towards an Islamic civilisation, society and actualisation of the religion of Allah, then Allah will help you—another point of hope. So the third element that exists is the component of hope.[98]

If we keep the bigger picture of the Revolution and the event of the creation of the Islamic Republic in mind, partial views about them will not misguide us. Sometimes a partial viewpoint and not seeing the continuous journey, from the beginning to the end, misguides a person. A person may even lose the way and forget the objective. We are not saying you should not have a detailed look at the specifics. We do not deny the importance of keeping an eye on the specifics, such as planning details. Planning and observing the various and different parts are having a partial view. We are saying you should not let this focus on the parts, sections, and dimensions make you negligent of the whole you are trying to achieve. Observing the whole is very informative for us.[99]

Leadership provides a solution for those problems that have none. This is regardless of which Iranian government

---

96. Surah Muhammad – Verse 7.
97. Surah al-Nisa – Verse 122.
98. 22/05/2019 – In a meeting with a group of university students.
99. 03/05/2008 – In a meeting with university professors and students from Shiraz.

or which part of the government it is. Pay attention to this. Wherever the enemy's propaganda makes the people pessimistic about the government, the role of the Leader here is to clarify the reality for the people and expose the enemy's conspiracies. Have you not seen over the last few years what they have done with the government, with the politicians and those in places of responsibility, and how they have tried to propagate lies and use various tricks so that the people feel hopeless?

Wherever they try to create hopelessness within the people, leadership comes and gives hope. Wherever they try to make an international political conspiracy against the nation of Iran, the leadership takes a step forward. It places the entirety of the Revolution in the face of the conspiracy. Wherever they try to create differences between the different sections of society, it is the leadership that comes and becomes a source of unity and an obstacle to disunity.

When they have tried to reduce participation in the election booths and make the people feel hopeless about giving a vote, the leadership has become an example for the people and has stated that participation in the elections is a duty. In the places the people have trust, they enter and produce an epic result. When it comes to expressing views on the issues of the Revolution, the eyes of the people are looking towards the leadership.

At the time of Imam Khomeini, we experienced this repeatedly. By the grace of Allah, the enemies fell face-first to the ground every time. After the passing of Imam Khomeini, with the people's aid, will, and cooperation, tens of times, the strong attachment between the people and the leadership has been able to land a solid punch on the faces of the enemy. Therefore, it is natural for them not to get along with the leadership and have deep-rooted hatred; this is not unusual. However, it needs to be a powerful leadership. Suppose the leadership is lethargic and absent, is unaware of the situation anywhere, and has a mind that can be changed easily and be taken towards making mistakes effortlessly. In that case, such weak leadership does not have that much importance. However, suppose there is to be a strong leadership that Islam asks for, the people want, the revolution demands, and the constitution legislates. In this case, they will show their opposition to such leadership. They have a right to be opposed. I am not surprised that they have targeted the leadership.[100]

One of the jihads is the intellectual jihad. The enemy may make us negligent, misguide our thoughts and force us to make errors and mistakes. Anyone who puts effort in the path of clarification for the people and becomes an obstacle to misguidance and misunderstandings in the face of the enemy's actions has carried out jihad. That too, is a jihad that is considered essential today. From this angle, praise

---

[100]. 26/11/1997 – In a meeting with the Basij on the occasion of 'The Basij Week'.

Allah, our country is the centre of jihad today, and regarding this, we have no worries.

From this viewpoint, most of my burden is to observe where the embers of jihad are dying out and with the help of Allah, I do not let them. I follow where mistakes are being made and try to stop them. This is a fundamental responsibility of this humble servant. I am not worried about the existence of jihad in the current situation of our country. You must know this! There is an eloquent point in the Quran that forces us to contemplate. The Quran explains we should observe and learn from the history that has passed.[101] Suppose today we are not able to understand the situation. In that case, it is possible fifty years later, ten years later, or even five years later, the Islamic society will reach a stage like the one that was present at the time of Imam Hussain (a). This can be avoided if sharp eyes can see to the depths, trustworthy guardians can show the path, the people of intellect can guide, and the strong determinations support this movement. Then, the mighty trenches are built, and the impregnable fortresses are created that no one can infiltrate. However, the same situation [as Imam Hussain (a)] can arise if we do not take control. That is when all the blood sacrificed would have been wasted.

In that chapter, the situation reached such a low that the grandchildren of those killed and sent to hell in the Battle of Badr, at the hands of the Commander of the Faithful (a),

---
101. Surah al-An'aam – Verse 11.

Hamza (a) and other commanders of Islam, usurped the pulpit of the Messenger (s) and in front of that very pulpit, struck the face of his beloved.[102]

Reliance Upon Allah and the Divine Traditions

There are laws governing this world that materialists do not recognise and do not see. *"Allah's precedent with those who passed away before."*[103] In another place: *"[It is] Allah's precedent that has passed before."*[104] The traditions of Allah are a reference to divine laws. These laws exist in this world and every corner of existence, for example, the natural laws; the law of gravity, governing the stars, the sun, the moon and the coming and going of the moon and the sun in the night and day. Just like these, some laws exist in society too. These sets of laws can not be seen by the eyes of the materialists, but they exist. Once we have prepared the grounds for these laws, God Almighty establishes them. For example, fire burns; however, you must first create the grounds for it. You light the fire up and put a dry piece of material over it; it will catch fire. Create the grounds, and then the natural laws will do the rest. The grounds must be prepared.

We have a vast front of the enemy standing opposite us. This vast front of the enemy consists of the heads of the Zionist regime, the leaders of the American government,

---

102. 09/06/1996 – In a gathering of officers from the 27th Muhammad Rasulullah (s) Battalion.
103. Surah al-Ahzab – Verse 62.
104. Surah al-Fath – Verse 23.

other hands and elements of the world's arrogant powers, the Takfiris, and ISIS. See how vast this front is! A huge congruent spectrum. All are enemies of the Islamic Republic. There are some whose hearts shake when their eyes set upon that front. This is because they are negligent of the divine traditions. This hatred, and other animosities, existed against the Revolution, yet, the Revolution was victorious. Today those animosities remain. Today, if you too acted upon creating the necessary conditions, you too will be victorious.[105]

Faith in God and trust in the divine promises will make us steadfast in the face of the enemies' schemes. This is the divine promise: *"Allah will surely help those who help Him."*[106]. Whoever aids the religion of Allah, whoever brings forth their forces to the battlefield for the sake of success, prosperity and reform, God Almighty will not leave them alone, and He will make them triumphant and victorious. Our experiences point towards this too.[107]

Strengthening Faith and Spirituality

If we wish for this movement to continue with the same speed and for it to be effective, we must build ourselves. We must become like sheets of Iron. We must strengthen our faith and increase our insight and awareness.[108]

---

105. 09/01/2016 – In a meeting with he people of Qum.
106. Surah al-Hajj – Verse 40.
107. 26/11/2003 – In a meeting with government officials.
108. 04/05/2011 – In a meeting with thousands of teachers from cross the country.

This faith is an astonishing capital. Praise Allah, all of you are faithful children brought up in faithful families. You need to bring into practice this faith you currently have by adding purified actions on top of it and avoiding sin. You should carry out good actions in their best possible form as much as possible. Among the sins, avoid most the ones that are related to a person's selfishness. Avoid those sins most which include the oppression of others. A person should avoid those inappropriate words that they may use regarding another. A person should avoid these to the extent that even their thoughts are cleared. All of these actions are purer. These are those actions which, in turn, increase the faith of a person. Faith is such that if it is accompanied by action, then that faith itself increases daily. The same goes for awareness. When accompanied by purified actions, that awareness continues to grow. *"Whoever is wary of Allah, He shall make for him a way out [of the adversities of the world and the Hereafter]."*[109] *"Whoever has faith in Allah, He guides his heart"*[110] Allah guides their heart. This verse is what I had in mind. Piety and self-accountability guide a person's heart and makes their faith deeper rooted.[111]

---

109. Surah al-Talaaq – Verse 2 and 3.
110. Suraah al-Taghbun – Verse 11.
111. 26/06/1999 – In a meeting with a group of injured students from the incident of Kuwee University.

Maintaining Ethics

Expand Islamic etiquette in society. My dear ones! One crucial matter to consider is the protection of Islamic etiquette in our speech. Today, unfortunately, it is gradually eroding, especially with the spread of online spaces. Foul language, ill speech, etc., must be stopped in society. Some today are doing this or are negligent towards this, and it is on the rise in society, especially through some media channels, whether audio, video or online. You must act in a manner in your presentation and work that does not spread this foul language and ill speech. The school of the Aa'ima (a) and the Alawi and Fatimi school of thought are far from these things. Observe the fiery sermon of Lady Zahra (s) in which she outlined her critique with two fiery speeches. One of these was in the mosque amid a sea of men and one to the women of Medina. They are full of important content and protest for the sake of lofty Islamic concepts that Lady Zahra (s) felt were under threat. However, in these two passionate, significant and lengthy sermons, you do not find one use of foul language or insults. Every word was weighty and momentous, and her statements were eloquent and persuasive. This is how to act. In our expressions and talks, nothing should be present but knowledge; there should be no back-biting, insult, foul language or ill-speech. You must teach the people this in terms of speech and action. Look how important this is that the Commander of the Faithful

(a) says: "*I dislike you starting to abuse them.*"[112] When some in his army used foul language against the army of Mua'wiyah. He told them not to use foul language and ill speech. This is Alawi and Fatimi ethics.

The fundamental point in our gathering we need to contemplate is that we have a heavy responsibility that is burdensome, dangerous, and valuable that we must pass and fulfil. Fulfilling this is what our efforts should be towards; this is only possible by observing piety. If we observe piety, our work will happen correctly. Our work will progress, fulfilling the necessary conditions and remaining free from flaws and holes made due to the corruption of those actions, and it will reach its intended objective. Piety leads to correct understanding as well as clarifying and acting correctly. Success is inevitable and assured if a person understands correctly and can explain and work correctly. This is why the faithful are invited towards piety more than anything else in the Quran and the narrations. We need piety more than anyone else as we have a heavy responsibility, and a part of the nation's power is in our hands. If we do not have piety, then this national power that each individual here holds a piece of would not be spent rightly. Therefore, the most critical issue for us is that of piety.[113]

Some with political objectives and others with religious goals carry out character assassinations of political, religious

---

112. Nahj al-Balagha – Sermon 206.
113. 2/11/2003 – In a meeting with Government officials.

and revolutionary individuals and even those related to the seminary and even respected scholars. What is this? This neither follows the logic of the Shariah nor the logic of those with sound reason, rather, the Sharia and the intellect disagree with this. If someone believes an individual is heading in what they believe is the wrong direction and they disagree with it, the way to resolve this is not by ruining or insulting their characters or by mentioning their names; instead, it is by clarifying. From the start, the Revolution came into existence on the foundation of clarification and the clarification of realities. When someone defines light by itself, darkness will also be defined. There is nothing wrong with highlighting the darkness too. However, mentioning names and ruining respected individuals is not logical. If someone aims to stop and destroy a misguided path, this is not the way, and that objective will not be reached. The position of the Shariah regarding this is known too. This method is not always free from unintentional slander, lies and accusations. The Quran states: *"When you [first] heard about it, why did not the faithful, men and women, think well of their folks."*[114] Why do you not have positive thoughts for one another? Why do you not assume correctness? Let us say you do not accept someone. Build your arguments regarding the matter you disagree with; however, resorting to ruining their character is an evil act.[115]

---

114. Surah al-Nur – Verse 12.
115. 31/8/2006 – In a meeting with members of the Guardian Council.

We must tend to our own ethics too. The importance of ethics is more than the importance of action. The environment of society has to be one of brotherhood, mercy and optimistic assumptions. I disagree with a society having an atmosphere of negative assumptions and ill intentions. We must get rid of these habits within us. Unfortunately, today it has become a norm for newspapers, the media and various communication channels to accuse one another. This is not good and is increasing, spreading and becoming more complex daily. This is not good; it makes our hearts darkened and darkens the atmosphere in our lives. There is no harm in the sinner seeing their mistake; however, the environment should not become one in which sin is spreading, slandering others and accusing them despite lack of evidence. I must state this here too. In the courts, according to Shariah, if an accuser says something about another individual, this has no weight. Whatever the accuser states about themselves in court, however, does hold weight.[116]

The Ruling of Back-biting With the Pen or Modern Media

We can not generalise the back-biting issue and say that it is always impermissible or permissible in all cases of reform. We can not say because we wish to reform society, we can attack person X, Y or a movement as a whole and start back-biting. Those who do start doing this do not stop at back-biting either. You can observe this yourself. Sometimes

---

116. 20/9/2009 – Sermon of Eid al-Fitr.

they bring stuff for which they are unsure whether it fits the definition of back-biting. Sometimes it may be slander, libel, uncertain statements or insults. It can not be said that the perpetrator intends to reform; therefore, these things are permissible for them. The only exceptions that exist are those mentioned in our jurisprudence books. Those instances with exceptions [for back-biting] need to be confirmed.
]This is very important. Something that we really need to be attentive towards and also explain and teach the people about is to be attentive towards this. Just feeling an act might be an allowed exception should not mean you have a free hand to say whatever comes to mind, whether by their hands, their pens, or their web blogs. All modern mediums are included in this ruling. Reading a web blog is like reading something on a paper, book or letter. It is like hearing words spoken. Listening to back-biting is inclusive of all these examples. It is not just about hearing it from your ears; reading a letter would also be [considered listening to back biting], and we have presented and emphasised this in our discussion on listening.

The camera holds the same ruling. Imagine if someone sees something being said and records it with their camera, then they go and show it somewhere else; this would still be considered back-biting. What difference is there? We must be attentive towards this. The environment needs to be made into an ethical environment. If we wish to reform society, it is not just through those who back-bite; there are other ways. Over here, we have spoken about back-biting, let alone slander, insults etc., that are worse.

This humble servant had the opportunity to deliver a public talk during one of the occasions, and I stated that the Quran says: "*When you [first] heard about it, why did not the faithful, men and women, think well of their folks*"[117]. When you heard slander, why did you not give each other the benefit of the doubt? This means you should reject slander from the beginning. If an individual came and slandered another person or said something about another person, regardless of whether it is slander or back-biting, why do we accept it? The term *lawla* in the Quran, and generally in Arabic, has various meanings. It does not just mean why, like when we say why we did not carry this out. It is a why with an emphasis. It suggests why as in woe be upon you, why have you not carried this out - *why did not the faithful, men and women, think well of their folks*. Why do you not give each other the benefit of the doubt? Why do you not think to assume positively of each other?

A person can critique as long as it is logical. So much can be spoken of openly, that would not be considered back-biting. A person can critique. It is understood that today in our society, we have a correct movement on the truth and a movement of falsehood that uses different methods to destroy society and deviate from the Revolution. There is no doubt about this. Some individuals are heading these movements. What

---

117. Surah al-Nur – Verse 12.

need is there for people to slander those individuals? What need is there to back-bite about these individuals? There is so much said openly; present that which is available openly, clarify it, explain it and shed light on the matter. There is no need to back-bite in a way that makes us justify it by saying, 'We are back-biting to try and reform them.'

Abstaining From The Propagation of Rumours

Some do not heed advice, whether in the media or other various elements. They do not wish for us to advise them. It is unknown who decides the policies of some of these press outlets, apparatuses and media organisations and where these are decided. Their bread and butter are from creating divisions. However, for those wishing good for the nation and are inclined towards presenting the truth, my advice is not to get involved in these minor and non-fundamental issues. Creating and spreading rumours is not correct. A person sees that the nation's officials, those who have taken the burden of this country upon themselves, are slandered, and rumours are created about them openly. It does not matter whether this is regarding the President, the Speaker of the House, the Head of the Expediency Council or the Head of the Judiciary; they are all officials of the country. The nation's officials have been given a responsibility; the people must trust them and think positively of them. Rumours must not be spread; this is precisely what the enemy wants. The enemy wants to spread rumours and make the hearts feel adverse about one another and the officials.[118]

Other foreign and biased television channels may speak against someone, claiming they have betrayed and made mistakes somewhere. However, if we end up propagating the same, we have done an injustice, which is unacceptable. When have biased media outlets ever cared about us? When have they wished for the truth about us to be broadcasted that they will come and say the truth in this particular case? They speak, say stuff and make claims. It can not be said that this is transparency. This is not transparency; in fact, this is muddying the waters. Transparency means that the officials in the Islamic Republic clearly present their performance in front of the people. This is what transparency means, and this is something they must do.

However, we have no right to attack a person with slander due to claims that have not been proven. Even if those claims are valid, they should not be expressed until they have been established. A person accuses another, and then that person blames someone else. They bring an example from the biased English media, and then they find someone who charges the whole system of acts that are not in accordance with the Islamic system's status. The status of the Islamic System is much loftier than what some accuse it of. These accusations are more worthy of themselves. Slandering an individual is

---

[118]. 25/11/2009 – In a meeting with the Basij.

a sin, and slandering an Islamic System, a whole collective, is a much greater sin.[119]

Maintaining Etiquette in the Online Space

The social media and the internet have unfortunately resulted in individuals speaking against one another and speaking ill of each other without any fear. Planning for this matter needs to be undertaken by the officials too. However, primarily we, the people, need to tie ourselves to Islamic etiquette. We should restrict ourselves to the law. These words of mine should not be used as an excuse for some to go and name the revolutionary youth as extremists and used to rebuke them. I consider all of the passionate youth of this country and the faithful revolutionary youth as my children, and I will stand behind them. I will support the faithful, revolutionary and passionate youth. That said, I advise everyone to act per Islamic etiquette and obey the law. The manifestation of the Revolution is enshrined in the law of the Islamic Republic.[120]

The Difference Between Critique and Bad Etiquette

Critiquing, asking for reform, and the people's demands to be met, are good things. Illogical fault-finding, exaggerating, slandering, insulting and spreading unfounded rumours are wrong. We must differentiate between the two. In my

---

119. 20/09/2009 – Sermon on Eid al-Fitr
120. 20/04/2012 – In the shrine of Imam al-Ridha (a).

opinion, this is one of the issues we must ask forgiveness for wherever we have fallen short in the past, and we must not allow it to continue through our negligence.[121]

Distinguishing Primary from Secondary Priorities

If you lose your concentration or focus, become negligent, get busy with other work, and cannot foresee what the enemy wants to do, you will definitely suffer a blow. The enemy is not sleeping; they are awake. *"The warrior should be wakeful because if he sleeps the enemy does not sleep."*[122] If you lose their attention and become negligent, this does not mean the enemy has also lost attention. It is possible that they are focused, and they will strike you. Therefore, we must keep our focus. When we speak, advise and emphasise to the officials and the people not to busy themselves in matters of secondary importance, it is for this reason. For this reason, we repeatedly advise the press, broadcasters, newspapers and internet outlets, which are becoming more common these days, not to introduce incorrect words and content that keep the people's minds occupied.[123]

Observing the Laws

I believe that we must act according to the law, regardless of whether it is for our benefit or harms us. You may not accept many of the laws approved in parliament; you may not accept

---
121. 30/10/2005 – In a meeting with government officials.
122. Nahj al-Balagha – Letter 62.
123. 08/01/2013 – In a meeting with the people of Qum.

many bills passed by the government. However, we must act in accordance with that very thing we may disagree with, and there is a logic behind this. The logic is that a bad law is better than lawlessness and breaking the law. It is not logical to suggest that we only accept the law whenever it suits us, and then whenever it does not, we reject it. I believe that the law must be the yardstick.[124]

One crucial work, among other vital responsibilities, is cultural work. We have many flaws and holes in our cultural work. There are many places where the enemy can infiltrate from concerning cultural work. The official governmental bodies, alongside the vast public bodies, are responsible for carrying out this work. 'Fire at will' means to carry out cultural work that is voluntary and upstanding. What we have said means that youth, the people of intellect and those with willpower progress cultural work themselves, using their capacities across the whole nation. They need to recognise the infiltration areas and work in opposition to them. 'Fire at will' does not mean lawlessness, obscenities, and giving opportunities to those making thoughtless claims against the nation's revolutionary movement. More than anyone, the revolutionary forces must be mindful of the national order, peace, and laws and not give an excuse to the enemy to abuse the state of the country. These matters need to be of concern primarily for the revolutionary forces, which are

---

124. 12/01/2004 – In a meeting with provincial heads from across the country.

compassionate, considerate, and affectionate towards the movement of the nation toward its objectives.[125]

All of you must consider that when we say a *Basiji* has value in their work and day-to-day living environments, and that they have respect and pride, it is because their ethics and mannerisms must be such that they attract the respect and love of the people. You have to be an exemplar of etiquette. You must be humble, well-mannered, merciful and disciplined in upholding the regulations. This incorrect perception of a *Basiji* being someone who does not uphold the regulations needs to be taken away. This is not the case; the opposite is the truth. The person who maintains the regulations is more *Basiji* than the one who does not. Why? We understand the *Basiji* to be someone willing to sacrifice more for the Islamic system than anyone else, and regulations are the absolute necessities for correctly managing the system. Therefore, in your day-to-day life and work environment, be attentive towards upholding etiquette, regulations, order and discipline. Understand that your existence for the Revolution is like an unending treasure source. So long as the Islamic Revolution and the system of the Islamic Republic relies upon these feelings, faith and sincerity, God willing, this reliance will always remain; no enemy at any level can cause harm to this Revolution or the Islamic Republic.[126]

---

[125]. 26/06/1989 – Sermon on Eid al-Fitr.
[126]. 27/06/1989 – In a gathering of a group of Basij from across the country.

The meaning of 'fire at will' that we spoke about[127] is this: All of the youth and the faithful groups in varying fields must carry out whatever work they are capable of in accordance with the laws and expediency of the country. They should not be waiting for anyone.[128]

Importance of Researching

Giving explanations, first and foremost, requires clarification and understanding. We must first understand before we can clarify. Therefore, attaining an understanding also becomes obligatory, necessary, and unavoidable. We must increase ourselves daily. What we know is not even a piece of straw compared to the desert. It is not even a field compared to the desert. What do we know? Every book a person opens, we see an ocean of content inside it which our empty containers need. Where is our depth? Where is our capacity? Where is the opportunity to understand everything? Nonetheless, we still have to strive.

In the face of what we should know and what knowledge the people need, we know nothing. We must study and research. I do not wish to oblige people to take lessons, but we must increase our study, research, contemplation and

---

127. For example in statements made during a meeting with university students from across the country on 07/06/2017.
128. 18/02/2019 – In a meeting with the people of Eastern Azerbaijan.

pondering so that we can present. Then, a duty upon all scholars is the responsibility to clarify.[129]

Clarification vs the Illusion of Clarification

If differences of opinion exist, I advise strictly that the respected gentlemen do not present their differences of opinion among the people. This is because when the differences in economic opinion are reflected upon the people, they have a real-world effect on the economic environment. Those theoretical difficulties are translated as real-world difficulties in the people's work market and their economic environment. If problems exist and differences of opinion exist, these should be resolved within the government and not be reflected upon the people.[130]

Two Impressions of Clarification Regarding the Relationship Between Iran and America

Two incorrect ideas are being injected into the thoughts of our people. On the primary level, America and the Arrogant Powers are the sources for this injection; on the secondary level, it is done internally by some individuals. I do not wish to generalise in my accusation, but some of these individuals are connected to special American institutions' linked to the spying and intelligence communities. Some are not

---

129. 22/12/1991 – In a meeting with a group of scholars from the province of Bu Shahr.
130. 28/08/2021 – In the first meeting with the President and the Cabinet of the 13th government.

connected to this; they are tired, regretful, and have latched onto the pleasurable scent of this world. The first group lends these two incorrect ideas to the second group and uses various pulpits and channels to propagate and spread them. This is done in the universities, outside universities, in the press, and by various other means. I wish to correct these two mistaken ideas.

The first [incorrect idea] propagated is in regards to the statement of Imam Khomeini: Whatever you have to protest about, direct it towards America![131] (This is a rule which still applies today). They say this statement was based on emotions and arrogance and had no logic behind it. They wish to propagate this. They wish to say that those of our youth, revolutionaries, and officials who oppose America and expose their conspiracies are fanatics. [They wish to say] what they do is based upon ignorant zeal and emotion. This is what they are trying to present. This is when the reality is 180 degrees the opposite. This statement that was made: "whatever you have to shout about, direct it towards America", has solid logic behind it. The logic behind it is that the foundations of American politics are based upon excessiveness and interference. The history of America, 250 years of which have passed, shows this to us. Initially, it was less so; however, approximately from a hundred years ago, or a bit less than a hundred years, this has significantly increased.

---

131. Sahifa-e-Imam – Vol 11 P 121.

Generally, American politics has looked to safeguard internal security by interfering in nations worldwide, capturing regions and infiltration. This is how they act; this is their politics. They implemented this political strategy in the Westerns Asia region, in Iran at the time of the *taghut* and in our neighbouring countries. Upon this matter, they would test their strength in relation to the Soviet Union. The Soviets would pull in one direction, and they would pull in the other. America had infiltrated Iran. Moments worth of negligence would have meant the enemy, which had been kicked out the door, would have returned from the window. However, Imam Khomeini did not allow this to happen and became an obstacle.

When they said to stand against America and, whatever capacity you have to shout, direct it at America, it means to defend your values. Not just values specific to Muslims; it is the defence of humanitarian values. Today, according to the admission of the Americans themselves, the American government and the American system are lightyears away from humanitarian values. Did you see the debate between the two nominees of the American presidential elections?[132] Did you see the realities they brought to their tongues? Did you hear it? They exposed America. They said many times over what we have said, and some refused to believe it; they have said it themselves. What is fascinating is that the one who spoke frankly was liked more by the people. As that

---

132. Donald Trump and Hillary Clinton.

man spoke more frankly and openly, most Americans leaned towards him. The opposite person said he was trying to work in a populist manner. Why was it populist? Because the people saw his words and saw that they were correct. They saw his comments in the reality of their lives. Humanitarian values have been decimated and trampled upon in that country. Racial discrimination exists there. A few days ago, this man stood up in his political campaigning video and said if you are walking down the streets of New York, Chicago, California etc., and you are coloured, black or brown, you can not be confident about your own life a few minutes down the line. Have a look at this! This is being said by someone who expects to walk into the White House a few days later and govern America. This is what racism in America is.

He spoke about the poverty faced by the Americans. He said 44 million people in America are hungry. He said, and so have others, that less than 1% of people in America own 90% of American wealth. Humanitarian values have been trampled upon there; discrimination, divisiveness, racism and the trampling of Human rights. When you chant 'Death to America!', you mean death to these issues. When Imam Khomeini says, 'Whatever you want to shout about, direct it at America!', you mean death to these issues. It is for these issues Imam Khomeini made this statement.

All the above on one side and on the other side, in those initial days of the Revolution, they established the grounds to inflict a dangerous strike upon the nation of Iran. They gave refuge to Muhammad Raza in America so that they could protect him, ready the grounds, strengthen his elements in Iran, and then use him to repeat what they did in 1953, 25 years before the Revolution. In 1953, Muhammad Raza fled Iran. The English and the Americans worked hand in hand and entered the country secretly using various embassies. They gained refuge, armed their assets, readied them, made use of the people's negligence in those days and returned Muhammad Raza. This very return led to 25 years of life being beaten out of this nation and the people going through hell. They wished to do this again; however, Imam Khomeini was able to obstruct this. He became a dam, awakened the people, and the nation of Iran woke up. Therefore, these anti-American slogans and the shouting directed at America are not based on emotions, ignorance or stubbornness but on logic. It relies upon logic and intellectual reasoning. If today the nation of Iran gives anti-American slogans, and if it has given these slogans for the last thirty-odd years, it has been based upon robust logic. Our dear youth and those who write, speak and hold various platforms, must know and pay attention to this, whether in the press, universities, classrooms or other platforms.

During those years, we also had an 8-year war with Saddam. The Americans stood firm behind Saddam and helped him in any way they could. The Americans showed their animosity towards us in a particular way after the war, in another way before it, and in another way during the war. During the issue of JCPOA, they showed their animosity and after the JCPOA in another way. A few days before they showed it, this individual[133] who was carrying out the negotiations on behalf of America stood up and said bluntly we would sanction Iran, even after the JCPOA. This was broadcasted on our television too. The stand of the Iranian nation in the face of America relies upon sound logic. So, the first error was that they wanted to present the people's stand against America as being one based on stubbornness. The reality of the situation is the opposite. The people stand against America based on logic.

The second incorrect and erroneous idea that is also being injected, one side by the Americans and from the other side by those internally, is more dangerous than the first. It is that if we compromise with America, the problems of this nation will be resolved.

This is one of those extraordinary mistakes that are extremely dangerous. They say that if we compromised with America, the problems of this country would be resolved. Tens of reasons can be provided for why these words are lies and deceptive. Compromising with America will not resolve the country's issues in any way, whether economic, political, security-related, or ethical problems. They will get worse. Ten to fifteen reasons can be counted and listed regarding this issue. The most recent reason is the issue of the JCPOA. How often throughout the negotiations did I say

---

133. John Kerry.

that they are unfaithful liars and will not remain upon their words? Now you can see it! Today I am not the only one that says they are unfaithful. Our nation's respected officials, the negotiators themselves, say this. The ones that put in so much effort negotiating for a year and a bit; they went, sat, stood up, ten days, fifteen days, twenty days away from the country, they put in all that effort around the negotiation table, they are the ones that are saying this.

In this meeting of foreign ministers in New York just last month, our respected foreign minister also participated alongside their foreign minister.[134] Our foreign minister stated an extensive indictment against them. He noted the things they should have done and did not and also stated those which they should not have done but then did. He presented an indictment and a statement of claims; they had no response. This is what they are like. We are supposed to compromise on Syria, Hizbullah, Afghanistan, Pakistan, Iraq and internal affairs with who? With those who do not surrender their animosity, even for a moment. Their objective is to ensure this nation does not progress. Their aim is to ensure this country's economic problems are not resolved. Then you expect them to come and help resolve your problems?

Firstly, the person standing in front is a liar, fraudster, who is unfaithful and someone who sticks daggers in the back. At

---

134. The first sitting of the Foreign Minister of Iran and the 5+1 group after the implementation of the JCPOA.

the same time, they offer their hand; according to what they say themself, whilst they hold a stone in the other hand to hit over the head. Secondly, how does America wish to resolve the problems of this country? America itself is in crisis; why do they not say this? All the important organisations around the world that judge these matters, even the Americans themselves, are saying this. America is facing a crisis; an economic crisis, an international crisis, a political crisis and an ethical crisis. They are in crisis themselves. Today the debt the American government owes is close to its total gross production. This is a sign of being in crisis. The economists say this too. They say they are in a state of crisis whenever a government's debt comes close to its gross production. This is the state of America currently. Its debt is almost sixty-something per cent of its gross production. Who do they wish to help? It wishes to exploit so that it can recover itself. Is it going to come and help the economy of another country? This is from an economic point of view.

From a political viewpoint, it is also in a state of crisis. I say this with certainty. Without exception, today, at any point of the world where the people rise and move against the despots, government, or state, they have the slogan of 'death to America'. There was a day when the slogan of 'death to America' belonged only here; however, now in Western Asia, Eastern Asia, even in Europe, Latin America and in regions of Africa, when the people rise, the first slogan they chant is against America. This is the political state America finds itself in. Is there a crisis more significant than this?

America had a plan for Western Asia. You do not remember, although it is not from very long ago, maybe ten to twelve years ago; however, you, the youth, will not remember that day. The American Foreign Minister said, 'We will create the New Middle East'. During the issue of the 33-day war, they brought forth the name of the New Middle East. What was meant by this New Middle East? They call the region of Western Asia the Middle East. The New Middle East refers to the area between Pakistan and the Mediterranean. All the countries in this area are known as the Middle East. America had drawn up a comprehensive plan for this region revolving around Israel to hold it in its fist. This is what was meant by the New Middle East. Today that Foreign Ministers New Middle East is such that they are stuck in Syria, Iraq, Lebanon, North Africa and Libya. On the issue of Yemen, they got involved and are now stuck. This is the state of American international politics at the moment. Is there a more significant crisis, and they wish to come and help you? [How are] they going to come to resolve the nation's problems?

We stand in opposition to this. Thanks to Allah, it was His work and His blessing upon this nation that He gave courage, insight and steadfastness. [The people] tolerated the difficulties, and the faithful men and women of this nation were able to act in a manner that led to the nation of Iran holding its head up high in Western Asia. Iran stands out in between Iraq, Syria, Lebanon, Yemen, and the Persian Gulf region. The Americans are facing an economic crisis, political crisis, international crisis and an ethical crisis, whether this is in terms of sexual ethics or financial corruption. These are words they are saying themselves and are publishing in their press. Although what is being said is a lot less than the reality. The two [American] presidential candidates, one of whom will go to the White House and become the President, do not speak without measure. Both are bad; however, they are working together to expose America and destroy America's reputation, and they have been successful too. How does this country expect to come and help Iran? Why is this incorrect thought being injected into the people's minds that if we compromise and resolve our issues with America, our country's problems will be resolved? No! Compromising with America will not reduce the nation's problems but increase them. If we have a political or economic crisis, we must resolve these problems ourselves; you must resolve our problems, you, the youth.[135]

Combination of Clarification with Action

Create connections, speak, inform, get informed, give motivation and get motivation. Explain the realities about the arrogant powers, oppressors and those opposed to this

---
135. 02/11/2016 – In a meeting with university students and professors.

front for those brothers who have newly entered the arena. You have thirty years of experience. Those that cannot clarify should invite people with their actions. "Invite people using other than your tongues."[136]. The tongue can invite people, but the invitation by one's actions is better and stronger.[137]

For the revival of Islam, Imam Khomeini walked upon the same path that the Holy Messenger (s) walked upon; the path of the Revolution. Movement is the principal foundation of a revolution. A directed, considered, connected and tireless movement overflowing with faith and sincerity. Just speaking, writing, and clarifying in a revolution does not suffice. Instead, traversing, advancing trench by trench and getting yourself to the objective become the primary principles and axis around which you revolve. Speaking and writing are also at the service of this movement until the goal is reached. The objective means the governance of God's religion and the disintegration of the satanic non-divine strength. "*It is He who has sent His Apostle with guidance and the true religion that He may make it prevail over all religions though the polytheists should be averse.*"[138][139]

---

136. Mishkat al-Anwar – P 46.
137. 23/09/2011 – In a meeting with those working for organisations facilitating Hajj.
138. Surah al-Saff – Verse 9
139. 31/05/1990 – In the message for the 1st commemoration of the passing away of Imam Khomeini.

Being Timely

A key point in the matter of Qum that I have stated repeatedly and will continue to repeat is that the people of Qum, in that instance, acted promptly. Every time work happens promptly, it leaves an effect, or the effect is amplified. If that same act had not occurred, if it was left to stale, time had passed, and then it was carried out, it would not have an effect, or the effect would be little. The skill of the Qummies was that they understood the point straight away; they understood the enemy straight away and gave a response at that very first moment. If they had not responded after that evil conspiratorial act against Imam Khomeini [the following events would not have occurred]. Suppose they would have passed the responsibility around, said, 'we will do it [at some point]', or, 'we will do it tomorrow', or, 'we will do it a month later', the following events would never have taken place. An obligation has its own time, and that action must be carried out at its allotted time. The best time to carry out an obligatory act is in its first instance. Some do not carry out the obligation at all. They say, 'who cares?'. Some do carry out their responsibility; however, they do it late. Some carry it out after the time has already passed. For example, the Tawwabeen; the Tawwabeen did not come at the time they should have, which was Ashura. They came when the time for work had finished.

Another example is the uprising of the people of Medina under Abdullah ibn Handhala. They came and stood against

Yazid, carried out an uprising and overthrew the governor of Medina; however, they were too late. When they heard that Hussain ibn Ali (a) had left Medina, they should have thought about this then, but they did not. They started thinking about it too late, almost a year after. The result of which has been written in history. They were massacred, decimated, annihilated and were unable to achieve anything. Work must be done at the correct time. If we wish to work at the right time, we must understand the obligation and what work needs to be done to carry it out promptly.[140]

Why do you say, may the peace of Allah be upon Ammar? Ammar did not make a mistake and understood correctly at the most sensitive time.[141]

There were some from the elites who did not go to Karbala. They were not able to go. They were not ordained with the divine opportunity. However, they were forced to join the Tawwabeen later. What use was it? Once Imam Hussain (a) has been killed, you have lost the son of the Messenger (s), the atrocities have been committed, and the momentum has started to decline, what was the point? In history, it has been written that the number of Tawwabeen was a few times larger than the martyrs of Karbala. The martyrs of Karbala were all killed in one day. The Tawwabeen were also all killed in one day. However, the effect of the Tawwabeen was not even one-thousandth of the impact of the martyrs

---

140. 08/01/2017 – In a meeting with the people of Qum.
141. 21/08/1991 – In a gathering of scholars from the Loristan province.

of Karbala! This is because they did not act when they should have. They acted on their own time. They were late in making the decision, and they were late in their diagnosis.

Despite knowing that Muslim ibn Aqeel was a representative of the Imam, why did you leave him alone? He had come, and you had also given your allegiance to him. You also accepted him. I am disregarding the layperson here; I am speaking specifically about the elites. In the late afternoon, at the beginning of the night, why had you left Muslim alone to the extent he had to seek refuge in Tau'ah's house? If the elites had not left Muslim, and, for example, they would have reached a hundred people, those hundred people could have surrounded Muslim. They could have turned one of their houses into the headquarters. They could have made a stand and defended. Not only was Muslim alone, but it took hours to arrest him. The soldiers of Ibn Ziyad attacked numerous times. Muslim alone was able to fight them back. If a hundred people had been around him, would they have been able to arrest him? The people would have gathered around him again. Therefore, it was the elites who fell short at this stage and did not protect him.

Observe! No matter which direction we walk from, we will reach the elites. [The impact of] the decisions, diagnosis, rejection of worldly benefits, and steps towards Allah of the elites at the necessary time [is valuable]. These are the factors that can save us and protect values! The essential steps being taken at the required times. It has no benefit if you contemplate and the time for action has passed. In Algeria, the Islamic Front in that country had won the elections. However, a military government took charge due to the instigation of the Americans and others. On the first day, the military government took control; it faced no opposition. If on that day and in those first few hours of the military government, officials of the Islamic Front had brought the people onto the streets, military power would not have been able to do anything and would have been annihilated. I also sent this message to them. As a result, we would have had an Islamic government today in Algeria. However, they did not take any steps. They should have made a decision promptly, but they did not. Some got scared, some became weak, some created divisions, and some started fighting over the Presidency.

On the afternoon of the 7th of February, 1979, martial law was declared. Imam Khomeini told the people to come out onto the streets. If Imam Khomeini had not made that decision, then Muhammad Raza would be in charge of this country today. If they had come with their military power and the people would have remained in their houses, they would have massacred Imam Khomeini alongside all those in the Refah Islamic Seminary. Then, they would have slaughtered and destroyed the people of other areas. They would have killed five hundred thousand people in Tehran, and the matter would have been resolved, just like in Indonesia, where they killed a million people and resolved the issue.

Till today that person is still in charge and remains honoured and respected! As if nothing had happened! However, Imam Khomeini made the necessary decision at the required time. If the elites enact orders promptly and without the passing of time, history would be different, and more Hussain ibn Ali's will not be dragged to more Karbalas. If the elites understand incorrectly, late or understand but differ, Karbalas will be repeated throughout history.

Observe the Afghans! Their heads were calculated individuals; however, their elites spread across society did not respond. One said, today, we have to take care of some other stuff. One said the war is now finished, leave us be, let us get to our work and go and do business. It only took a few years for them to gather thousands. So, if this is how they want to act, then many Karbala's will be repeated in history.

God Almighty has promised that if people were to help Him, He would help them. If someone moves for the sake of Allah, victory will be written for them. Success is not given to everyone! When a collective moves, there will be martyrdom, difficulties and trials; however, there is also a victory. *"Allah will surely help those who help Him."*[142]. It does not say we will grant victory; no one will even break a nail. *"...they fight in the way of Allah, kill, and are killed."*[143] They will

---
142. Surah al-Hajj – Verse 40.
143. Surah al-Tawbah – Verse 111.

kill and be killed; however, they will attain victory. This is one of the divine traditions of God.[144]

Steadfastness and Insight

If you become hopeless and tired quickly, work can not progress. You must not lose hope; you must keep moving. Think about this! This Revolution was founded after a lengthy fight. The incidents in 1978 and 1979 did not occur over an hourglass. They had started many years before, in 1963, the battle had begun. Those who had carried out these duties over the testing years by clarifying, explaining, expanding, strengthening the intellectual sources and clarifying the grounds did not have it easy. They had to face difficulties. They had to face imprisonment; in those days, challenging a police officer meant imprisonment! Opposing the head of one of the city councils carried much more difficulties. Let alone someone trying to expand on the positions of Islam concerning standing against the system. These were difficult and required effort, imprisonment, trials and solitary confinements, yet, they made a stand and fought. This struggle led to one spark in 1978 and 79 from which the nation entered a new chapter. If you remain steadfast in the manner I have mentioned, creating a narrative and readying the minds, these efforts will serve you when necessary. [Remaining steadfast upon this struggle] can

---

144. 09/06/1996 – In a meeting with the commanders of the 27th Muhammad Rasullullah (s) Brigade.

mobilise people's mindset towards a reality that they can then demand. When the people demand it, the officials have no choice but to accept it. Therefore, remaining steadfast is necessary. We emphasise this heavily upon university activism as those active in the universities must remain steadfast and stand firm.[145]

In the realm of clarification, what does this look like? I say that in a city, what is expected of a Friday prayer leader is not just that they can prepare a talk and then go to the pulpit and present it. We expect more from them. The expectation is that we must be like a doctor that finds the illness, understands it and then puts in their effort to gather the required medicine, which they then place upon the wound or give to the patient to eat.

Our duty is not just to say; we have said it now, and whoever wants to act upon it can act upon it! This attitude does not belong to an era where the government is in the hands of the Muslims, an era in which governing the affairs of the society is upon our shoulders, especially not during a period in which the enemy is using all its efforts to remove Islamic concepts. Our duty is not just to say the content and feel like if it works, it works, and if it does not, then it does not; we just have to say what we have to say! This is not what our duty is. Our words must enter the hearts. *"and the Apostle's duty is only to communicate in clear terms."*[146] . It

---
145. 02/07/2016 – In a meeting with a gathering of students.
146. Surah al-Noor – Verse 54.

is unacceptable for us just to throw words into the air; if someone catches it, they catch it; if they do not, then they do not. If they understand it, they understand it; if they do not, then they do not. This is happening and it is as a problem.[147]

In the past, I have repeatedly said that if a nation loses its analytical ability, it will be deceived and suffer defeat. The companions of Imam Hasan (a) could not analyse. They could not understand the situation and what was happening. The companions of the Commander of the Faithful (a), those who had broken his heart, were not all those who held animosity. However, many of them, such as the Khawarij, could not analyse. The analytical ability of the Khawarij was weak. You would find an incompetent, mischievous and outspoken individual, and they would sway the people in one direction and lose the indicators. When you are on the highway, you must keep an eye on the signs. If you lose the signs, you will quickly make a mistake. The Commander of the Faithful (a) stated: "*And this banner will be borne only by him who is a man of sight, of endurance*"[148]. First, you require insight, intelligence, and the ability to understand and analyse; then, you need steadfastness, resistance and resilience. A person's heart must not quickly tremble from whatever they face. The path of truth is a path of difficulties.

---

147. 16/09/1991 – In a meeting with Friday Prayer leaders from across the country.
148. Nahj al-Balagha – Sermon 173.

All satanic characters through history, including our time, have added to this falsehood, blocking the path of the Commander of the Faithful (a) and the servants of God. It is not an easy job; it is difficult. Tolerance, steadfastness, capacity, a reach into internal strength and internal motivation is necessary to traverse the truthful path. That being said, life becomes pleasurable when a person can locate the truthful path. It becomes a life in which there is no injustice, suppression, forcefulness, or control of Satan upon the actions and thoughts of a life full of spirituality.[149]

Keep Repeating

When you have concluded about one of the important fundamental issues of the Revolution, turn this into a discourse, and for example, publish it in a journal. There are a large number of you. Many of you are Friday prayer leaders or known individuals in your provinces or centres and have a platform. Many can speak to the people, gain an audience, and state and repeat until it becomes a discourse. Discourse refers to that thought common among people, and naturally, this brings them closer to action. This issue is the same. The issue of presenting national problems to internal systems for their resolution must become one of the evident and apparent ideas among the people. This must be

---

149. 15/04/1991 – In a meeting with the General public.

said so much, proven so much, clarified, and repeated that it becomes a definite discourse among the people.[150]

The fourth point is the creation of a discourse. Look at the talks of Dr. Sattari regarding the issue of knowledge-based sciences and economics and knowledge-based organisations and the emphasis given to them; other friends also alluded to this. This is due to a discourse that has lasted for ten to twelve years. When the discussions of breaking the front lines of knowledge, or the production of knowledge are presented, pursued, and spoken of in universities, they are transformed into a discourse. The result becomes that when this humble servant sits here sometimes and a collective of university students and professors come, and they also present the same words that we spoke about as material, this shows a discourse. This is good. When this happens, you can expect knowledge advancements to occur. Today we have many achievements in space, nuclear, nanotechnology, biotechnology, and other fields. We have made significant gains. These advancements have been a result of the creation of discourses. When discourses are created, everyone will start to think of the issue. As if a broad highway is completed, and everyone wishes to travel through it. Therefore the creation of discourses is essential. However, just by repeating the term 'the Resistance Economy', discourse will not be created. This word should not be repeated in a manner that

---

150. 21/09/2017 – In a meeting with the Head and members of the Assembly of Experts.

leads to what it means being forgotten. It must be presented alongside clarification and explanation.[151]

Practical Strategy and Compassionate Guiding

It has to be a sensible, popular, and disciplined movement. When I say disciplined, it means it should not be turbulent or chaotic. Sometimes popular movements are accompanied by turbulence and chaos; they have no value. If [the movements] wish to be correct, organised, and intellectual, they require a few things:

A practical strategy is ultimately necessary for every era. Our point of discussion is here. Is what is the practical strategy for someone who is a youth to enter the arena. The issue of having a practical strategy, requires guidance, focus, follow up, and persistent activity to advance this great caravan of the people and, more importantly, the youth. Who is responsible for this? Who is responsible for creating focus, creating a plan of action, finding a strategy, presenting the strategy, and planning? This is the responsibility of the circles of the middlemen. This is not the responsibility of the Leader, the government, or any other institutional body. This is a responsibility of the collectives from the nation itself. Praise be to Allah; today, they are not few in numbers either. We have intellectual geniuses in various needed fields among the youth and among our officials. They can sit, plan and

---
151. 24/08/2016 – In a meeting with the President and members of the Cabinet.

give guidance. University groups and experienced and active collectives in the cultural and intellectual fields are among these types of groups. The more active they are in these fields, the more effective they become. The reigns of work are in the hands of those who are active. Laziness, lethargy, sluggishness, and such vices are of no use.[152]

Mannerism

In the opinion of this humble servant, the things that are of utmost importance are the thoughts and hearts of your audience. Firstly, the thoughts, and secondly, the hearts. By thoughts, we initially mean the foundation of beliefs needs to be strengthened in the youth. Youth are in the midst of acceptance and transformation; they are in the midst of change. The tools that have an effect are many in today's world. The intellectual foundation of youth must be strengthened so that not only are they not affected by negative, opposing, and spiteful influences, but they can also have an effect on their environments. They must spread light and make their surroundings aware of Islamic understanding and sources. They should be proactive on this path and be a progressive force. In terms of thoughts, they must reach such a state.

When we speak about the heart, it is because for man to reach their peak and be grounded upon the straight path,

---

[152]. 22/05/2019 – In a meeting with a gathering of university students.

in reality, the intellect alone is not enough. Apart from the ideological dimension, the dimensions of the heart and spirit are also necessary. A state of obedience, humility, remembrance, and repentance towards Allah is essential for a person. If this exists, many shortcomings can be compensated. If this does not exist, intellectual strength, the strength of reasoning, and protesting, in many situations, will not help a person. The heart of the youth must be softened through advice, beautified guidance, and good mannerism. They must be familiarised with humility, intercessions, attention [towards Allah], and [His] remembrance. Prayers and divine remembrance must be clarified for them correctly. These become the support for that intellect. If this happens, then intellectual steadfastness becomes unending. In the practical field, this softness of the heart, attention, and remembrance, comes to the aid of a person. This is what keeps a person strong. This is something necessary. These two things need to be strengthened in the youth.

Classes for Islamic teachings must be established. Teachings that are convincing, using topical language in accordance with the thoughts of university students and the terminology they use, must be presented. These are obligatory duties that can not be rejected. This is one example of speaking at the level of the people. Speech must happen in the language of university students. Speech must use terminology that is understandable for university students. How many examples are there of terminology being effective in one environment; however, it is not effective in a different environment? The difference is almost the same as speaking two different languages. Honestly, the difference in terminology is like differences in language. It is like someone coming to a gathering of Persian speakers and giving a talk in Gujarati. No one will understand anything. Suppose a person is unaware of the terminology and environment of the youth and the environment of the universities, and they do not use this terminology. In that case, the path of creating an intellectual connection will be closed, and their effectiveness will decrease. Therefore, it is essential to speak in accordance with the people.

I do not wish to use the word Tarbiyyah for beautified guidance (maw'idhat al-hasana) as the word Tarbiyyah is more general. Aside from speech-related issues, issues about mannerisms are also necessary for beautified guidance. *"Invite the people using other than your tongues."*.[153] Good mannerisms soften the heart, destroying animosity and bringing those with animosity down on their knees. Good mannerisms include good etiquette, humility, honesty in speech, truthfulness in holding a position, frankness in speaking the truth, and a long-term view of material and worldly affairs. These things are indicators of sincerity in ones action. If, by God's grace, we can have sincerity in our actions, naturally, this would show itself in our mannerisms and speech. So, the best way to carry this responsibility out is,

---

153. Mishkat al-Anwaar – P 46.

firstly, to have a tongue that advises and guides in a brotherly and sometimes fatherly manner, and secondly, to have good mannerisms and actions.

In my opinion, one of the things which will help you is what the Commander of the Faithful says about the Holy Messenger (s): "The Prophet was like a roaming physician who has set ready his ointments and heated his instruments.".[154] We must not be imprisoned behind a desk or in a room. Turning into an environment of office workers is not for the benefit of the collective of scholars. Regardless of our other responsibilities, this position of a scholar, which is in closeness with the people, going among the people, speaking the people's language, and hearing the people's pains, must not be lost.[155]

It is not necessary to exaggerate and it is not necessary to speak against reality. Present whatever we have correctly, pleasantly, and eloquently. This will attract the hearts and will affect the people.[156]

Special Attention Towards the Online Space

Today, the online space is an opportunity for work. The enemy uses the online space differently; however, you dear

---
154. Nahj al-Balagha – Sermon 108.
155. 11/07/2010 – In a meeting with members of the Organisation of the Leaders Representatives in Universities.
156. 26/09/2016 – In a meeting with with members of the committees responsibly for the commemoration ceremonies for the Martyrs of Kahgiluye, Buyerahmed and North Khorasan.

youth should use it in this manner: use it to create hope, advise towards steadfastness, advise towards the truth, use it to create insight, advise toward tirelessness, against lethargy and remaining stagnant.[157]

Courage

We do not just need courage in action; we also need courage in understanding. Deep understanding requires courage. If courage did not exist, we would have holes in our knowledge. Sometimes a person has an incorrect understanding of what is general and sometimes an incorrect understanding of what is specific. Having a correct understanding of Islamic sources, Islamic topics, and those matters which are the external manifestations of those general teachings, meanings, and the general and specific areas of understanding requires courage. If we do not have courage, then fear of our wealth and lives, fear of reacting in the face of the enemy, and fear of the environment and its pull will lead us to say, "they will speak against us if we talk". If we speak, then they will stick this label on us. These fears leave the understanding of a person incapacitated. Sometimes, one cannot understand the matter properly due to these fears and considerations. They are not able to understand the issue accurately and resolve it. It leads to mistakes happening. Therefore, *"and fear no one except Allah"*, is essential. In this verse: *"such as*

---

[157]. 11/03/2021 – In a televised speech on the occasion of Eid al-Mabath.

deliver the messages of Allah and fear Him, and fear no one except Allah, and Allah suffices as reckoner."[158], it is understood that the condition for propagation is being fearless. *"...and fear no one except Allah"*. You say, 'If I end up saying this, I may be tricked in this world. *"and Allah suffices as reckoner"*. Leave the calculations to God, and let Him make the calculations for you. The difficulties will be resolved if we replace the fear of people's judgment and their various perceptions with the fear of Allah. This is because fearing Allah is piety. If we place this to one side and replace it with the fear of the people, then the Furqan that God Almighty speaks about will not be attained. *"If you are wary of Allah, He shall appoint a criterion for you."*[159] This Furqan comes out from piety. The truth becomes apparent to a person through piety. In my opinion, this matter is essential. The issue of fearing for your wealth, life, the words of people, your honour, rumours, slanders, and such, is critical. The matter is so essential that God Almighty addresses the Messenger (s) and warns him about it: *"When you said to him whom Allah had blessed, and whom you [too] had blessed, 'Retain your wife for yourself, and be wary of Allah,' and you had hidden in your heart what Allah was to divulge, and you feared the people though Allah is worthier that you should fear Him."*[160] You should not take into regard the words of the people, the slandering that will happen, and the

---

158. Same as above.
159. Surah al-Anfal – Verse 29.
160. Surah al-Ahzab – Verse 37.

acts they may commit [against you]. *"though Allah is worthier that you should fear Him."* In my opinion, one of the things that made these various victories for Imam Khomeini easy to accomplish was his courage. Courage led to his academic, spiritual, political, and social victories, and [courage led to] the gravitation of the people's hearts towards that noble personality, which was extraordinary. The courage of that noble individual was that he did not take regard on anything. The seditionists like to place the fear of themselves in the hearts of the elite, replacing the fear of Allah. *"—Those to whom the people said, 'All the people have gathered against you, so fear them.' That only increased them in faith, and they said, 'Allah is sufficient for us, and He is an excellent trustee.'"*[161] Meaning they are repeatedly saying to us, *"All the people have gathered against you, so fear them."* The reply is *'Allah is sufficient for us, and He is an excellent trustee.'*. And the result is this: *"So they returned with Allah's blessing and grace, untouched by any harm. They pursued the pleasure of Allah, and Allah is dispenser of a great grace."*[162]. This feeling, understanding, and spiritual reality results from this – *"and Allah is dispenser of a great grace."* Therefore, this courage must exist.[163]

Courage is a virtue that is very lofty and very constructive. The effect of courage on the battlefield is that a person does not fear danger, enters a dangerous field, uses his energy to

---

161. Surah Aal al-Imran – Verse 173.
162. Surah Aal al-Imran – Verse 174.
163. 24/09/2009 – In a meeting with members of the Assembly of Experts.

carry out his duty, and ultimately, the result is victory over the enemy. This is what laypeople understand of courage. However, there are many arenas aside from the battlefield where courage can show itself. The effect of courage in those fields is more important than the effect on the battlefield. Examples of this are the arena of life, the clash of truth and falsehood, the arena of teachings, the arena of the clarification of realities and the arena of holding various positions that may occur in different situations throughout a person's life. Courage in such an arena shows its effect too. When a courageous person sees the truth, they pursue it with no fear of anything. The vastness of the enemies does not become an obstacle for them. However, one with no courage is not like this. The issue is that, at times, the foundations of truth-hood crumble due to the lack of courage in people, especially if those people hold positions and status in society. In other words, sometimes truth becomes an untruth due to the lack of courage shown by a person who does not express their opinion. Falsehood triumphs over the truth. If courage in etiquette, society, and the arena of life are present, which is a better form of courage than the one on the battlefield, then such a problem would not occur.[164]

---

164. 09/02/1996 – In a Friday Prayer Sermon.

Lack of Expediency

In the environment of sedition, some have misunderstood this narration – *"During sedition, be like an adolescent camel who has neither a back strong enough for riding nor udders for milking."*.[165] They have thought its meaning is that when there is sedition in the air, and the situation becomes unclear, you are supposed to stay away. In no way is staying away implied in that statement. It means that when such a time occurs, the seditionist should not be able to use you in any way, using any means *"neither a back strong enough for riding nor udders for milking."*. They should not be able to ride you, nor should they be able to milk you; you have to be careful.

Observe the effects of the Battle of Siffeen. In the Battle of Siffeen, you had Ammar on one side busy giving speeches to this part of the army, then to another part of the army and various groups. That was indeed a time of sedition. Two Muslim groups stood opposed to each other. It was a great sedition. A group was doubtful [about what was happening]. Ammar was continually busy illuminating the situation. These speeches he gave to various groups have been recorded in history. On the other side, you had individuals who were among the companions such as Abdullah ibn Mas'oud who, it is narrated, came to Imam Ali (a) and said, 'Oh the Commander of the Faithful...', it means they accepted him as the Commander, "...we have doubts about this war. Send

---

165. Nahj al-Balgha – Saying No.1.

us to fight at the borders so that we do not get involved with this fighting.". Sometimes staying quiet, staying away and not speaking in itself helps the sedition to grow. At times of sedition, everyone must clarify and have insight.[166]

When some individuals hear these words, no doubt out of sympathy, they will say, 'I wish so and so would not have said these words today.'. It was my duty to say those words. I must say these words. The responsibility of this humble servant is greater than others. The other gentlemen need to say these words too. Our honourable Imam Khomeini broke through the front lines. Wherever he saw a distortion taking place, he would clarify the issue with all his strength and without consideration. If these innovations and mistakes had occurred in his time or had they become common in his time, he would have spoken without a doubt. Some have latched onto these issues and will be offended. They will say, 'Why has this person shown such a lack of affection towards those issues which are liked by us.'. This is the tone they will use to remember these matters. Although most of them are faithful, truthful and sincere people; however, they are making a mistake.[167]

---

166. 24/09/2009 – In a meeting with members of the Assembly of Experts.
167. 07/06/1994 – In a meeting with a gathering of scholars from Kehgiluye and Buyerahmed.

Far From Agitation and Commotion

Consider clarification as fundamental to your work. This humble servant sometimes sees a group, an individual, or a youth who is probably pure and faithful oppose another person or a meeting. They start creating commotion and turmoil or start shouting slogans. I am opposed to such actions. They bear no fruit. This is something that I have been advising all those who are involved in such activities for a while. For example, they go to a gathering because a particular speaker is giving a talk, and because they do not accept them and may even be correct about the speaker, they ruin that gathering. No, this has no benefit. There is a benefit in clarifying the issues and in carrying out work correctly and intelligently. This is what has benefits. Sometimes some do this out of spite and then blame the faithful and revolutionary youth, be careful of this too.[168]

Far From Creating Sedition and Honesty

Clarification can take place in many different forms. It is not a desired form of clarification when it creates conflicts. If it is in a form that leads to increased awareness among the people and the creation of pathways to solutions for the officials, then this form of clarification is greatly desired. There is no problem with this either. Clarifying stances is good; however, as I have mentioned, this clarification can

---

168. 23/05/2016 – In a meeting with the Imam Hussain (a) Military Academy.

take up two forms. The form which leads to the creation and expansion of corruption should not happen. However, clarifying realities in a manner that increases the people's and the official's awareness and makes the officials grateful is desired. Sometimes a person says something which may be filled with criticism, yet, the officials are thankful to them. Repeatedly officials have come to me and stated that the critique I had mentioned had made their job easier and has abled them to carry it out. They may thank you for presenting the criticism. Personal interests should not be taken into account over here. This is not the place for hesitations [in taking and giving criticisms]. What needs to be considered is the truth, our duty and that one day we have to stand in front of Allah and give an answer. We must be attentive to the questioning of God.[169]

Avoiding the Creation of Negativity

If criticism is to take place, it must consider the above. If this happens, then I imagine the discussion of whether or not we should criticise, or whether this is counted as disparagement and stubborn annoyance or not, shall decrease. This is because when the intention is for reformation and progress, this intention itself shows its effect.

It is not a bad idea if we take a general, collective and public look at the matters faced by the country through this

---

169. 10/03/2016 – In a meeting with the Head and members of the Assembly of Experts.

lens. However, in this overview, we must observe realistically. We should not force error upon ourselves and look from a pessimistic lens. We have positive points; we also have negative points, and we must see both of these. At times, just the negative points are emboldened. Unfortunately, today we can see that it has become fashionable among some officials and political elites to observe pessimistically, have a negative outlook, be blind towards the positive points and lean solely upon negative points. On the media, and other than the media, the creation of negativity is repeatedly happening. It has reached an end where when challenged, they say, 'Why are you not letting us show the reality? You keep saying it is presenting a darker image and such things; we want to show the realities!'. No, this is presenting a pessimistic outlook. Let's say, for example, a unit in a production chain has developed a problem, and you wish to report on it with a realistic lens; this is good, but alongside it, report the positive as well.

If these positive points are presented, then the affairs of the nation will be understood in one manner. If these positive points are not mentioned, this nation's affairs will be understood differently. If only the negative points are seen, and they do exist, this does not mean it is looking from a realistic lens. This will not present an accurate understanding of the country's state, leading to hopelessness. This itself leads to damage being caused in society.

I do a quick review of around ten to twenty newspapers daily. Some of these newspapers have four to five headlines which are enough to shake the hearts of someone weak. Negative, negative, negative and negative! They enjoy doing this. It may be due to political objectives, or the objective is to attract readership; whatever it is, we do not know, and we do not wish to accuse anyone; however, this reality exists and is wrong. Allowing a negative outlook to take precedence is against having a realistic outlook, leading to hopelessness.

The opposite is also true. Giving precedence to a positive outlook without considering any negative points is also misleading. It creates an acceptance within a person, which is an acceptance that is based on falsehood. This is also wrong. The negative points must be seen alongside the positive points. [For example], these are works that this country and system have been able to carry out, and these are the ones they have not been able to do. Both of these have to be seen next to each other. Therefore, if you wish to observe the country's situation correctly, you must see both the positive and negative points next to each other.[170]

Innovation

We must innovate. Gather all your human and intellectual resources so you can present the truth through new methods, using contemporary language, with new arguments and

---

170. 05/08/2011 – In a meeting with Government officials.

beautified. One thing can be said in two different ways. Even one text can be presented in two different ways. If you have a strong and wise piece of text and give it to two separate people to read, one may read it in a pleasant manner that reaches the heart and those listening can understand it and enjoy it. Another person may present that exact text, making the listeners restless, annoyed, tired and bored. Even if we deliver content others have created, we can present it in various ways.

Go back and find a better method [to present ideas]. You can create new content. Do not think that whatever must be said has already been said. According to Saa'ib: "You can speak for a lifetime about one strand of the hair of the beloved". Until the reappearance of the Imam of our time (a), we can present hundreds of thousands of words of new material from the sources we already have. After his reappearance, we are unsure what the situation will be like. Do not think all the wheat has been ground, tools have been put back, those who have passed have spoken every word, and the matter is put to rest. This is not true.

There is a lot still to be said, and new ways of thinking can be envisioned in our logical and technical jurisprudence, our greatest skill, and we have advanced a lot in it. A person does not need to reach the level of Allamah Hilli before they can present a new idea. Individuals of a much lower level can also speak about new ideas if they are focused and have worked on them. [There is also a lot to be said in the fields of] exegies of the Quran, the Principles of Belief, Ethics, Etiquettes, Politics, Strategy, and other subjects.[171]

Being Skilful

A critical duty we all have, whether it be this humble servant, government officials, or managements in various fields, is to introduce the status of the teacher to society. This has not been done. The teacher's station and the teacher's position that this humble servant has understood and believed in have not been understood in society. The issue of livelihood is essential; there is no doubt of this; however, if the matter of the teacher's station is not more important, it most definitely is not less important. The teacher's station will not just be understood by us stating it. If I say that the teacher's station is lofty or that it is the station of the Prophets (s), this will not nurture the public understanding of the notion. Speaking about this is not enough; it requires work. Society must understand that a teacher is a point of reference. A teacher has a lofty character. Teaching is a sanctimonious job. This must be presented using various types of arts, by writing books, creating movies, writing poetry, and using other effective methods.[172] Until now, this has not been done. One of the essential tasks that need to be pursued in the

---

171. 26/04/1993 – In a meeting with officils from the Organisation of Islamic Propagation.
172. 09/05/2018 – In Farhangian University.

Education sector itself, alongside other sectors such as the Cultural sector, media, and others, is this issue.

What position a teacher holds must be known, and honouring the teacher must be actualised. It must be present in classroom texts, stories, and novels. Having an eloquent tongue can revolutionise every topic, especially complex matters. It is not a bad idea that I expand upon the question posed by this young daughter at the beginning of the session. Whatever those like me say about the Revolution, we will not be able to explain the lofty realities of it unless we enter the arena equipped with skilful speech. A skilful tongue can clarify and explain significant events and illuminate the minds. Therefore, just like you have indicated, it is entirely correct. The arts can play such a role.[173]

Many tools of propagation exist in the world. Unfortunately, most of these have not been blessed by our valuable realities. We must make use of our skills for the clarification of our realities. The feature of the arts is that they can clarify the realities with a beautified, pleasant, colourful, and adorned vision.[174]

Making Use of Emotions

Throughout the ages, the jurisprudence, philosophy, theology, and teaching of the Shia has managed to protect

---

173. 02/02/1999 – In a question and answer session with the youth.
174. 02/06/1997 – In a meeting with those facilitating the commemoration ceremonies for Imam Khomeini.

itself. [This is despite] the distortions, doubts, and the creation of quasi-scientific information supported by oppressive policies and the Pahlavi treasuries, which were busy furthering their biased objectives. [The Shia ideology] has managed to protect itself, take itself towards perfection, and expand and strengthen itself in the hearts and minds of millions worldwide, not just in Iran. Indeed, the most effective factor has been the sturdiness and originality of this school of thought. However, there are places where intellectual integrity is not enough by itself. Another element is required. It is the same thing which becomes the support for sincere faith. That factor is correct emotions based upon correct teachings. This love of the Aa'ima (a) and Ahl al-Bayt (s) is the same element that the Quran itself leans upon, *'except the love of [my] relatives.'*[175]. This attachment to the words of the Ahl al-Bayt (s), their guidance, and solution-providing indicators in all issues is the essential factor that has been able to protect this sound and sturdy ideology from harm. Scholars and thinkers who have subscribed to money, force, power, desires, and other stumbling blocks are not few in numbers. That which can keep scholars and lay people away from these stumbling blocks is inspiring faith mixed with emotions. This has protected the Shia.

Imam Khomeini stated, "The month of Muharram is when blood was victorious over the sword." How? You, dear youth, were not present in the street in those days. In this big

---

175. Surah al-Shura – Verse 23.

world, many changing events and political transformations happened in the 20th century. In 1917, there was a federal revolution in Russia. In the following one or two decades, various subsequential political transformations took place in different corners of the world through the shedding of large amounts of blood, bloody coup d'état, intimidation, or grand military mobilisations. Nowhere had an event occurred in which the nation, with its own bodies, hearts, and emotions manifested in its slogans, without arms and with its sheer volume, controlled the society in a manner that the powers opposed to it could not withstand. This was until the Revolution of Iran.[176] The intellect, philosophy and reasoning are the pillars of religion; there is no doubt about this. However, an intellectual or philosophical school can't take hold, grow roots and remain throughout history without being watered with emotions and heartfelt faith.

This is a feature of religions. This is what differentiates them from other ideologies and other various philosophies. [Religions] can attract people's faith. Faith is different to knowledge. Faith is different from reasoning. Faith is different from philosophy. Faith is an act of the heart. The place of faith is in the same place as emotions and sentiments. Faith means sacrificing your head and heart; it means giving your heart. Therefore the heart finds its role. This is how emotions have protected religion throughout history.

---

[176]. 31/08/2000 – In a meeting with Basij university students participating in Tarh-e-Wilayat.

In the war of philosophies with one another, no philosophy can resist religious and monotheistic philosophy. This is especially true for a philosophy Islam codifies—however, this is not the issue. Many know the Islamic sources and teachings and even know the realities; however, they have not been able to give their hearts to those realities. Think about the rightfulness of Ali ibn Abi Talib (a) at the beginning of Islam. Do you think those individuals who heard the Prophet (s) speak about the realities of Ali ibn Abi Talib (a) did not understand? They knew. We have in our narrations that they heard from the lips of the Messenger (S); they had knowledge. However, they lacked faith in what they knew and what they had found out. Meaning they had not given their hearts. What obstructs the development of faith? Many things, this opens up a much broader discussion.[177]

Embracing the Islamic Revolutionary Thinkers

One essential point during clarification is that only content which is certain and correct and sourced from the teaching of pure Muhammadan (s) Islam should be presented to the audience. The Leader of the Revolution has repeatedly emphasised using the statements of Imam Khomeini to get to the teachings of the Islamic Revolution. In reality, the words of Imam Khomeini are the original source [on this matter]. In the same line of thinking, following

---

[177]. 05/07/2007 – In a meeting with Eulogists on the birth anniversary celebration of Lady Zahra (s).

the statements of Imam Khomeini, the statements of the Leader of the Revolution are valuable. They are overflowing from the teachings of the pure Muhammad (s) Islam, and due to his closeness with the thoughts of Imam Khomeini, they form the best explanations for the teachings of Imam Khomeini. In addition, his thoughts gained added value due to almost 80 years of struggle and the importance of his macro-management. From another perspective, the benefit of being up-to-date and observant over matters in the present era sets his thoughts apart from other Islamic revolutionary thinkers. However, despite everything that has been said, due to humility, you do not find any open invitation from him to the audience to study and research his own words. After the leaders of the Islamic Revolution, other revolutionary thinkers such as the honourable martyrs Syed Muhammad Baqar al-Sadr, Muttaheri, Beheshti, Mufatteh, Bahonar, and the late Allamah Tabatabai, Allamah Muhammad Taqi Ja'fari, Ayatullah Misbah Yazdi and Ayatullah Jawadi Amoli are among those that can be leaned upon. The Leader of the Revolution also invites the youth in his statements, directly or through mentioning their traits, to study these honourable personalities' publications.

The issue of rejecting the system of domination is among the primary key phrases. The issue of freedom is among the keywords. You should outline freedom correctly. The issue of justice is one of the keywords as well. And there are other such keywords too. You should explain these keywords. My advice to student groups is that they should clarify these primary and fundamental keywords correctly. [To do this] they should use Imam Khomeini's statements.[178]

One of the friends asked how we could get ahold of the viewpoints of Imam Khomeini. In my opinion, this is very apparent. Imam Khomeini's opinions are a compilation; luckily, the statements of Imam Khomeini have been recorded, and what is there is what is there. Just like how you can deduce the speaker's thoughts from their texts, [you can deduce the thoughts of Imam Khomeini from his texts], however, using the correct method of deduction. The proper process of deduction is by looking at all the words and placing them alongside each other. Some words there are general, and some are specific. Some are absolute, whilst others are conditional. The words must be compared with one another and matched, and the collective of these words makes up the viewpoint of Imam Khomeini. It must be said that this is not a straightforward task. However, it is obvious what needs to be done. It is an act of ijtihad which falls upon the shoulders of you, the youth. Working groups should sit and, in various fields, deduce Imam Khomeini's opinions, which can be attained from his statements.[179]

---

178. 07/06/2017 – In a meeting with a group of students.
179. 28/09/2008 – In a meeting with a group of students.

Sometimes in some corners of our speeches, there are valuable words; unfortunately, for the most part, they are not considered and appear invisible![180]

The second word of advice is to strengthen one's ideological principles. This is very important. Thankfully, there are many broad-minded individuals among you who think and work on many matters. Still, youth environments, including universities, have been subject to certain detriments since long ago. There are two significant detriments jeopardising youth environments: one is passivity, and another is deviation. Passivity means feeling that your hands are tied, that you are of no value, and you have no hope of being able to face difficult events. This could be remedied with the previous word of advice: when your spiritual relationship with God is strengthened, you will not remain passive in any way. Deviation, ideological deviation and deviation from one's principles – are remedied with the same advice.

Notice that at the beginning of the Revolution, we had youth who were Muslims and had entered the arena for the sake of Islam. Still, they joined up with false synthesised groups because they had a shaky ideology and because their ideological values were not solid for whatever reason. They changed from pious, healthy, Islamic and religious youth to people who aimed guns at their own compatriots. They shot at other youths, the elderly and shopkeepers, and they committed those horrible crimes. Because of their weak

---

180. 02/06/1997 – In a meeting with a group of students.

ideological basis, they joined up with those corrupt groups and were pushed into those paths. And they finally ended up being under the flag of Saddam. They finished up in those places. All of that originated from ideological instability.

And there were other individuals at that time – I knew many individuals: before the Revolution, I was familiar with many youths who were members of different groups – who stood firm because they had correct ideological principles. They would read Shaheed Motahhari's books and be familiar with Allamah Tabatabai's viewpoints and Shaheed Sadr. Therefore, they had a solid ideological and intellectual basis, so they stood firm.

However, some of them had shaky principles and were unfortunately lost. And some people used to carry out revolutionary activities at the beginning of the Revolution but regretted their actions later. They were "the regretful". One of the problems of our Revolution is the issue of these regretful individuals: those who were revolutionaries one day but regretted being revolutionary later on.[181]

According to the report I have received, book reading has not been prevalent among student groups. This is something that I have always advised. I want to repeat: you need to read and know. If there is time, God willing, I will speak about this again. You should launch book-reading initiatives. You should read books and study. In my previous meetings with students,

---

181. 17/05/2020 – In a televised speech with the representatives of various University student groups.

I frequently talked about the books of Shaheed Motahhari[182], but I do not want to say that you should merely read his books. You, your academic committees and your seniors should make a list of studies. You should develop, design and define a curriculum for different places and groups of students and carry out tasks like this. This is an essential course of action.[183]

The matters being discussed currently by Iranian thinkers in the field of Islamic issues, general Islamic teachings, such as the thought of the Shaheed Motahhari, is multiple times deeper and more substantial than what other famous intellectuals around the world have presented, such as the Muslim Brotherhood, Syed Qutb, Rasheed Ridha, Abdeh and others. In society and other general Islamic discussions, the thoughts of the Late Allamah Tabatabai and the Shaheed Motahhari, these Shia thinkers, have been more substantial than anyone else. Specialised discussions such as Jurisprudence, Gnotisicsm, and Philosophy have their own place.[184]

In the face of this hostility and this front, our dear and eternal nation must strengthen its identity. [This nation needs to strengthen] its personality and identity elements and should also increase its inner strength. This is a definite need.

---

182. For example, in a meeting with a group of students and representatives of University student groups on 06/08/2012.
183. 22/05/2019 – In a meeting with a group of students.
184. 15/04/1990 – In a meeting with the organisers of the World Ahlulbayt (a) Assembly.

What gives identity and power to a nation and a movement? First of all, having a firm ideological infrastructure. Many countries that had a revolution and later hegemony, arrogance, oppression and tyranny, have returned from their path after a short time; some after five years, some after ten years. They ended up taking the course of their predecessors and behaved like them. [The reason for this] was that they did not have a firm ideological infrastructure.

When you see foreigners use specific terms, unfortunately, some inside the country also repeat them. This is what we mean by de-ideologicalisation. The main enemy of hegemonic powers is this fundamental ideological infrastructure, which is Islamic. This infrastructure is based on Islam and has been explained in detail in Imam Khomeini's statements. If you look at the large volume of books containing Imam Khomeini's statements, you will see this Islamic ideological infrastructure is completely luminous. Our late Imam Khomeini's wealth of statements is a rich source of information in this regard.

Besides these statements, valuable lessons from our revolutionary thinkers are also available to us: thinkers such as Shaheed Motahhari, Shaheed Beheshti and others up until now. These thinkers have derived this infrastructure from the Holy Quran and Islamic sources. Of course, I firmly believe that the intellectual forces of the Islamic government should complete and continue this path. They should improve, promote and update this ideology daily, as new responses are needed with the emergence of contemporary issues. They should provide these responses for those who desire it, for researchers and youth.[185]

By the grace of God, today, the Islamic system is proud to have outstanding academic and spiritual personalities—for example, this dear and lofty personality, the respected Agha Misbah. By the grace of God, this work is also due to his blessing. I have known him for nearly 40 years and have a heartfelt attachment to him. He is a jurist, philosopher, thinker and expert in the fundamental matters of Islam. Suppose God has not given the opportunity for the current generation to benefit from the likes of the late Allamah Tabatabai, or the Shaheed Motahhari. By the grace of God, in that case, this dear and lofty personality fills the hole they left in our time. I truly praise God and thank Him that our society, especially the young generation, is attracted to him. Wherever I gathered information from, all across the country, I was informed that our young generation has an intense affection for him, believes in him and values him. This is also a great blessing from God and a reason for the success of this work. When a person enters the arena with a divine spirit and objective, this is how it turns out.

I was delighted when informed that the late Allamah Ja'fari would be commemorated. The reason is that after the demise of this great personality – a very active individual

---

185. 17/02/2021 – In a televised speech with the people of Western Azerbaijan.

in scholarly, propagational, religious and artistic areas – no proper work had been carried out that befits his status. It is common to commemorate the name and memory of great personalities in society – it is better to do so during their lifetime, if not, at the least, this should be done after their demise – so that others benefit from the scholarly and existential identity of those personalities.

Chapter 3
Methods and Types

- *Compiler's notes*

One of the most essential elements in clarification is selecting the best and most appropriate processes and methods given the audience, conditions, time and place. The Supreme Leader of the Revolution, whilst stating the importance of online space for the illumination of the public minds, he has also stated the importance of real-world spaces and written forms of communication. Following are some of the points he has mentioned regarding this; however, they do not leave those striving on this path needless of thinking about, creating and using new methods. They are presented more from the perspective of being examples in the arena of clarification.

Methods are essential. In this verse – "*Invite to the way of your Lord with wisdom*"[186] – the method has been stated. Words with wisdom mean words that are robust, free from doubt and uncertainty and not weak. Wisdom contains all of these – "*with wisdom and good advice and dispute with them in the best manner.*"[187] – Discussion, debate, the coming together of minds, addressing the hearts and the minds, with a tongue

---

186. Surah al-Nahl - Verse 125.
187. Same as above.

that is clear and speaking in a brotherly manner are all very important.

My dear ones! Among the things considered essential for propagation is the ability to answer the audience's questions. Suppose a youth sits in front of us and has ten or twenty questions on their mind, and let's say we speak for an hour, but none of their questions is answered. According to you, would this speech be considered successful? Of course not. We must answer those questions on his mind that he has not asked, been unable to ask, or does not consciously recognise he even has them. How can we answer them? This can happen if we receive questions from him and know what is on his mind.

For this reason, I repeatedly advise the excelling youth and scholars to connect with the young generation. Connect with the young generation, request their questions, and understand their thinking and what they want when they sit in a sermon delivered by a scholar. Not to see what they expect you to say but to understand what they expect to be clarified. Understanding the needs [they have] is essential.[188]

Considering the Audience

Paying attention to a real audience. The online space is a good thing, it is an opportunity, but it isn't sufficient. Some have just stuck to the online space, Twitter and other

---

188. 24/12/1997 – In a meeting with a group of scholars.

platforms, to send their message. This has no benefit; a real audience is necessary, round-table discussions are necessary, speeches are necessary, publications are necessary, discussions between two or three people are necessary, and analysis meetings are necessary. Sit in this manner with your audience and other activities [of this nature].[189]

Nothing will replace face-to-face discussions. [For example] the age-old tradition of our scholars sitting on the pulpit and speaking to the people in person. There is one effect in this act. That sister of ours spoke about different electromagnetic effects. There is no form of impact of electromagnetics in human-to-human and face-to-face interactions. This act has an effect. Many issues, doubts and questions in the minds of the young generation will be answered in the explanations provided by the officials. Doubts and uncertainties will be resolved. When I was physically more able, I would participate in universities more. Even now, if I can and have the time, I would like to join in various universities. Now, however – *"Allah does not test a soul more than its capacity"*[190] – I do not think the youth have much of an expectation anymore of me and those of my age with my duties; however, the nation's officials can and must participate. Right now, from where I am, I advise the officials that they should participate in

---

189. 07/06/2017 – In a meeting with a group of university students.
190. Surah al-Baqarah – Verse 286.

university student meetings. They should come, hear and speak to the university students.[191]

Using Indirect Methods

Sometimes, in movies, the role played by tangents or side stories has a large impact. For example, in a television series, a lady with a good, attractive and positive personality observes her hijab and takes care of it. This is a secondary detail but leaves a significant effect. Or for example, someone with an attractive personality goes and prays at a sensitive time. This humble servant is not saying that you must show prayers, bowing down and prostration. Sometimes it's artificially forced in, and the person recites – *far from defects is my Lord, the Most High* – incorrectly; they do not know how to replicate it. This is not what I am saying. However, you can show just enough, so it is known that they will pray by rolling up their sleeves for ablution. Sometimes these secondary and side actions play a huge role in affecting the youth. There are thousands of examples of this nature. We do not have enough time right now, and you also do not need me to give you different examples. So do pay attention to the role of these secondary actions, especially concerning the religious field.[192]

---

191. 06/08/2012 – In a meeting with a group of university students.
192. 04/02/2003 – In a meeting with IRIB officials.

Formation of Gatherings

One of the responsibilities of the University students' movement is striving to understand, meaning to contemplate. In my opinion, one necessary task is the formation of well-planned widespread intellectual gatherings in which the collective of university students, alongside students from the religious seminaries, sit and contemplate various matters. Spreading thoughts and disseminating correct ideas can lead to the fruits we expect from the arenas of knowledge and technology and the advancement of the sciences. By using a correct movement heading in the right direction, we could flourish and bring new ideas into the arena.[193]

The physical and intellectual presence of the collective of university students in the country's public matters is necessary. Both intellectual and physical presence is necessary. [Intellectual presence can be achieved using] the student media channels, student gatherings, expression of views in this gathering and other such gatherings, and expressing your opinions to institutions and ministries related to the issue. For example, if you are an economist, speak to economic institutions. If you are in the cultural field, write a letter, give proposals and your opinions to the cultural organisations. Announce the positions you hold. [Physical presence refers to] times when participating in a gathering may be necessary. Under no circumstances will I

---
193. 28/09/2008 – In a meeting with university students from across the country.

reject some student gatherings regarding various issues that arise; in fact, I approve of them—for example, the issue of Bahrain or when other such matters come up. However, I am against extremism, unconsidered acts and incorrect decisions in these gatherings by an individual or a small group that get the crowd enveloped in emotions, and suddenly the collective begins to support them.[194]

Bodily - or, as you say, physical – presence is also sometimes necessary. Holding gatherings is essential. There is nothing wrong with gatherings. Of course, they should be legal. As, sometimes, the law might be too strict in some cases, and it might be flawed. This is alright. Not everything happens as we wish. Your gatherings are good. You should hold gatherings on essential matters and by adopting the correct method. If some have a rally against the JCPOA in front of the Islamic Consultative Majlis, I do not think there is any reason behind this course of action. How much time do the members of the Majlis have? The correct way to hold a gathering is to rent a hall where 500, 1,000, 2,000, or 10,000 students can gather. Two or three students who have studied the matter well beforehand should go and speak reasonably. This is important. The opinions expressed there will reach members of the Majlis, government officials and the Leader's representatives. Such gatherings are important.

Of course, this does not mean you should disrupt their meeting. I have said this before, and I would like to repeat it

---

194. 06/08/2012 – In a meeting with university students.

now, and I will say it tens of times more that I am opposed to disrupting others' meetings, no matter what kind of meeting it is. Disrupting others' meetings is a useless and sometimes harmful course of action. The least is that it is futile and, at most, harmful.

What is the necessity of doing this? They have held a meeting there and are speaking against such a revolutionary principle. Very well, you too should announce that you will hold a meeting one or two days after that here – they will be there, and you will be here or in the hall that I referred to – and that you will discuss the matter. You should invite and gather students, discuss the issue and put an end to it. This will be good. You will find some individuals who are willing to listen to you. There are such individuals. After all, students are after knowing the truth. So, physical gatherings are excellent, and there is nothing wrong with them. However, they should observe the rules; as mentioned in the meeting, this should be planned correctly. Officials of academic affairs should help with this as well.[195]

Formation of Intellectual Committees

We need intellectual committees at two places. One is at the top, and another is grassroot. The Popular Voluntary Mobilization Forces (Basij) have numerous and various layers. For example, when these youth say to us in such meetings

---

195. 02/07/2016 – In a meeting with representatives from students bodies nd university students from across the country.

that they have the enthusiasm and should be sent there [to Iraq, Syria, Palestine and Lebanon] and when they complain why we do not do so, this is a layer of the hard war. A hard war needs intellectual committees to formulate the boundaries and clarify who should go, when, and how they should go. A soft war also requires intellectual committees. Soft war is a vast arena developing daily alongside online efforts, and it is much more difficult than hard war.

In a hard war, bodies roll in dirt and blood, but souls fly towards paradise, but in a soft war, if – God forbid – the enemy wins, bodies become fat and remain whole, but souls descend into the depth of hell. This is the difference between a hard war and a soft war. So, the latter is much more difficult. The soft war needs intellectual committees.[196]

Knowledge-Based Circles

Standing up or taking the pulpit to speak to the people between or after the two prayers, using a board to write narrations on and clarify issues for the people, and forming an ideological chain with the youth of the mosque to explain different matters and answer their questions are tasks that are common these days. This is based on the feeling we get from reading reports from others' opinions – and these tasks were not common in [the old] days.

---

196. 23/11/2016 – In a meeting with the Basij.

At that time, public prayer leaders were satisfied with saying daily prayers and then leaving the mosque. Meanwhile, they could answer one or two religious questions if there were any. But there was nothing more than that. Today, the quality of such tasks should be enhanced daily.[197]

Using Media and Online Platforms

The arts are the best tool to use for these teachings and these issues. Unfortunately, the enemies of Islam, Iran, our honour and our dignity have used the arts with ill intentions. They continue to do so. They have used poetry, visual arts, stories, cinema, exhibitions and other branches of the arts to batter righteousness, destroy Islamic and spiritual realities and virtues and promote materialism and the squandering of wealth on material pleasures. Who is supposed to repair this? You, the youth! Suppose the revolution and the Islamic society are not able to make use of the arts honourably. In that case, it will be unable to transfer the secrets of their hearts to the audience, and it will be unable to establish a connection with them.

For example, imagine a society that takes away the possibility for the virtuous and those with correct thinking to give speeches, and they are not allowed to speak. You can see how great the harm would be. Just like this, and in some ways even more significant harm, is suffered by a society

---
197. 21/08/2016 – In a meeting with Friday prayer leaders from the province of Tehran.

unable to use the arts. The arts can reflect those matters that a simple and standard presentation can not. This is especially true for future generations, and also, this is true for the current generation.[198]

In my estimation, the events of these few years have not been properly covered by the journalists. Be it the events of the military war or events that have taken place in other arenas, for example, in the arena of various processions and the remarkable presence of the people in multiple arenas. Many books should have been written [about these years]. Many pictures, visual arts, cinema, exhibitions, stories and other forms of artistic effects should have been used so that the greatness of the presence of the people would be apparent to those who had not seen it with their own two eyes. You and I have seen it with our own eyes; when the reports come in from places where we were not present, we can observe that many points were hidden from our attention.[199]

One matter is the issue of content production. We require processes that create content. In the arena of content production, we can not be content with coincidences. We have data banks; however, we must sit, contemplate and make a plan about this issue, the issue of content production. We

---

198. 23/10/1991 – In a meeting with the families of the martyrs, those injured at war, other segments of society alongside officials from Tehran, Shehdaad Kerman, Qom and officials and students from the Arts University.
199. 11/11/1993 – In a large gathering to the officials of the Basij from across the country.

have thoughtful religious youth, valuable individuals who can produce social content and religious seminaries whose hands are open to doing whatever work they want in this field. As I stated, we have some university students, too, outstanding youth in this arena. Alongside this, we also have data banks. These must be used. Strengthen the systems for content production; we require this.[200]

---

200. 23/01/2018 – In meeting with the Advisory Council for Cyber Space.

Chapter 4
Subjects in Need of Clarifications

- *Compiler's notes*

Those striving in the arena of propagation see themselves as duty-bound to propagate and clarify in any arena in which they know a need exists. In this chapter, we will list some topics which the Supreme Leader of the Revolution has specified need to be regarded in this clarification. Under each of these topics, we have entered the Leader's explanation for them. However, not all the topics that need clarification are restricted to these subjects. The subjects mentioned in this chapter are also not all equal in importance. Some are important, and some are more important. Some are always present and continuous, whilst others are seasonal. It is possible that a topic has to be prioritised at this particular time. For instance, the Supreme Leader of the Revolution considers the need today to be the clarification of the realities of today's world, country and the enemy, as well as opposing the movements of distortion. One way the Leader of the Revolution has presented for us to understand what is needed now is to see the points the enemy has focused their propaganda efforts on. What follows is an explanation of this in his own words.

Sometimes there is a need for propagation in society on a topic that the people themselves are not aware of. However, you know this need exists. For example, you listen to the enemies' propaganda and understand that you must consider that to be the focus of your propagation and bury the enemy's false propaganda. To do this is to take care of a need that exists.

My dear ones! One of the ways the enemy does a service for us is precisely this. They show us through their propaganda exactly what we should be focused on. You have to work in opposition to those very points. The enemy tells us they are sensitive about this topic, and we must therefore focus on that exact point. That said, we do not act as reactionaries to the enemy's actions. This is just a logical and intelligent outlook.[201]

Fundamental Beliefs[202]

Three issues play a significant role in strengthening the country: one is the issue of science and technology, another is the issue of the economy, and the last is the issue of culture. We should make investments in these three areas because they are key elements. Our administrations, our officials and our influential personalities should be active in each of these three areas.

---

201. 24/12/1997 – In a meeting with a group of scholars.
202. For further reading, refer to The Islamic Belief System: Reclaiming the Narrative translated by Ahlulbayt Islamic Mission published originally as *Tarhe Kulliyye Andisheye Islami Dar Qur'an* by Sahba Publications.

Subjects in Need of Clarifications

Of course, the issue of population is significant as well. As was pointed out, the population issue plays a vital role in national capacity. Some of the gentlemen in this meeting emphasised this issue which is entirely correct. An increase in the young generation and the largeness of the country in terms of the population plays a very significant role in improving capacity.

The cultural issue is the most important element, particularly at the level of popular beliefs. As you can see, they [the enemy] are making considerable investments in this area. It was pointed out in this meeting that significant funds are allocated to establish influential networks for satellites, the Internet, mobile phones and the like. They are spending a lot of money to influence people's beliefs and get people out of the circle of Islamic influence and values.

The antidote to these plots is that we can prepare descriptive and compelling plans for people's beliefs at different levels. Our scholars, cultural organisations, propagational institutes, spokespeople and IRIB should be able to establish and deepen these beliefs in the people's minds. Of course, the direct relationship of the scholars with the people is an irreplaceable factor. Nothing can replace this direct relationship between scholars and the people. Even the IRIB, a comprehensive network, cannot replace the direct connection of scholars and religious thinkers with the people.[203]

---

203. 04/09/2012 – In a meeting with members of the Assembly of Experts.

Today, religious enlightenment is the most essential armour an Islamic society can wear and use to face enemy attacks.[204]

Notice that in the present time, the propaganda orientation of our enemies is not only to abuse, curse and make political accusations against the Islamic Republic. Today, our enemies are fundamentally challenging the Islamic Republic with issues that form the basis of the Islamic Republic. As they put it, they are theorising a philosophy against the Islamic Republic. They are creating ideological and intellectual grounds to promote the philosophy that the world of arrogance – headed by America – should dominate the world.

All the things related to the people's faith, the legitimacy of Islam, the Holy Qur'an and divine rules, the unity of religion with politics and specific principles of the Islamic Republic are being challenged by them. They are seriously pursuing this challenge. The opponents of the Islamic Republic are not a bunch of thugs who gather together on the Radio and on TV to talk political nonsense. They have hired intellectuals: individuals who have intellectual ideas – whether religious or political. They are spending money, presenting ideas and thoughts and injecting them into our society. In the face of this, anger, weapons, and force are useless. In the face of the notion that "nothing can match iron except for iron",

---

204. 01/05/2005 – In a meeting with a group os scholrs from the province of Kerman.

we should act with reason. The enemy uses the arts and modern propaganda tools to promote their ideas. And the main target is our youth.

They bring their thoughts into newspapers and different media. They even get them into those media connected to the Islamic Republic in ways our media do not understand. These media sometimes publish their ideas as well. They bring some people to the press under the false names of philosophers, politicians, intellectuals and the like. And such individuals wrestle and fight against the well-established principles of the Holy Qur'an, and they try to question them. This is clear - *"To such deceit let the hearts of those incline, who have no faith in the hereafter. Let them delight in it, and let them earn from it what they may"*[205]. Those whose hearts are potentially prepared for such things will use these ideas, and some ignorant and naïve individuals – who do not have the capacity for scholarly complexity – will accept them. Today, the critical responsibility falls on our distinguished personalities.

Agha Amini quoted Agha Sayyid Ahmad Khatami (may God preserve him) as saying that illogical and unfounded ideas are promoted regarding religious lamentations. However, I want to say that it is not confined to lamentations. We should observe precision in expressing divine teachings, the teachings of Ahlul Bayt (a.s.), the hadiths we narrate, the narrations we quote, and the qualities we ascribe to the Imams and the teachings that we want to be committed to. We

---
205. Surah al-An'aam – Verse 113.

should observe precision in all these areas. In Jurisprudence, our scholars have placed great emphasis on and attached great significance to the reliability of such and such narrators, even when it comes to trivial and unimportant matters. They used to discuss such issues at length to see whether such and such narrators were reliable or not. Their purpose was to ensure that the narrated document was devoid of any doubt. It was to see if it was a reliable document and – when they could trust it – to issue a peripheral and third-degree edict about the issue of cleanliness or other religious matters. We attach such significance to these matters. So why should we trust any hadith, narration, statement and claim on the issue of divine teachings and the issue of intellectual and emotional matters? This is not acceptable.

Precision in narrating and recounting and in what we want to give to the people as food for thought is necessary. This is a major condition. This should be thought upon. As I said before, this is a challenging task that cannot be carried out only by holding a meeting, issuing warnings and establishing associations. This requires firm determination on the part of seminarians and scholars so that they pursue and insist on it. They should not show fear in the face of a possible backlash.

A few years ago, we spoke about bloodletting in this meeting. This issue is a clear example of "al-ghay" [meaning error: it comes from a Qur'anic verse that says, *"Truth stands out clear from error"*][206]. Several great personalities spoke

---

206. Surah al-Baqarah – Verse 256.

about this issue. They showed their honourable nature and accepted what we said. Many people, too, accepted it. However, we saw that some voice was raised from a corner of the country saying we opposed Imam Hussain (a)! Does "the Light of Guidance and the Ark of Salvation" mean that we should perform an undoubtedly problematic act from the perspective of Sharia that is clearly forbidden? We should cast out such light so that our young generation becomes more interested in Islam.

You should take a look at the youth's inclination towards Islam. This inclination is spiritual and very valuable, but it can come and go like a wave. If we want this wave always to be there, we should strengthen the youth's intellectual makeup. We have so many sources. Our youth read Dua Abu Hamza – this was pointed out by Agha Meshkini as well – and Dua of Imam Hussain (a) on the Day Arafah, but they do not understand them. "Oh God, bestow upon me a heart whose enthusiasm helps it get close to You" [from Dua Sha'baniyyah]. There are many prayers, principles and profound statements like this in supplications such as Dua Sha'baniyyah and Sahifa al-Sajjadiyyah. We must explain these supplications to the youth so that they understand and read them with keen interest and with the enthusiasm that they usually have.[207]

---

207. 08/09/2005 – In a meeting with members of the Assembly of Experts.

The Most Important Principle in Religious Teachings

Our friends made excellent points regarding the Islamic aspect of the paradigm. The first issue that has to be taken into consideration is the starting point - the issue of monotheism. - *"To Allah, We belong, and to Him is our return."*[208] - The most critical problem of the modern world - the most alluring example of which is in the west - is that it has strayed away from God, faith in God, and commitment to this faith. Of course, people may appear to have faith in God, but they are not committed to this faith. If this issue of the starting point is resolved, many other issues will be resolved as well. *"Whatever is in the heavens and the earth declares His glory."*[209] *"For to Allah belong the Forces of the heavens and the earth, and Allah is Exalted in Power, Full of Wisdom."*[210]. When people come to believe this issue, this divine glory and this monotheism it will provide them with an inexhaustible power source. *"He is Allah, besides Whom there is no god - the King, the Holy, the Giver of peace, the Granter of security, Guardian over all, the Mighty, the Supreme, the Possessor of every greatness. Glory be to Allah from what they set up (with Him)."*[211] When one believes in monotheism like that and manages to extend this belief to the framework of one's life, humanity's fundamental problem will be solved.

---

208. Surah al-Baqarah – Verse 156.
209. Surah al-Hashr – Verse 24.
210. Surah al-Fath – Verse 7.
211. Surah al-Hashr – Verse 23.

The second essential issue is the Day of Judgment and divine accountability - death is not the end of everything. The fact that there is divine accountability is essential. "*So he who has done an atom's weight of good shall see it, and he who has done an atom's weight of evil shall see it.*"[212] A nation with this belief and includes these Qur'anic verses in its plans will witness an essential change in its life. Believing that the consequences of one's actions extend beyond one's material life makes self-sacrifice and jihad meaningful and logical. The issue of jihad is one of the most excellent tools religions use - and it is particularly highlighted in Islam. Jihad should be accompanied by self-sacrifice; otherwise, it will not qualify as jihad in the first place. Self-sacrifice is something illogical within the framework of material wisdom. There is always the question, "Why would I sacrifice myself?" Faith in the Day of Judgment makes self-sacrifice logical and reasonable. When we believe that none of our actions will go unnoticed, all our efforts will be recorded, and we will see them in front of our eyes in our "real life" in the hereafter, then we will not feel regretful if we lose something to fulfil an obligation - even if that something is our life, our children and our dear ones. "*And this life of the world is nothing but a sport and a play. And as for the next abode, that most surely is the life.*"[213] These things should be included in the paradigm of progress and should become meaningful in the progress of a society.

---
212. Surah al-Zilzal – Verses 7 and 8.
213. Surah al-Ankabut – Verse 64.

Therefore, the main issues are the issues of monotheism and the Day of Judgment.

The next issue is the lack of a clear line between the world and the hereafter. "The world is the farm for the Hereafter."[214] I think some of our friends mentioned the same point as well. This is very important. The world and the hereafter are not separate from one another. They are two sides of the same coin. "*And indeed hell surrounds the unbelievers.*"[215] The disbelievers are living in hell, but they do not realise this. They will realise it when hell appears in a material form. They are not aware of what they are. And we fail to see them for what they are because we are blindfolded, but when death wakes us up, we will see their real nature. This is the meaning of the lack of a clear line between this world and the hereafter.

The next issue is Islam's view of man and the centrality of man. This issue has an extremely vast meaning in Islam. It is clear that the Islamic view of man is entirely different from the conception of man in materialistic western philosophies, 19th-century positivism and similar other schools. The Islamic conception is one thing, and the western conception is quite another. The two sides define man in entirely different ways. Therefore, the centrality of man in Islam is completely different from that of man in those materialistic schools. Justice, security, welfare and worship

---
214. Irshaad al-Quloob – Vol 1, P 89.
215. Surah al-Tawbah – Verse 49.

- all these things are supposed to bring about happiness for man. The issue of happiness is limited to the individual, but this does not mean that one should ignore other people's conditions and not do anything for them. *"And whoever keeps it alive, it is as though he kept alive all men."*[216] According to a tradition, an Imam was asked what the Qur'anic verse means. He said the most probable interpretation is that one should guide someone onto the right path. It is clear that this is an obligation everyone should fulfil. However, from an Islamic perspective, a priority for man is the obligation to deliver himself. We have a duty to save ourselves. Our salvation lies in the fulfilment of our obligations. Of course, social responsibilities, administration of justice, fighting oppression, establishing a righteous government and fighting corruption are all preliminary steps towards that salvation. Therefore, this is the most important goal; everything else is just a preliminary step. The establishment of an Islamic community is a preliminary step. Justice is also a preliminary step. *"That mankind may observe right measure."*[217] It has been mentioned in the Holy Qur'an that this is a goal of divine prophets. Undoubtedly, justice is one of the goals, but it is a medium-term goal. The ultimate goal is the salvation of mankind. This has to be taken into consideration.

Man has obligations to fulfil. He has free will and is faced with divine guidance. *"Have We not given him two eyes, and a*

---

216. Surah al-Ma'idah – Verse 32.
217. Surah al-Hadid – Verse 25.

tongue and two lips, and pointed out the two conspicuous ways to him?"[218] Man is free to choose between being guided and misled. Man commits himself, his society and those around him. From this perspective, democracy is not only a public right but also an obligation. That is to say, all people are responsible for playing a role in governing their society. It is unacceptable to say, "This does not concern me." No, the well-being or corruption of a country and its government concern everyone living there. That is to say; people have a responsibility to play a role. This is one of the essential elements that should be considered from an Islamic perspective.

Government is the next issue. Again, Islam has exceptional views in this regard. From an Islamic point of view, individual qualifications are an essential issue when it comes to government. Based on the level of one's involvement in management, one should have the necessary qualifications and consider oneself qualified. Otherwise, his rule is unlawful. Avoiding arrogance, extravagance, and selfishness are essential issues in government. *"Surely he was arrogant, (and) one of the extravagant."*[219] God says this about Pharaoh. That is to say, the problem with Pharaoh was that he was arrogant. Therefore, for a ruler, being arrogant is a negative characteristic. A ruler does not have the right to behave arrogantly. If someone is arrogant by nature, he does not

---

218. Surah al-Balad – Verse 8.
219. Surah al-Dukhaan – Verse 31.

have the right to accept power. Also, the people do not have the right to accept him as the ruler and leader of their society. A selfish person wants everything for himself.

Selfishness is the opposite of self-sacrifice. Self-sacrifice means depriving oneself of everything for the sake of others, and selfishness means depriving others of everything for the sake of oneself. Arrogance and selfishness are among the negative characteristics of government. Speaking about the Umayyad dynasty, the Commander of the Faithful (a) says in Nahjul Balagha that they were not qualified to rule because public wealth was exclusively in their hands. However, public wealth belongs to the people. They also considered the people as their slaves. And they manipulated God's religion the way they wanted. Therefore, Islam has its own view of government. This has to be included and observed in our long-term paradigm of life.[220]

Mahdawiiyah and Awaiting the Re-Appearance

When colonialism entered our region during the past century, one of the matters that troubled colonialism was the belief in Mahdawiyyah! In the document I saw, the heads and commanders of colonialism suggested they needed to do something so the faith in Mahdawiyyah would gradually disappear among the people. At that time, the French and English colonisers were present in some African countries. No matter where the colonisers came from, they judged that

---

220. 01/12/2010 – In the first sitting of The Strategic Thoughts.

until the belief in Mahdawiyyah existed among these people, they would be unable to control these countries completely! Now you see how important the belief in Mahdawiyyah is!

There are several features in the belief in Mahdawiyyah which work like blood in the veins or a soul in the body. One of them is hope. Sometimes, powerful and vulgar hands bring weak nations to the point where they completely lose hope. When they lose hope, they won't make a move. They think it is futile and it is too late. They believe they cannot confront the powers because they won't succeed. This is the spirit of despair. This is what colonialism seeks. Today, the global Arrogant power wants Muslim nations, including the dear Iranian nation, to get afflicted with the spirit of despair, so they say, 'We cannot do anything; it is useless!'. The Arrogant Powers want to inject this among the people by force. What for? So they can take enthusiasm and hope away from the human community, which advances with hope and turn the people into the living dead. So they can do whatever they want! They cannot do whatever they want with a living and enthusiastic nation. To an unconscious, dazed, isolated nation anyone can inject anything they want; they can do anything they want to them. Whereas, with a strong, enthusiastic, intelligent, active nation, they cannot do whatever they want.

Those living in the Islamic Republic's neighbourhood cannot do whatever they want with the Islamic and revolutionary nation of Iran. It is a nation that is awake, and is aware of its strength and honour and knows how to act with the world in a manner that is worthy of it. The result of this you can see too.

If a nation had no movement and believed in no values or future for itself, the enemy could easily come and make a plan for them, advise them, make decisions on their behalf, and execute those plans! They would be able to interfere with no obstruction. This can only happen due to a lack of movement. This lack of movement is due to a lack of hope. That is why they try to make people feel hopeless. You must know this.

Today, understand that every breath taken or voice that creates hopelessness within the people is in the hands of the enemy, regardless of whether they know it or not. Every pen that writes a word on paper intending to create hopelessness and despair within the people is linked to the enemy, regardless of whether the owner of this pen knows it or not. The enemy is making use of them.

The belief in Mahdawiyyah and the noble existence of the Promised Mehdi (a) keeps hope alive in the hearts. At no point would a person who believes in this lose hope. Why? Because they know that there is a bright ending that is certain. They try to reach that end. There is no futility.

This is our belief. When they realise they cannot take this belief from the people, they try to ruin the minds of people. How do they distort this belief? They say that when the Imam (a) returns, he will fix everything. This is how this belief is ruined. They transform a motivational engine into a stick in the wheel. They transform a powerful medicine into a dangerous and sleep-inducing drug.

What do you mean the Imam (a) will come and do everything?! What is your responsibility today? You must prepare the grounds so that this lofty personality can come and carry out his work on the prepared soil. It is not possible to start from zero! Society will have the capacity to accept the Promised Mehdi (a) if it has prepared and has the capability to do so. Otherwise, the same will happen as what has occurred throughout history with all Prophets (s) and the Awliyyah.

Why were many of the Great Prophets (s) unable to purify and beautify the world of evil? Why? Because the grounds were not ready. Why was the Commander of the Faithful (a) in his time, even in the short time of governance he had, unable to dry the roots of evil? [This was despite having] that divine strength, that knowledge linked to the divine treasures and unparallelled will and determination, with all the virtues and illuminated characteristics, and all the praises of him by the Messenger (s).

The people removed that lofty personality from the journey. "They killed him in the mihrab whilst he was in worship because of the severity of his justice."[221]. The punishment the justice of the Commander of the Faithful

---

[221]. From the book: Imam Ali (a); The Voice of Humanities Justice by George Jordak and translated by Syed Hadi Khusroshahi – Vol 1, P 62 and 63.

(a) was for his life! Why? Because the grounds were not favourable. They had made the grounds unfavourable. They had made the soils fertile for wanting the desires of this world. Those who had created a front against the Commander of the Faithful (a) in the middle and end of the Alawi government were those whose religious grounds were not sturdy and whose makeup was not in accordance with the religion. The lack of readiness leads to such catastrophes!

If the Imam of Our Time (a) returns to a world that is not ready, the same thing will happen again. The preparation must be made.

Therefore, we can prepare the grounds. When these grounds are spread, by Allah's will, the foundations for the Imam's (a) re-appearance will also be set, and this long-awaited desire of humanity and the Muslims will be actualised.[222]

I would say that Mahdawiyyah is among the fundamental subjects of religion. It is comparable to prophethood: this is the kind of importance we should attach to the issue of Mahdawiyyah. Why? Because Mahdawiyyah represents what all prophets were sent for - namely, building a monotheistic world based on justice using all the capacities Allah the Exalted has bestowed on humanity. This is the era that will come after the re-appearance of Imam Mahdi (a): the age in which monotheism and genuine spirituality will be dominant over the entire life of human beings, the era in which justice

---

222. 16/12/1997 – In a meeting with different segments of the public.

will be established in the real sense of the word. This is why the Prophets (s) were sent.

I have repeatedly said that the movement carried out over many centuries by humanity in the shade of the teachings of divine prophets is a movement towards the broad road which will be built after the re-appearance of Imam Mahdi (a). This road will lead humanity to lofty goals. It is as if someone guides a group through mountains, valleys, marshes and thorny bushes to reach the main road. The rest of the way will be easy when they reach the main road. The straight path will be marked out. It will be easy to move ahead. When they reach the main road, they will not stop pushing forward. No, when they reach the main road, they will start moving towards lofty divine goals because human beings enjoy an inexhaustible capacity. Humanity has moved through difficult paths and cleared various obstacles to reach this main road. This main road will be built after the re-appearance of the Imam of the Age (a). It is the world that will be made after the re-appearance of Imam Mahdi (a). In a sense, the movement of humanity will start from that point.

If Mahdawiyyah did not exist, it would mean all the efforts by the divine prophets, all prophetic missions, and the jihad of the divine prophets were futile. Therefore, the issue of Mahdawiyyah is essential. It is one of the central divine teachings. For this reason, as far as I know, in all divine religions, there are teachings essentially the same as Mahdawiyyah. But these teachings have been distorted

Subjects in Need of Clarifications

and blurred over time, and it is not clear what they are trying to say.

The issue of Mahdawiyyah is among the undeniable Islamic realities. That is to say, Mahdawiyyah is not limited to Shia Islam. All Islamic denominations accept that the world's end will come when Imam Mahdi (a) establishes ultimate justice. There are valid narrations by the Holy Prophet (s) and Islamic luminaries in different denominations of Islam. Therefore, there is no doubt in this regard. However, Shia Islam has an advantage over other denominations because the issue of Mahdawiyyah is not ambiguous in Shia Islam. The issue of Mahdawiyyah is not convoluted and unintelligible in Shia Islam. It is clear. Mahdawiyyah has a representative, and we are familiar with this representative. We know his characteristics. We know his ancestors. We know his family. We know when he was born. We know the details; this familiarity is not based on Shia narrations alone. There are non-Shia narrations that clarify the details for us. Followers of other Islamic denominations should pay careful attention to understand this evident truth. This is the kind of importance that should be attached to the issue of Mahdawiyyah, and we are better qualified to work on this issue. It is necessary to carry out scholarly and accurate work in this regard.

The issue of waiting [for the re-appearance of Imam Mahdi (a] is an integral part of Mahdawiyyah. It is one of the key concepts for understanding religion and the general movement of the Islamic Ummah towards the lofty goals of Islam. Waiting means expecting an event that will definitely happen. This is the meaning of waiting. Waiting means that this future is definite. This is especially true if we are waiting for a being who is completely ready. This is a critical issue. We are not waiting for somebody who has not been born yet. No, we are waiting for somebody who exists and is present among us. There are certain narrations according to which people can see him, but they do not recognise him. In certain narrations, he has been likened to Prophet Joseph, whose brothers used to see him. He was present among his brothers, and he used to sit beside them, but they could not recognise him. It is such a clear and motivating truth. This facilitates waiting. Humanity needs this waiting, and the Islamic Ummah needs it even more. This waiting puts responsibilities on the shoulders of human beings.

When a person is sure of such a future, he must expect it and be prepared for it. As the Holy Qur'an says: *"And certainly We wrote in the Book after the reminder that (as for) the land, My righteous servants shall inherit it. Most surely in this is a message to people who are devout."*[223] Those who worship God can understand this message. Waiting requires that we prepare ourselves. We should know that a great event will happen, and we should always expect this event. We can never say that the event will not occur in a few years, and we can never say that the event will happen in the near

---

223. Surah al-Anbiyyah – Verse 105 and 106.

future. We should always wait for it. Those waiting should get closer to the characteristics that will be expected in the era being awaited. This is the requirement for waiting. If there is supposed to be justice, truth, monotheism, purity and worship in the era we are awaiting, then as the people waiting, we should get closer to these things. We should become familiar with justice. We should prepare ourselves for justice. We should prepare ourselves to accept the truth. These are the requirements of waiting.

One of the things that the essence of waiting requires is that we should not be satisfied with the status quo and the level of progress we have made so far. The requirement is to make efforts to increase our progress and spiritual characteristics daily. These are the requirements of waiting.

As Agha Qara'ati said in his report, thankfully, certain people are doing scholarly work on the issue of waiting. It is necessary to pay careful attention to scholarly and accurate work on the subject of waiting and the era after the re-appearance of Imam Mahdi (a). It is also necessary to avoid unscholarly and ignorant work in this regard. Unscholarly and ignorant work - the kind of work that is not based on knowledge and valid documents and sources about the Imam of the Age (a) - is among the things that can be highly dangerous, and it can prepare the ground for false claimants. Unscholarly and undocumented work based on fantasies and illusions rather than valid sources and documents pushes people away from the state of waiting and prepares the ground for false claimants. It is necessary to avoid such things seriously.

There have been false claimants throughout history. As mentioned in this meeting, certain claimants try to make a sign apply to themselves or others. All these things are wrong. Some information said about the signs of Imam Mahdi's (a) re-appearance is not definite and has not been mentioned in valid and documented narrations either. They are based on narrations that are not solid, and we cannot rely on them.

Moreover, it is not easy to apply valid narrations. There have always been certain people who have tried to apply the poems of Shah Nimatullah Wali to different people in different centuries, and I have seen some of these people. His descriptions have been applied to a particular person, and after a century or so, the same descriptions have been applied to another person. These things are wrong and misleading. When there is deviation, the truth will be sidelined, and it will be a tool to mislead people. Therefore, it is necessary to avoid unscholarly work seriously, and we must prevent surrendering to rumours. Scholarly, firm and documented work is something that experts should do. Everybody cannot do such work, and it is up to experts on narrations, Rijal and Philosophy. Only such experts can step in and do scholarly work in this regard. It is necessary to take this issue as seriously as possible so that the path is opened up for ordinary people. The more hearts become familiar

Subjects in Need of Clarifications

with the matter of Mahdawiyyah, and the more we feel the presence of Imam Mahdi (a.s.) among ourselves and increase our relationship with him, the better it will be for our world and our progress towards the goals.

Some of our supplications are valuable and, in some instances, reliable documents. It is very good to ask Imam Mahdi (a) to act as our intercessor. It is very good to pay attention and get close to him. This closeness does not mean those who claim to meet or speak to Imam Mahdi (a) in person are correct. Not at all. The majority of the claims that are made in this regard are either lies or illusions. I have seen such people. Some of them were not liars: they suffered delusions and spoke about their delusions as if they were the truth. We must not surrender to such people. The right way is the logical way. Tawwasul [seeking spiritual intercession and connection] to Imam Mahdi (a) is done from a distance. Imam Mahdi (a) listens to our intercession, and by Allah's favour, he will fulfil them. The fact that we address him from a distance does not really matter. Allah the Exalted conveys greetings and messages to Imam Mahdi (a). This intercession and this spiritual closeness are very good and necessary.

I hope Allah the Exalted will hasten the re-appearance of Imam Mahdi (a). I hope we will be among his followers both when he is in occultation and when he re-appears. By Allah's favour, we will be among the soldiers who will fight alongside Imam Mahdi (a), and I hope we will be martyred for his cause.[224]

Values and the Constitution[225]

The clarification of our sources of values and the strengthening of our constitution are also important. The constitution is like the pillars and foundations of a structure. The pillars and foundations are necessary to create a large and grand building as they give the structure a general form. These pillars and foundations are like a constitution. The normal laws take care of the work needed inside this structure—the separation of the rooms, the walls and the interior design. The values are like the materials that make up this structure. All pillars and all the works that take place inside this building, whether they regard the constitution or the normal laws, the values are what they consist of. The values are what they are formed and made out of. We have this constitution and this sturdy foundation. In these twenty-four – twenty-five years, a lot of effort has been placed into beautifying the interior of this grand and imposing structure. We can present a sturdy and beautiful construction to the world. All the enemy's efforts have been made so that this example can not be presented to the world. Therefore they attack the pillars and foundations of this structure so that it

---

224. 09/07/2011 – In a meeting with teachers and alumni specialising in Mahdawiyyah.
225. For further reading refer to *Surat Wa Seerat e Inqilab*.

Subjects in Need of Clarifications

collapses. The normal laws are connected to the foundations and pillars. To change and modernise those normal laws, it is not wise or logical to mess around with the foundations. The pillars are never destroyed to alter a piece of decoration. To change the formation of the rooms, you do not destroy the foundations. The foundations must be protected.[226]

Other central points the enemy has been working on are the values and foundations of the revolution. The enemy wishes to destroy people's faith in their hearts and minds on that factor which brought about this great miraculous movement approximately nineteen years ago. [This factor] has protected [the movement] till today and led the war to end, benefitting Islam and the Muslims. We must be very protective of this. They wish to create doubts in the people towards the foundations and principles of the revolution and make them disbelieve and have misgivings regarding this great movement and the foundations of the Islamic Republic. Their hatred is not with individuals. Their animosity is not with a specific label. Their hatred is against the foundation of this great movement. Their hostility is towards the revolution. If someone does not understand this, how negligent are they?[227]

---

226. 06/08/2003 – In a meeting with Government officials.
227. 24/12/1997 – In a meeting with a group of scholars.

Governance of Religion[228]

There has been an insistent effort, mainly by political and materialistic powers, to reduce Islam to matters only related to the individual and belief. This effort has existed for a long time. I cannot specify a specific date and say such efforts started from that date. But this effort has been pronounced in the Islamic world since about a hundred or a hundred-plus years ago.

This effort doubled after the formation of the Islamic Republic. They also try to make it look like it is not a political effort and make it look like an intellectual effort. As the westerners say, they have been attempting to "theorise" it. Thinkers, writers, activists and the like are commissioned to write about this and prove that Islam has nothing to do with social issues, matters concerning life and fundamental issues regarding humanity. [They are tasked to write] that Islam is a belief in the heart, a personal relationship with God, and a series of individual actions based on that relationship. They introduce this as Islam. They insist on proving this in the minds of their audience.

They want this inwardly political and allegedly intellectual tendency to liberate essential areas of life and social relations from Islamic interference. In managing society and building civilisation, they say Islam has no role in building human

---

228. For further reading refer to the book *Siyasat* published by Islamic Revolution Publications and the book *Hukumat wa Wilayat* published by Sahba Publications.

civilisation; it has no duty, and there is no place for it. They say Islam has no role in the management of society. It has no role in the distribution of power and wealth in society. They claim the society's economy and various other social issues have nothing to do with Islam.

The same applies to war, peace, domestic and foreign policy, and international issues. They sometimes say, "Do not turn diplomacy into ideology. Do not connect it to ideology." They mean that Islam should not comment on foreign policy and international issues. Islam isn't effective in spreading goodness, establishing justice, confronting evil and oppression and combating wicked forces in the world. They say Islam is neither an intellectual reference point nor a practical guide in these critical areas of human life. This is what they insist on.

Now, the reason for this insistence and its starting point are issues that are not related to my speech today. I want to say that, first of all, this genuinely anti-Islamic movement is mainly launched by the great political powers of the world. They are the ones who are active and working in this field, and they try to promote this using their intellectuals.

Islamic texts explicitly reject this, and we Muslims should pay attention to this matter. When I say that we should do our duty, I primarily mean we should promote and express Islam's view about itself and the areas of human life it cares about, gives an opinion on, works on, explains, promotes, and expresses. This is the first step. Then, we should try to put these into practice.

Islam states that the field of activity of this religion is the entire scope of human life, ranging from human emotions to social, political and international issues and including issues related to all of humanity. This has been clearly explained in the Holy Qur'an. If someone denies this, they have not paid attention to the words of the Qur'an.

A verse in the Qur'an says: *"Oh you who believe, celebrate the praises of Allah, and do this often and glorify Him morning and evening."*[229] - This issue relates to one's beliefs and emotions. Another verse states: *"Those who believe fight in the cause of Allah, and those who reject faith fight in the cause of evil: so fight against the friends of Satan."*[230] - This is another verse. So - *Celebrate the praises of Allah* - and - *Fight against the friends of Satan* - means that this entire vast scope is covered by religion.

One verse addresses the Holy Prophet (s) saying: *"Stand to prayer by night, but not all night, half of it or a little less or a little more and recite the Qur'an in slow, measured rhythmic tones."*[231] - In another verse, God tells the Holy Prophet (s): *"Then fight in Allah's cause, you are held responsible only for yourself, and rouse the believers."*[232] - This means that all these areas of life, ranging from standing to pray by night, supplicating and

---

229. Surah al-Ahzab – Verse 41 and 42.
230. Surah al-Nissa – Verse 76.
231. Surah al-Muzzamil – Verse 2 to 4.
232. Surah al-Nisa – Verse 84.

shedding tears, to fighting and showing one's presence on the battlefield, are areas where religion is active, and the Holy Prophet's (s) life confirms this.

Regarding financial rules, the Qur'an says: "*But give them preference over themselves, even though poverty was their own lot.*"[233] - This is a personal matter. Elsewhere, it says: "*In order that it may not merely circulate between the wealthy among you.*"[234] - This is about the correct distribution of wealth, which is a matter entirely related to society. Elsewhere, it says: "*That men may stand forth in justice.*"[235]

The Prophets (s) and the Friends of Allah have come to establish justice. One verse says: "*To those weak of understanding make not over your property, which Allah has made a means of support for you.*"[236] - In another verse, God says: "*Of their goods, take alms, so that you might purify and sanctify them.*"[237] - All aspects of financial matters are mentioned in the form of general rules and general guidelines. Of course, there should be plans for implementing these rules, but these are the general rules and guidelines mentioned. In other words, Islam has spoken about all these matters.

The Qur'an also has verses about security and the safety of people in society: "*Truly, if the hypocrites, and those in whose hearts is a disease, and those who stir up sedition in the city, desist*

---

233. Surah al-Hashr – Verse 9.
234. Surah al-Hashr – Verse 7 and Verse 9.
235. Surah al-Hadid – Verse 25.
236. Surah al-Nisa – Verse 5.
237. Surah al-Tawbah – Verse 103.

not, We shall certainly stir you up against them"[238]. - Another verse says: *"When there comes to them some matter touching public safety or fear, they divulge it. If they had only referred it to the Messenger"*[239] - These verses mean that Islam has an opinion in all essential aspects of social life. The verses I have mentioned are a small part of those in the Holy Qur'an. Hundreds of such examples can be seen in the Qur'an.

A person interested in and familiar with the Qur'an and its rules understands this is the Islam that Qur'an introduces. The kind of Islam that the Qur'an defines and presents is an Islam that is involved in all aspects of life and that has opinions, viewpoints and demands. We should know this and respond to those who try to deny this evident truth.

As social issues and essential tasks need to be done, such as building a society and civilisation in Islam, Islam also attends to the issue of governance. It is not the case that Islam would demand social order but then not clarify the subject of leadership for religious and worldly affairs. When religion becomes a system related to the individual and society and becomes a system that has opinions and speaks about individual and social issues, then it is necessary to determine who is at the head of this society and what characteristics this head should have. Thus, religion must appoint an Imam.

---

238. Surah al-Ahzab – Verse 60.
239. Surah al-Nisa – Verse 83.

If you look at the Qur'an, there are at least two verses in which Prophets (s) are described as Imams. One of them is: *"And We made them Imams, guiding men by Our command, and We sent them inspiration to do good deeds, to establish regular prayers."*[240] - Another verse that mentions God appointing Imams is: *"And We appointed, from among them Imams, giving guidance under Our command."*[241] - This means a prophet is an Imam, leader and commander in society.

That is why Imam Sadiq (a) stood up among the crowd gathered in Mina and shouted, "Oh people, the Messenger of God (s) was indeed an Imam."[242] For people to understand what the correct religious status of the Holy Prophet (s) was, he stood up among the crowd and shouted this. Well, this is one issue. Throughout Islam, religious intellectuals, scholars, writers, researchers and university professors have the duty to explain this because the enemy heavily invests in promoting the opposite viewpoint.

Of course, our task in Iran is even heavier in this regard. This is because there are more possibilities here for us to work on this. The country's officials should explain this, especially in cultural fields and people with essential podiums available in some areas of society. It is not the case inside the country that we do not need to explain this issue now that an Islamic system has been established in the Islamic Republic. No,

---

240. Surah al-Anbiyya – Verse 83.
241. Surah al-Sajda – Verse 24.
242. Al-Kaafi – Vol 4 P 466.

currently, falsehoods are being promoted in our country in this regard, and certain things are being said.[243]

Clarifying the fundamental thought and the foundational theory concerning the Islamic Republic, namely the governance of Islam in every affair of our life, is a general duty for the Islamic seminaries. It is a responsibility for each person, individuals of high esteem in the seminaries, enlightened scholars and thinkers up and down the country, in various cities, to do this. They should clarify this with reasoning and logic, considering their various audiences.

It may appear that this issue is one of the self-evident and apparent truths. This is undoubtedly the case for those in a religious environment and those aware of the Islamic sources. The governance of religion in every aspect of life, not just the hearts and personal acts, is one of the unshakable truths of all divine religions, not just the sacred religion of Islam.

Therefore you can see in the Qur'an how the great divine Prophets (s) were in a state of combating against the [non-divine] governments, powers, rebellious leaders and those who dominated societal affairs. Who were the Prophets' (s) first enemies in the societies they were sent to? It was the people who had a say in the future of societies and the lives of [people living in that] society. If religion was only to be used in the heart's solitude, the soul's depth and other

---

243. 24/10/2021 – In a meeting with guests of the Islamic Unity Conference and a group of Government officials.

places of privacy, such as a house or places of worship, then there was no need for the oppressors and the non-divine rulers to oppose it. Why did they oppose them? The first who should have fought the Prophets (s) should have been those who were busy in worship and the pious [of other religions]. Then why does the Qur'an say: *"We did not send a warner to any town without its affluent ones saying, 'We indeed disbelieve in what you have been sent with.'"*[244] – Why were the wealthy elites the first to oppose? Why were the rulers, the non-divine leaders, the powerful and the politicians the first to oppose the Prophets (s)?

For no other reason but this, the Prophets (s) would invite those societies to social order and a new system of politics, which was other than the system of politics governing those lands. This order they strove for is what governance looks like when taken to its completion. Political, social and economic systems are all manifestations of that order. They opposed the foundations that were ruling over those societies. Therefore, they were forced to wage jihad, strive and mobilise armies. In the Qur'an and our narrations, we can see this being indicated: "The first to kill in the way of Allah was Ibrahim (a)."[245] – Striving in the path of Allah and fighting for the sake of Allah, according to our narration, is attributed to Ibrahim (a), and this is aside from the issue of idols that Ibrahim (a) had dealt with during his childhood.

---

244. Surah al-Saba – Verse 34.
245. Nawadir Rawandi – P 23.

In Islam, this is evident too. The first task carried out by the Holy Messenger (s) was the formation of a government governing the affairs of the society. No one from the Muslims sees this differently. This is one of the evident truths.

However, over centuries, practically a distance was created between the political and religious institutions. This distance was the natural effect of governments' greed and the tyrants' rebelling in society's affairs. They were not able to adhere to the religious principles. First and foremost, the tyrants and rulers were offenders; how could they be those who invite towards religion? In the apparent, they showed religion but did not stand by their words. Therefore, the religious and governmental institutions separated. The command of Wilayah and Imamate was transformed into a Sultanate. [Islam governing] is a part of the Islamic obligations, as is evident by the narrations, history and words of the companions. It is a part of the apparent truth in Islamic teachings.

In the last few centuries in Europe, the institution of the Church dominated politics and government. They did not govern; however, they would infiltrate. With their regressive, false, restrictive views, they would pursue scholars, professors and opponents that would present anything new and other issues mentioned in European history. The Europeans came and presented the theory of the separation of the state from religion. They said religion must be kept aside entirely, and governance should be completely free

Subjects in Need of Clarifications

from religion. Governance was presented as an issue that should be in accordance with prevailing norms and has no relation with religion and religious principles. This was the thinking of the Europeans born out of the situation that existed between the state and religion in Europe. If one were to look at the case in the Middle Ages, one would see how unfortunate the situation was.

After that, they introduced this into the Islamic countries as they felt if there was anything that could resist the colonial movement in the 19th century when it was at its peak and capturing Islamic nations, it would be this religion. They saw this in Iraq, and India, from a different angle in Iran and other Arab countries in North Africa. They promoted the idea of religion having nothing to do with politics and that it must be removed amidst the thinkers in the Islamic environments. Islamic thinkers such as Sayyid Jamal al-Din, his students, and scholars in India, Iran and Iraq responded by opposing this theory. They fought against the idea of religion's separation from politics for a hundred years. After that, the Islamic movement began, and the respected Imam Khomeini, with his steady and logical intellect, brought this matter to a close: Islamic Governance. This reached a level which meant that despite the centuries or more worth of work carried out in the Islamic countries to separate and isolate religion, religion became the axis around which everything in these nations revolved. This was a result of such a great revolution. [This religion] did something that none of the leftist or left-leaning schools of thought could have done. It brought the nation to the forefront, strengthened its will and revived human characteristics and identity within the people. It gave the people the spirit of jihad and struggle. It gave them idealism. It took them out of stagnation. This school of thought did something which none of the other schools of thought, inviting towards struggle, revolution and reassessing the wrong state of the world, could do. They never even thought such a thing would be possible.

In such a situation, [this religion] brought it to reality. Therefore, if someone imagines [the inseparability of religion and politics] as part of the obvious truths of the faith, that is the case. Religion is for governing the day-to-day affairs of people. This is in the Qur'an, the Messengers (s) life, the lives of the Messengers (s) successors, and the lives of the Muslims, in the words of the Aa'ima (a), and this is one of the apparent truths. It is not such that religion comes to solely govern the beliefs and the internal connection of the heart and then leaves the lives of humans in every dimension of their life in the hands of other religions and other methods aside from the methods provided by religion. [Or, in the hands of] methods that are man-made, ignorant, rebellious and born out of lowly oppressive selfish and arrogant desires. Such a thing is not possible. Religion is for the establishment of justice. Religion is for the governance of virtues. How is it possible that it hands over people's lives to those with vices and objectives born out of vices, just like the pursuit of desires and wealth typical in this world? This is impossible. Therefore, this is an obvious matter. However, this very obvious matter is what some have started denying. They write about this.

In reality, those speaking and writing about the separation of religion from politics, under an intellectual guise, regardless of whether or not they wear the turban, are going back a hundred years. This is returning to a time when all of the Islamic nations were in a slumber of negligence. At that time, any thought or intellectual wave from the West and Europe could come and be accepted without any conditions.

In the face of such negligence, Syed Jamal, other intellectual figures, religious thinkers stood up until this reached the shoulders of our noble Imam Khomeini. They fought against this for a hundred years. He attracted all the hopeful hearts in the Islamic world. He made this reality as apparent as the Sun to the people. Now, some return to a hundred years ago, claiming to be academic in the guise of intellectuals. They say words that had already been spoken a hundred years ago from conquered, startled, weak and west-toxified intellects. They came, but the Islamic scholars rebuked them and removed them from the minds of the people. In reality, [the ones now] are nothing but a return to a hundred years ago.

Should we just let this issue go considering it is nothing more than a return to what has already passed? No! Should we do nothing about it just because it is a false idea? Indeed, we should! Even a false idea may become widespread. A wrong idea can also find a place in the hearts.

Today, this is the objective. Today, the most fundamental responsibility that rests upon the Islamic Seminary as a collective and on the shoulders of individuals with greater capacities on an individual level is the creation of ideas and the production of Islamic thought. [It is their responsibility to] clarify and strengthen the solid Islamic fundaments and remain steadfast in the face of doubts in the people's minds injected by the enemies of Islamic governance. The enemies do this to make up for the heavy defeat they faced at the hands of Islam. However, they will not be able to. This idea has spread globally; the concept of the governance of Islam and the complete authority of religion in governance in a particular region. Even the non-Muslims have been attracted to this thought in some areas of the world. In Islamic countries, aware scholars, intellectuals and youth, alongside religious university students, have also been attracted to his idea.[246]

Be wary that the Islamic government Imam Khomeini spoke about and that you wish to prove, explain, clarify and describe does not change into a non-Islamic government. This is the very point of contention between us and our opposition around the world in the intellectual arena. If someone has a Muslim name and governs, they do not oppose them. However, what is sensitive for them is when

---
246. 10/09/2001 – In the beginning of his Dars al-Khaarij.

religion becomes the authority governing society's affairs. Therefore we must pay close attention to this point that Wilayat al-Faqih brought, presented and initiated as an Islamic government. It must be understood as a government of Islam, religion and Shariah.

Our jurists and intellectual elites may try and refine our jurisprudence which has its weaknesses and many shortcomings. This is a different discussion, and this work must be done. However, the issue that needs to be presented, and this was definitively the view of Imam Khomeini, too, is that the environment of the society needs to be filled with Islamic Shariah, jurisprudence, laws and actions. He would not accept anything else. I once spoke to him about Wilayat al-Faqih and told him that we had discussions with some intellectual elites and friends before the revolution. Some of them stated that Islam does not present a specific Islamic method in the field of Economics. Whichever way can help attain Islamic objectives, such as justice, can be considered Islamic. However, we believed that this was not the case. Islam has made the boundaries clear, established a method and created a framework for Islamic Economics, which must be followed. He replied and said, "Yes, this is correct.". I do not wish to use this story to prove these words are correct. I want to document that this was the viewpoint of Imam Khomeini and that he would not be persuaded by anything less. In places where the discussion regarded the secondary rulings, he would also emphasise them as Islamic and jurisprudential law. He remained like this till the end. Concerning *ghina* or music, he presented a new discussion. That is what his jurisprudential foundation was like. For this issue, he presented jurisprudential evidence. What is said in *Makaasib* varies from this in certain aspects. However, his discussion was based on jurisprudential foundations and not on the foundations of worldly necessity, inclinations or expediency. Someone may disagree with the general or specific points of this view, which is fine; it is their viewpoint; however, the stance of Imam Khomeini must not be distorted. You must be very careful that the perspective of Imam Khomeini is indeed derived in a manner that is apparent in his words, books and character. This is an essential point; I believe this is a historic responsibility and a trust placed on your shoulders.

The second point is that the foundations of an Islamic government presented a new discourse to the world. Indeed, in this case, the revolution carried out a revival which left the rivals dumbfounded. This was not comparable to some of the things they tried to compare it to afterwards. It had no resemblance to what it was being compared to. What is written in the constitution, in the words of Imam Khomeini and the culture of the revolution under the title of the governance of Wilayat al-Faqih, is something completely new in the world. It may be said that the term Wilayat al-Faqih is an Arabic and scholarly term belonging to the seminarians and the books; in fact, this concept is very new and modern and means having someone at the head of the government that we know can not err. This is very important. Observe where the difficulties of the world stem from. We wish to place someone at the head of the government that we know will not err. We may make a mistake, and he ends up committing an infringement. Any time we realise they have infringed, we will understand that their presence in this appointment is inappropriate. They and the people accept this. This is a very novel point in the sources of governance in the world.

They created controversy around this and said this thought is old and regressive. At the revolution's victory, there were possibly tens of governments that had undergone coups in which military officers had come with their boots and guns and taken the government for themselves. All those governments had been accepted and received official recognition; no one had anything to say about them. However, they all had something to say about this Islamic government, Imam Khomeini and this incredible movement! This was because new words had been spoken in the world that had the power to work with prevalent political yardsticks and cultures. The pressure from this event was certainly more than the pressure felt from the force of Marxism and Communist governments in their initial phases. However, after ten to twenty years, they reached their peak due to the propagation, actions and attractions the Marxists exhibited. However, in the starting phase, without a doubt, the pressure from this [Islamic Revolution] was more than the strength and force felt from them [Marxists and Communists]. Why? Because suddenly, worldwide, whichever country the Muslims resided in, they felt a sense of identity, character, acceptance and agreement towards it [the Islamic Revolution].[247]

The Islamic Republic

The Islamic Republic has something new to say. This new concept is made up of the people and divine values. Both of these must be twinned with each other to form movements and societies. This is what we say. Divine and spiritual values alongside the will of the people, not imposed on the people. This is the new concept of the Islamic Republic, understood by the term Islamic Republic itself. We are a Republic, and we are Islamic. This must be clarified, and you have an arena to work on this, and you can start moving.[248]

The idea of religious democracy is what can help these countries. Religious democracy is based both on democracy and religion. Religious democracy, which resulted from the novelty of our benevolent Imam Khomeini, can be a prescription for all these countries.

Of course, Sunni religious scholars - including Shafi'i scholars in Egypt, Maliki scholars in other countries of that

---
247. 24/01/2000 – In a meeting with members of Imam Khomeini's Academic Congress.
248. 28/12/2011 – Advice to ambassadors and political representatives of Iran outside of Iran.

region and Hanafi scholars of certain other countries - might not believe in absolute Wilayat al-Faqih. That is fine. We do not insist that they should accept our jurisprudential principles. Religious democracy can take on different forms. We should clarify and explain the principles of religious democracy to them. We need to present these principles to them as a gift. The people of these nations will undoubtedly like religious democracy. This is our duty, and we need to do it to prevent the enemies of the people of these nations from exploiting the vacuum that has been created. They should fill this vacuum with Islam.[249]

The Islamic Republic has been oppressed. Let me tell you - I have repeated this for many years - that the Islamic Republic is a government that embodies all the principles of spiritual power. The Islamic Republic is powerful, but it has been oppressed. Being oppressed and powerful are not contradictory. There are several reasons why the Islamic Republic is considered oppressed. One reason is that the Islamic Republic's enemies have levelled various allegations against it to prevent its ideology from being spread among the great Muslim communities. They have resorted to different allegations - from ideological and intellectual allegations to allegations against various denominations, politics, and executive affairs. They criticise us for acting, talking, and thinking the way we do. They have been repeating these allegations for thirty years. The officials in charge of hajj,

---

249. 08/09/2011 – In a meeting with members of the Assembly of Experts.

whose hearts are brimful of faith in the Islamic Republic, shoulder a great responsibility in this regard. This great duty is to explain the realities to your Muslim brothers exposed to these types of propaganda. You must clarify the Islamic teachings and principles of the Islamic Republic for them.

The Islamic Republic is an "Islamic" republic system. Most of our people are Shia Muslims, but the Islamic Republic comprises both Shia and Sunni Muslims. The reason is that our Sunni compatriots and many Sunni Muslims living across the world supported us before and after the Islamic Revolution and during the Sacred Defense era. They stood up for us, and some gave their lives for this cause. That is the reality behind the Islamic Republic.

In the Muslim nations of Africa, Asia, and different parts of the world, even in the heart of the United States of America, which has been our most spiteful enemy, there are some non-Shia Muslims whose hearts are brimful with love for the Islamic Republic, Imam Khomeini, and our great, determined nation. That is all because the Islamic Republic has been an Islamic republic. They are trying to turn this reality on its head. They are trying to slander the Islamic Republic as if it is opposed to different Islamic denominations. You must go and explain the facts. Our Muslim brothers and sisters worldwide must know that our country belongs to them. They must understand that the event which took place in our country was one that all Muslims would desire wholeheartedly. There are no Muslims who do not want the world to live under the rule of the Holy Qur'an. Our people live under the rule of the Holy Qur'an and Sharia in this country.

Is there anyone in Islam who is not profoundly dissatisfied with the domination and influence of the infidels and foreigners over Muslim countries? The hearts of Muslims are filled with pain, but they cannot talk. They are not allowed to speak. The Islamic Republic is the means through which the Muslim nations' stifled shouts are expressed strongly.

That is the reason why the arrogant powers are opposed to the Islamic Republic. That is the reason behind the US hostility towards us. We are expressing the heartfelt feelings of the Muslim nations. The few corrupt governments [that are currently ruling some Muslim nations] are not the whole of what we call Muslim nations. Muslim nations are tired of the US's domination, interference, and arrogance. Muslim nations are tired of American and non-American arrogance but cannot do anything about it. These feelings are expressed by the officials serving at different levels of the Islamic Republic's system. These are the clear realities that the Islamic Republic is expressing. You must express these realities across the world of Islam and the Muslim nations. All people must have access to these realities. These are some of the opportunities to clarify the realities of the Islamic Republic.[250]

---

250. 05/11/2008 – In a meeting with Hajj workers and officials.

Imam Khomeini and His Path

I am worried that the young generation, who are pure and ready to be present in the arena, do not understand Imam Khomeini. [I am worried] that we make the future generations feel needless of the love, understanding and relationship with this lofty personality. Therefore, I request proper and substantial work should be expected and pursued in this field and do not be content with anything less on this.[251]

Today, whatever we have appropriated as the objectives of this revolution, we must pursue using the same method of Imam Khomeini; with frankness, complete clarification and necessary courage and valour. This arena must be entered courageously. We must understand that what protects us in the face of the enemy, and what protects our independence, freedom and identity, is this.

Suppose this nation wishes to flourish, to reach the advanced sciences, and it wishes to advance in the various material fields of this world, such as business, agriculture and other arenas. In that case, this can be done by pursuing the path of Imam Khomeini. This is because this is the path of independence, returning to one's own identity, unearthing the hidden treasures in the chests of mankind and actualising the potential of these capacities.[252]

---

251. 02/06/1997 – In a meeting with those facilitating the commemoration ceremonies of Imam Khomeini.

252. 31/05/2005 – In a meeting with those facilitating the commemoration ceremonies of Imam Khomeini.

What is the yardstick for success in our revolution? This is an essential question. It is thirty years now that we have been moving on the path of this revolution. Our people have been insightful and courageous. They have shown that they are truly competent. You have been safeguarding this revolution for thirty years. But there is a danger. The revolution's and Imam Khomeini's enemies will not stand by and watch. They will try to bring this revolution to its knees. How? By making the revolution stray away from its path. Therefore, we must have a yardstick.

I would say Imam Khomeini and his path are the best yardsticks. Imam Khomeini is the best standard for us. Although there is a lot of difference between Imam Khomeini and the Holy Prophet (s), it would not be inappropriate to liken Imam Khomeini to the Holy Prophet (s) [in certain regards]. The Holy Qur'an says, "*Certainly you have in the Messenger of Allah an excellent exemplar for him who hopes in Allah and the latter day and remembers Allah much.*"[253] The Holy Prophet (s) is exemplary - in his behaviour and actions.

Similarly, in another holy verse, we read, "*Indeed, there is for you a good example in Ibrahim and those with him.*"[254] In this verse, the companions of Prophet Ibrahim have been mentioned so that no one can say, "The Holy Prophet (s) and Prophet Ibrahim (a) were infallible, so we cannot be like them." No, the Holy Qur'an says, "*Indeed, there is for you

---
253. Surah al-Ahzab – Verse 21.
254. Surah l-Mumtahina – Verse 4.

a good example in Ibrahim and those with him when they said to their people: Surely we are clear of you and of what you serve besides Allah. We declare ourselves to be clear of you, and enmity and hatred have appeared between us and you forever until you believe in Allah alone - but not in what Ibrahim said to his father: I would certainly ask forgiveness for you, and I do not control for you anything from Allah - Our Lord, on You do we rely, and to You do we turn, and to You is the eventual coming."[255]

This is true of our noble Imam Khomeini, who was a follower of the path of the divine prophets. Imam Khomeini himself is one of the most prominent yardsticks in his behaviour and words. Fortunately, we have access to his speeches. They have been compiled already. Imam Khomeini's will clearly delineated everything he had in mind about the future of the revolution. We must not allow these yardsticks to be distorted, concealed, or forgotten. Distorting these standards is like losing or breaking a compass we need on our journey. Imagine that you have lost your way in a sea or desert. You would be completely confused if your compass broke down. Presenting the views of Imam Khomeini inappropriately would be like losing your compass - we would lose our way. Everybody interprets the Imam's words the way they wish, and the ill-wishers are taking advantage of the situation - they present things to mislead the people.

The positions adopted by Imam Khomeini should be presented in a clear manner - just the way he expressed

---
255. Surah al-Mumtahina – Verse 4.

them. This is the criterion for the path of Imam Khomeini and the Revolution. Someone may explicitly say he does not believe in the Imam - this is a different matter. The followers and supporters of Imam Khomeini know how to deal with the people who openly say they do not believe in Imam Khomeini. But if this revolution is supposed to move forward on his path, everything should be clear, and the positions of Imam Khomeini should be clarified appropriately.

It is not right to hide or deny some of the positions adopted by Imam Khomeini just to please certain people. Some people wrongly think that we should play down some of the positions he adopted or try to hide them to increase the number of his followers and attract those who are against him. No, the identity and personality of Imam Khomeini depend on the positions that he used to express most eloquently and transparently. It was his positions that shook the world. It was his explicit positions that attracted a vast number of people to the Iranian nation. This tremendous global movement that you see in different parts of the Islamic world started in this way.

We should openly hold up the views of Imam Khomeini. We should explicitly support his positions against the arrogant powers, reactionary attitudes, western liberal democracy, and the hypocrites. Those who were in close contact with that great man accepted his stances. We cannot afford to hide Imam Khomeini's positions or try to play down what we consider radical just to please certain individuals. When

I was young, some people used to play down or ignore some of the Islamic teachings just to attract more people to Islam. They used to deny or hide such things as jihad, retribution, and hijab. They used to claim that retribution and jihad were not part of Islam just to attract a certain orientalist or a particular individual opposed to Islam's principles. This is a mistake. Islam must be presented in its entirety.

Imam Khomeini, minus the path of Imam Khomeini, is not the person under whose leadership the Iranian people laid down their lives, sent their children to fight to the death and sacrificed their lives and wealth. Nor was this that gave rise to the most incredible movement of the contemporary world. The Imam, minus the path of Imam Khomeini, would be an Imam without an identity. Taking the identity of Imam Khomeini away from him is not a service to him. The principles that he supported were expressed explicitly. These principles were reflected in the words, speeches, letters, and Imam Khomeini's final will- the summary of all his positions. These intellectual principles are the same things that gave rise to that splendid movement against Western plundering and America's unchallenged hegemony in the world. Whenever US presidents travel to Asian, Middle Eastern, and some European countries, the people hold demonstrations and shout slogans against them. Do you think those people were always like this? They were not. Imam Khomeini's movement, his uncovering of truths, and his positions disgraced the arrogant powers and Zionism and revived the spirit of resistance among the people of the world, especially in Islamic communities.

It is a mistake to deny the positions adopted by Imam Khomeini. Unfortunately, this mistake was committed by people who were once followers of Imam Khomeini or among the people who used to promote his thoughts. Some people stray from their path for various reasons, lose sight of their goals, and turn their back on their ideals. After advancing his goals for many years, some people stood up against them and said such words.

It behoves our dear brothers, youth, intellectuals, researchers, seminarians, and students to reflect on these characteristics. It would be good if they could work on them. Our knowledge of Imam Khomeini's path should not be confined to the text of his works and speeches - the texts should be explained and clarified appropriately.[256]

The Concept of Resistance

Propagate and promote the concept of resistance[257] in the face of the strong-armed enemy. Some should not think that because the enemy has a bomb, missiles, a propaganda apparatus and such tools, we should retreat. No way! The concept of resistance is authentic and correct. This is true in the theoretical and practical fields. It must be promoted

---
256. 04/06/2010 – Friday Prayer Sermon during the 21st commemoration of the passing of Imam Khomeini.
257. For further reading refer to the book *Andisheye Muqawamat*.

from both of these angles. In theory, this means to clarify. You, the youth, can clarify the concept of resistance among yourselves, in your environments and even in your connections with other countries and their youth. You can clarify the concept of resistance and that the objective of the Arrogant Powers is to dominate and control other nations. Clarify this for everyone; they must know this is the objective of the Arrogant Powers.

In the practical sense, we recognise the resistance movement to be the right of the youth. The youth in Iraq, Syria, Lebanon, North Africa, Sub-Continent and other areas are resisting America. It is their right; we know their right. The strengthening of these movements in a manner is strengthening the concept of resistance.[258]

Negotiating and Combating Arrogant Powers

Consider the following! Governments that the Foreign Office of America punishes, such as China, Russia and Turkey, during the time of the Welfare Party, do they not have a relationship with America? Do they not negotiate with them? All those that aggressively stand against America have political or economic ties with America. It is not such that a relationship with or negotiations with America will be an obstacle to animosity with America. Currently, some nations have embassies in America, and America also

---

258. 03/11/2018 – In a meeting with students.

has embassies in their capitals and are active. In terms of political and consulate-related business, they have relations; however, America describes those countries as part of their terrorist list.

They should not feel that if relations are established with America or negotiations take place, they will not hear even a peep from them against the Islamic Republic; no, this is not the case. Many nations have relations with America, and many of their relations in the appearance on the world stage are good, affectionate and respectful. Yet, at the same time, wherever America feels it necessary, it strikes and enforces economic blockade and sanctions!

The Americans are arrogant. Arrogant people and governments are always trying to beautify their words. Therefore, it is not such that having relations will be good for our country, and if we do not have ties, or if we do not have negotiations, then we will not face these problems, or if these negotiations take place, then these problems will disappear. America does not have the capability to create such problems, nor will a relationship or negotiations lead to a miracle leading to the removal of our difficulties. Neither of these is true. It is the nation's capability, the government's competence, our strength and our desire for respect that can stand against America and act according to our country's will and interests.[259]

---

259. 16/01/1998 – Friday Prayer Sermon.

The slogan to fight against the Arrogant Powers is a slogan that is alive. Despite what the Arrogant Powers propagate, the fight against them is possible and has a future. Today this is considered an obligation. Consequently, you, the youth, thinkers and enlightened individuals must find various methods of this fight.

Understand the enemy, the continuation of the enemy's ranks internally, the methods of the enemy and how that transforms and translates itself inside the country. Understand the continued presence of the Arrogant Powers inside the universities, schools, among society, in the nation's activities, institutions and propagation. The Arrogant Powers do not wish faith to be deeply rooted in this country and among the people. They want the people to be busy pursuing desires, they do not wish for Islamic virtues to be promoted, and they hope for Islamic vices to become common. The Arrogant powers want laziness and joblessness in the country and do not wish for there to be creativity, innovation and reform in economic, social and cultural affairs. They do not wish for there to be advancements in knowledge, research and educational classes.

Perhaps some people will do what the arrogant powers want due to their deceptive slogans. You must remain completely vigilant. This is our expectation of the young generation. Do not be content with shouting "Death to the Arrogant Powers" or "Death to America". This is just a slogan that is necessary and exists; however, this is not everything.

What is needed are those actions mentioned alongside these slogans. These slogans are a part of the work. You should gather around and speak to each other. When I said that the university and youth environments must be political, this is what it means. Fighting the arrogant powers is introduced as the flag and the path of this nation, which must be clarified and opened up.[260]

Identity

You should educate youth to have their own sense of identity. If society does not feel it has an identity, loud, authoritative voices will overwhelm them easily. He who resists is a person who has a sense of identity. Sometimes, this identity is national; sometimes, it is religious; sometimes, it is a humanitarian honour and other such things. Youth should be taught to have a sense of identity. Today, our Islamic-Iranian society, fortunately, enjoy a deep-rooted, historical, and resistant identity which has been shown in practice. We should transfer this to our youth. So, the issue of culture is essential. The cultural sectors should feel responsible, and they should work on this.[261]

My dear ones, intelligent, motivated and pious youth who have gathered in this collective and all you who want to play their part in the country's education, you should take

---
260. 30/10/1996 – In a meeting with a group of students.
261. 10/06/2018 – In a meeting with a group of teachers, elite students and university researchers.

this war seriously. There is a war in the present time. Some people wish to sing a lullaby to us, so we sleep and ignore the enemy's actions. In the arena of cultivating lofty, determined, courageous and purposeful individuals – in the arena of this great education and this great task – there is an ongoing war. Some people want the opposite to happen.

They do not want pious Muslims to develop these qualities. They are working in different ways. The issue of identity that I have always stressed is linked to this issue. Our students should grow and move forward with a sense of identity. When a young individual has a sense of identity, he will avoid deviation, betrayal, weakness, and laziness. The main problems that sometimes arise are because that sense of true identity does not exist in individuals. Others can pull them in any direction when a sense of identity does not exist. [Extract from a poem]: "Desires of others pull me in every direction like a wing, and so do my whims."

We are faced with our feelings, our emotions, inner motives and inner demons. From the outside, too, tens of hands pull us in different directions. The thing which prevents us from deviation is our commitment and our sense of identity.[262]

Notice that our people have beautiful dispositions. How our people behaved regarding the floods in the north and south was very beautiful. Those who are aware of the developments, Golestan, Khuzestan, Khorram Abad and Ilam

---

262. 09/05/2018 – At Farhangian University.

were the critical areas which suffered from the recent floods - and those who are aware of the presence and sacrifices of the people [that helped] know what a beautiful epic and glory our people created.

Well, you can include and describe this in your poetry. When you have such concepts in your poetry, it becomes the flag of national identity. It becomes the flag of your nation's identity no matter if you compose poems on Islamic, revolutionary and national teachings, moral values or about such events. When you compose poems on these issues, your poetry becomes a flag of identity. And my dear ones, identity is essential to every nation. A nation that loses its identity is easily squeezed and crushed in the fists of foreigners.[263]

The Economy of Resistance[264]

In the arena of Economic affairs they presented the concept of "Offensive Economics", that is not a problem. This humble servant did not think of "Offensive Economics". If an accurate academic explanation were presented in this regard, it might complement economy of resistance. What is wrong with that? We will also present that. What came to our minds was "The Economy of Resistance". The Economy of Resistance does not just have a repellent function. It is not such that the Economy of Resistance builds a wall around itself and

---
263. 20/05/2019 – In a meeting with a group of poets and people belonging to the cultural and linguistic fields.
264. For futher reading, refor to the book *Shu'aar e Saal* published by the Islamic Revolution Publications.

only functions to deflect and defend. No, this is not the case. The Economy of Resistance means an economy which gives a nation the capability and permission to grow and flourish, even at times of immense pressure.

This is a thought and a general understanding. You are students, professors and economists, very well, clarify and explain the idea of the Economy of Resistance using your language. Specify its boundaries, meaning an economy that ensures the growth and flourishing of a nation even under sanctions, hostility and animosity.[265]

The Objective and Aspirations of the Revolution[266]

Besides identifying the problems, we should delineate the goals of these revolutions; otherwise, there will be confusion. We should outline these goals. One of the most important goals of the Islamic Awakening is getting rid of global arrogance. We should announce this openly because it is wrong to think that global arrogance - headed by America - may get along with Islamic movements. Wherever Islam and supporters of Islam prevail, America does its best to destroy them while putting on a friendly smile. Regional revolutions have no other choice than to distance themselves from global arrogance. We do not say that they should go to war with America, but we say that they should determine

---

265. 06/08/2012 – In a meeting with university students.
266. For futher reading, refer to the book *Rawshanaye Aayendai* published by the Islamic Revolution Publications.

what the position of America and the global arrogant powers is regarding recent events in the region. They should do this correctly because they will be deceived if they do not understand their position accurately.

Today, global arrogance is ruling the world using money, weapons and science. But it lacks new ideas and a road map. This is a significant problem for the arrogant global powers today. It does not have any new ideas to help the people and intellectuals. But you do. You have Islam. We can delineate our goals and stand up against global arrogance when we have new ideas and a road map. In this way, their weapons, science and money will not be as effective as they were in the past. Of course, they will not be entirely ineffective, but we should think of ways to counter them.

We should delineate the goals of the Islamic Awakening. One of the crucial goals of the Islamic Awakening, which regional developments should pay attention to, is to preserve the pivotal role of Islam. Islamic principles and Sharia should be the pivot of everything. There is an all-out effort to claim that Sharia is incompatible with progress, change and civilisation. This is what the enemy says. No, it is perfectly compatible. Of course, many people in the world of Islam do not have enough knowledge of Islamic jurisprudence and have supported the enemy's claim with their dogmatic and old-fashioned ideas. These people are Muslims, but they are at the service of the enemy. There are such people in Islamic countries who are located near us.

They call themselves Muslims, but they do not have any new ideas or outlook on Islamic teachings. Islam is for all eras. Islam answers all the needs of human beings. We only need to develop the necessary expertise to find Islam's answers to all the questions of human beings. Some people do not have this expertise and only know how to excommunicate and drive certain people out of religion. And they call themselves Muslims. Sometimes we discover that these people cooperate with the enemy.

Another goal of the Islamic Awakening is building a governing system. If a governing system is not made in countries which have carried out a revolution, they will face dangers. Similar revolutions were carried out in North African countries about 60 or 70 years ago. In the mid-twentieth century, a revolution occurred in Tunisia, and certain people came to power. Similarly, a revolution and a coup were carried out in Egypt, and certain people came to power. The same thing happened in some other countries. But they failed to build a governing system. This resulted in the destruction of these revolutions and the complete political transformation of the individuals who had come to power as revolutionaries. There was a complete change in their political behaviour, and they turned their backs on their values. This happened in Tunisia, Egypt and Sudan during that time.

Around 1964, 65 and 66, my friends and I listened to Sawt al-Arab radio station - Sawt al-Arab used to be broadcast from

Subjects in Need of Clarifications

Cairo in Egypt. It was broadcasting the interviews of Gamal Abdel Nasser, Muammar Gaddafi and Jaafar Nimeiry, who had gathered in one place. We were being suppressed by the dictatorial regime of Mohammad Reza Pahlavi in Mashhad, but these fiery and impassioned speeches made us very enthusiastic and brought us great joy. Well, Abdel Nasser died, and you saw what his successors did. You also saw what happened to Gaddafi and Nimeiry. Those revolutions underwent drastic changes because they had no plans and did not build a governing system. There should be a governing system in countries that have revolutionised. They should make a solid foundation. This is one of the crucial issues regarding the Islamic Awakening.[267]

What is the logic behind transformation? In other words, which condition do we desire to reach in transforming? If this logic is not transparent and well-calculated, we will end up in chaos and turmoil. That is why we say, "Change our condition to the best of conditions" at the beginning of the year. A transformation should help us achieve the best of conditions.

A change in itself is not considered a value. A shift towards becoming better and progressing is a value, not in change itself. Therefore, we should find "the best of conditions". In my opinion, this is strengthening the main principles of the

---

267. 11/12/2012 – In a meeting with participants of the International Conference of University Professors from the Islamic World and the Islamic Awakening Conference.

Revolution and making the path towards the ideals easier. The great and principal ideals of the Revolution are justice, independence and Islamization of society. The movement towards these ideals should be facilitated and made easier. At present, we face many difficulties in this area, and there is a need for a transformational movement. Of course, these ideals, which should receive our attention and towards which we should move, have different levels. You should work on them in student meetings and debates to find their details and then explain them to the people.

Generally speaking, some ideals are the principal ideals of the Islamic Republic. They are long-term and mid-term ideals that play a fundamental role and should receive due attention: ideals such as the creation of an Islamic community, the administration of social justice and the establishment of independence, freedom and other such concepts.

Some ideals exist at more minor levels and constitute high-level ideals. For example, scientific progress is an ideal – it is definitely one of our ideals – but it is a constituent of a whole that will help form the Islamic community and independence.

Another ideal is strength in foreign policy which means protecting the country and the political system of the country from the network created by the arrogant powers and the system of domination. Strength in foreign policy was manifested at the beginning of the Revolution in the slogan "Neither east nor west". In those days, there used to be an Eastern superpower, namely the communist system, and another superpower manifested as the capitalist system. The slogan meant that the Islamic Republic should protect itself, and it did protect itself from entering into the network of dependence on those superpowers. This is also an ideal that should be preserved, pursued and improved every day. Another example is economic self-sufficiency, which is a minor ideal constituting the principal ideals.

Some of the other ideals that we are and should be pursuing and that we should pay attention to in our search for a transformation are, in fact, some policies whose goal is to run the country and to immunise the Revolution. For example, we could mention the creation of organisations such as the Islamic Revolution Guards Corps, Construction Jihad and Basij. These are some of the policies which form the body of the principal ideals.

We could also refer to the Islamization of universities, or, the transformation of the IRIB into a public university that educated 40 million people – the country's population in those days - and 80 million people – the population in the present time. This has been one of the ideals. It has been one of the things we have been pursuing and should be pursuing. There are other such ideals as well. Therefore, as you can see, the primary principles of the Islamic Republic that should be protected and facilitated exist at different levels. This includes loftier ideals, like forming the Islamic community;

mid-level ideals, like scientific progress; and lower-level ideals, like the organisational policies mentioned.[268]

You should not forget about idealism. You should not forget about idealism. What are ideals? Our ideals are achieving a just, free, advanced, religious, pious, wealthy, united, strong, powerful and independent society. These are ideals. For the sake of God, it is worth sacrificing one's life on the path of these ideals.

Sura an-Nisa says, *"And what reason have you that you should not fight in the way of Allah and for the weak among the men, women, and children"*[269]. Fighting for ideals is this. An edict of fighting has been issued to save the country and the weak. Of course, this verse is about fighting. Notice that this verse is about fighting, not jihad. Jihad is something, and fighting is something else. There is a general and specific difference between them. This is the basis of Islam. This is the orientation of Islam. One should move on the path of these ideals. Your goal is to attain the ideals I referred to – creating such a society. Therefore, you should not forget about idealism.[270]

Let us move to another word of advice. There are some key phrases which you should not forget:

One of these key phrases is "The people's role in the government". This is a key phrase. Some good and

---

268. 11/05/2021 – In a televised speech with representatives from various University bodies.
269. Surah al-Nisa – Verse 75.
270. 07/06/2017 – In a meeting with a group of university students.

revolutionary youths are surprised when they hear such and such a person keep saying, "You should participate in elections." They become upset with me because of my insistence on participation in elections. Dear youths, you should notice that the day when people turn their backs on ballot boxes will be a disaster! This is a disaster, and the enemy wants this. You should understand this from me as soon as possible. I have heard the whispers which desire to see the day when 90 per cent of the people refuse to vote.

They said that only 20-plus per cent of the people did not participate in the elections. However, the enemies say that this is not enough and that they should do something to make 90 per cent of the people veto the elections. This will be a disaster, and I see it. The presence of the people in elections is a great blessing! Democracy is one of the main keywords. You should not forget this. You want the people to vote for such a person and not vote for such a person. Well, you should do something to make this happen. However, you should not prevent people from going to the ballot boxes.

Another key phrase is "independence", which I mentioned earlier, which is also very important. The issue of 2030 – The 'Education 2030' agenda – is vital in this regard, and it is related to the point of independence. Some say, "We have taken the necessary precautions and rejected some parts of it." The issue is not about this. Let us assume that there is nothing concrete in this agenda which conflicts with Islam- of course, there are such conflicts, and those who think that we have not received accurate reports in this regard should not feel like this because our reports are accurate. What I am saying is that the educational system of the country should not be written outside the country. This is what I am saying.

You say that the agenda is not against Islam. Whether this is true or not, it does not matter. This is Iran, the Islamic Republic, and there are great people in this country. Should a few people at UNESCO, at the UN or in such an organisation write our educational plan? Why? This is related to the issue of independence. Independence extends to these issues.

Another key phrase is "rejecting the system of domination". "Freedom" is another key phrase you should delineate correctly. "Justice" is one of the keywords as well, and there are other such keywords too.

You should explain these keywords. My advice to student groups is that they should clarify these principles and fundamental keywords correctly. Make use of the statements of Imam Khomeini and such personalities to do this.[271]

Justice: One of the Most Important Aspirations of the Islamic Revolution

Question from a university student: Why are some officials apathetic to the problems faced by the people? What is His Eminence's opinion regarding the university students' responsibility on this issue? Should a university student

---

271. 07/06/2017 – In a meeting with a group of university students.

Subjects in Need of Clarifications

also stay quiet and apathetic towards the injustices and inequalities?

We have spoken about this issue. I do not believe university students must stay quiet and say nothing. I also do not believe that a university student should go out in the middle of the street to show themself. I believe that university students should demand the fundamental issues in the arena of pursuing justice. They must make common the idea of seeking justice among the people, their families and anyone else who is working in their field.[272]

The issue of justice is one of those messages that must enter the minds of the people. It should become a fundamental slogan near those who demand and love justice, whether social or economic justice. For example, we should not broadcast a film, a comedy or a statement that leads to apathy towards justice in the interest of other slogans. For instance, if one slogan is transformed into another without considering justice. This will undoubtedly be a decision which will not be in sync with the people, which is what this institution and parts of this collective must take as their yardstick, and with which they must be in sync.

What are the messages which we must reflect in the people's minds? In my opinion, one of them is the slogan of justice that I have mentioned. We must not compromise on the slogan of the justice of Ali. The people need Alawi justice;

---
272. 12/05/2003 – In a question and answer session with university students of Shaheed Beheshti University.

that is what they are thirsty for. Even those who never speak of justice or for whom justice works against them as they wish to be unjust. If an injustice happens towards them, they contest it. In reality, even they are thirsty for justice. I have stated before that all major slogans have conditions attached to them; however, this is not the case with the slogan of justice. Justice is unconditionally a need and demand of society. Unconditional justice may not be realised, nor are we people who have the ability to realise it; however, justice must be presented unconditionally so that it can be progressed as much as possible. The Late Allamah Tabatabai used to say that the Messenger (s), the Commander of the Faithful (a), and the friends of Allah are perched atop a summit, and they invite people to that summit. The Messenger (s), or the Commander of the Faithful (a), never invite the people to one step below where they are; instead, they ask them to come to where they are. They invite everyone to the summit, and it is this invitation to the summit that motivates the people to start moving. One of the people may take one step; another may take a hundred; another may reach the bend whilst another would reach the higher altitudes.

Therefore we should not delete that summit, keep it in mind and pursue it. When a person instils the concept of seeking justice in people's minds, keeps the pursuit of it alive and explains it logically and correctly; naturally, they will not get upset about attaining lesser justice as they know there is a higher level. Like when the Commander of the Faithful

Subjects in Need of Clarifications

(a) says to his companions: *"Certainly, you cannot do so"*[273]. Everyone knows that humans' capacity, spiritual foundations and even physical capabilities are less than the Commander of the Faithful (a), and it is not enough for them to reach that summit; however, the movement towards that summit needs to be kept alive.

Therefore justice and the pursuit of and beautification of justice are among those things that must not be forgotten. Observe Nahj al-Balagha, and you will see that, from top to bottom, it is full of justice. A serious belief of this humble servant is that many of our shortcomings today in reaching the country's revolutionary objectives and desired management are due to our lack of attentiveness towards justice.

We must change this culture dominating our thoughts, which goes for the people too. It cannot be that people feel that in life's challenges, there are no boundaries or objections that justice will not present in front of them and that they can go to whatever extent they want.

For example, a person attains unlawful and illegitimate wealth using unjust methods. For instance, over ten years, they get a few million Tuman. If we were to distribute that wealth, you would see that the salary you or this humble servant receive throughout your service is equivalent to the wealth this person gains in one day, week, or month. Yet, this person demands more! They demand more based on saying

---

273. Nahj al-Balagha – Letter 45.

how much service they have done to the nation and the value of how much production they have enabled. In their minds, justice plays no role, and they do not give any importance to the issue of justice, so they do not see how justice has been trampled upon, injustice has occurred and how the law has been broken. This is how this wealth has been attained.[274]

The Achievements of the Revolution[275]

The achievements of the Revolution are truly great and astonishing. Of course, we have not worked enough on delineating these achievements. Sometimes, certain things have been said in a speech or on television, but there is much more room for speaking about the achievements of the Revolution. The Revolution has made extraordinary and great achievements in the most vital parts of social life.[276]

Another factor contributing to the accomplishment of the lofty goals of a nation, which is also an essential factor, relates to the young generation. Our youngsters should strengthen their spirit of inquest, hope, self-confidence and the belief that 'we can'.

There is a common proverb among Arab nations which says, "The strongest proof that something is possible is its occurrence." Likewise, the strongest proof that the young

---

274. 04/02/2003 – In a meeting with IRIB officials.
275. For futher reading, refer to the book *Armghaan* published by the Islamic Revolution Publication.
276. 17/02/2021 – In a televised speech with the people of Western Azerbaijan.

Iranian generation can open new frontiers in science and technology and introduce innovations - something I have often emphasized over the past years - is the scientific and technological progress that Iranian youngsters are currently making in various areas.

We do not wish to exaggerate what has occurred and understand and present more than what has actually happened. However, these advancements exist, and they are occurring currently. The work in the Khwarizmi Festival, the universities and the Olympiads are the most substantial proof to show that this work is possible. Strengthen the belief in possibility in your minds. We have numerous examples of this in this country's practical arenas.

The majority of the people are not aware of these successes. I insist that these advancements reach the ears of the people. I have told the Government officials to do this, to tell the people. There was a day when we could not manufacture, unlike what we can do now. Those days are not that far away. It has just been these 25 years. Before the revolution, we did not believe we would be able to create energy plants, dams or even understand sophisticated technologies, let alone be able to produce them. However, today all of these exist.

Today, in critical arenas, we have made outstanding advancements. This is the movement and spirit of the revolution. This is the self-confidence the revolution has given. The revolution gave us an environment to use our capacities and gave us the possibility to think and be hopeful.

Strengthen this in yourselves, in your generation and your young collectives.

An Iranian can break the boundaries of knowledge today, limits that are very advanced limits and broad horizons. They can progress and create new boundaries. We do not expect this to be done, for example, over the next five or ten years.

Creating pessimism and saying it is impossible, or they will not let us, or there is no point, is a poison to this movement. There was a day when they came and created this poison and injected it into the cultural well of this nation. They came one day and said openly, we can not do it. During my youth, one of the common phrases heard was that the Iranians are not even able to produce a pitcher! This was the view of the politicians and heads of academia in those days. Many of the politicians in those days were from the universities. Their names are known. They used to say Iranians can not! This is not the case; Iranians can!

I was in a room similar to this, and I told youth like yourselves that they should put in the effort so that fifty years later, this nation should be feeding skills and academic opinions to all parts of human society. You should move with this intention. If you wish to reach there in fifty years, the work you are doing currently is not a lot. Steps must be taken, which definitely will be taken and must be hastened.[277]

---

277. 19/04/2005 – In a meeting with young inventors.

The Middle Path of Being a Revolutionary[278]

Some people have developed a particular habit. They constantly speak about "hardliners". Yes, being both a hardliner and a softliner – acting in an extremist or negligent manner – is bad. This is clear, but it is unclear what extremist and soft ideas are and what the middle ground is. These are not among the apparent issues, and they need clarification. This is because we receive a lot of news in this regard. When I take a look at different newspapers, I see that when some people speak about extremism, they mean revolutionary and religious orientations. However, you should not accuse religious and revolutionary orientations of extremism.

When defending our borders and national identity, laying down one's life and offering one's blood, they are the ones who step forward. Just because an issue arises that is not approved by some people, they should not immediately attribute it to revolutionary individuals. An example is the issue of the Saudi embassy, which was, of course, a very bad and wrong measure. Anyone who did it should know it was the wrong course of action. Should we undermine revolutionary people and revolutionary youth – who are both revolutionaries and who, on most occasions, have a greater understanding and are more intelligent and reasonable than many seniors and older adults: they understand and analyze issues well, and they are prepared to lay down their lives for

---

278. For further reading, refer to the book *Inqilaabi e Taraaz*.

the Revolution and Islam – with the excuse that such and such a course of action, which was wrong, was adopted?

I am saying this because I have an amicable relationship with youth up close and from afar. I was not too fond of the incident that happened to the British embassy a few years ago, let alone the one that happened to the Saudi embassy. These courses of action are not acceptable in any way. Such operations are wrong and are to the disadvantage of the country, Islam and everyone. However, they should not use this as an excuse to invade and criticize our revolutionary youth.[279]

The Country, Region and the Dominating System

If you observe their propaganda, you will see that regarding our dear, great and strong nation, which is also oppressed a the same time, they focus on a few points...

They wish to paint the future as dark and murky. The enemy tries to make the future seem dark, bleak and full of doubts about what will happen and where we will reach. The responsibility of the propagators of religion, spirituality and the true message is to give hope to the people and take away the feeling of despair. Hopelessness is the biggest enemy of a nation. Efforts must be placed to reduce despair in the people. Observe in the region what content is needed

---

279. 20/01/2016 – In a meeting with officials facilitating the elections.

Subjects in Need of Clarifications

by your audience. No matter what, become an obstacle to hopelessness, finding a place in their hearts.

The enemy wishes to have despair rule over the hearts; in one way or another, they wish for everyone to feel hopeless. [They create despair in a] student one way, teachers one way, workers one way, scholars one way, businessmen one way, government officials one way and more senior officials one way. Each of them has its method, which we are observing closely. They have methods which even create despair in the senior officials of a country. We meet officials from other nations; sometimes, they speak to us, and their hearts are full of despair. What can a person full of hopelessness do? We tried to take out this despair from their hearts and inject hope in its place. By the grace of Allah, our nation is hopeful and happy. Inject hope into the people.[280]

Another source of conflict is regarding having a correct understanding of the realities in Iran and the world. If you have a proper understanding of your own country's realities, this is to their disadvantage. They are opposed to accurate knowledge: they are fighting against it. What is their weapon of choice? The very dangerous weapon belongs to the media, particularly recently emerged media. By creating false images, they try to divert the thoughts of the Iranian nation. They portray both false images of Iran and of themselves.[281]

---

280. 24/12/1997 – In a meeting with a group of scholars.
281. 04/10/2018 – In a ceremony of tens of thousands of Basij in Azadi stadium.

The Reality of the Enemy and the Region

They also create false images regarding the conditions of the region. One of the false images that they create is that they are in a position of power -- while they are not in a position of power.

Now, their hard power is a visible type of power. In other words, they have money, military weapons, and media resources: their hard weapons. However, in international confrontations, soft power is the main criterion. Soft war power equals logic, reasoning, sensible arguments, and new discourse – a new discourse which plays a determining role in life. --It means presenting new ideas. The U.S. is extremely poor at soft war power. They have no new ideas to show. They have no logic. They only know how to bully others: their reasoning is poor.

Today, its liberal democracy is ridiculed around the world. Its methods of implementing liberal democracy – which they were once proud of – are being widely criticized by intellectuals from across the globe. That is why you are witnessing that the US – which enjoys atomic power, advanced technology, and significant sources of money – has been defeated in many parts of the world. It was defeated in Iraq, Syria, Lebanon, Pakistan, and Afghanistan. Today, one can envisage other defeats for the US.[282]

---

282. 04/10/2018 – Same as above.

The Reality of the Country

They have created another wholly false and deceptive image: that of Islamic Iran. It is an image they are trying to promote to shift public opinion worldwide. They also want to present it to us, the Iranian nation. They want to inject these false notions into us and convince us to accept the ideas they have spread about our country. By relying on the economic problems which exist in our country and which are realities, they are nurturing some erroneous notions in their own thoughtless and unintelligent minds.

Recently, I heard that the U.S. president has told some European countries' heads that they should wait two or three months longer; after that, the Islamic Republic "will be done." He has mentioned such things to them! --This reminds me of the statements made by the domestic servants of the US 40 years ago, four decades ago! They used to boost one another's hopes by saying that if they waited for six months, the Islamic Republic would be terminated. However, after six months, the Islamic Republic would still be here; they would say that they should wait another year: yet, the Islamic Republic would never be terminated! Forty years have passed since then, and that little sapling has become this enormous tree!

This wretched person wishes to bolster his hopes and those of his European partners by saying that if they wait for two or three months, the Islamic Republic will be gone. --This reminds me of the popular idiom: When the camel dreams of eating cottonseed, sometimes he eats them by the mouth-full, and sometimes he eats them seed by seed {meaning that American efforts to overthrow the Islamic Revolution and the Islamic Republic are foolish dreams that will never be realized}.[283]

The enemy has failed to know you! The enemy has been unable to understand the Iranian nation! He does not know the Revolution or the revolutionary and faith-based spirit! This mistaken analysis has misled the enemy throughout all these years, and he continues to be deceived! According to a saying attributed to the Infallible Imams (a): "Praise belongs to the God who made our enemies from among the fools." God has made the enemies of the Iranian nation from among the fools.

Of course, we have problems. Yes, we have economic problems. The dear youth and our motivated and pious people should pay careful attention. We have economic problems. We have an oil-based economy, which is a grave flaw in itself. We do not have a culture of economizing. The culture of economizing is very feeble among us: this is a flaw. Extravagance is a flaw; we have these flaws that are not unsolvable. The fundamental flaw is reaching a dead-end; thankfully, we have not reached a dead-end road. We do not have dead-ends.

---

283. [Participants chant, "O liberated leader, we are prepared!" The Supreme Leader responds, "May God increase your success. Thank you very much. May God preserve you all!"]

Subjects in Need of Clarifications

The fundamental flaw is that some of the country's youth presume there is no option other than seeking refuge in the enemy. --This is a flaw. Some people are trying to inject this idea into the minds of our youth. The enemy wants the people of Iran to conclude that it has reached a dead-end, that there is no option other than seeking refuge in the US, kneeling and submitting to the US. I wish to explicitly say this: I want to explicitly state that those who promote this thought, which is favoured and advocated by the enemies inside the country -- are the ones betraying the country. This is a betrayal of the country. If we promote this notion – one that the enemy favours – that there is no option other than to seek refuge in the enemy, this is the greatest betrayal against the Iranian nation! Of course, this will not happen (submitting to the enemy). By Allah's favour and grace, with your help, I will, with all my power and energy, not allow this to happen to our country!

This is the image that the enemy is creating (dead-ends). --This is a deceptive image of his own condition and that of ours. These are false images with which the Iranian nation and our public opinion are being inundated, with the aid of thousands of television, radio, and Internet networks. This is a false image, but what is the actual image? The real image is that you and all the youths of the country should know today's position of the country and your people. --This is the first condition for you to exert your influence.

First of all, today, great politicians worldwide, experienced and sensible political brains, are praising the people of Iran for their 40 years of resistance. --This is a reality. This is something that we see clearly and transparently. We are aware of this, and I am proclaiming it to you. Experienced politicians -- even in the US and in Western and European countries which do not have good relations with us – are applauding the people of Iran because they have been refusing to retreat for more than 40 years in the face of enemies' pressures and because they have made outstanding achievements and turned themselves into a world power. --This is praiseworthy.

A few years ago, I quoted a statement from a chief Zionist military official who said, "I do not have a good relationship with Iran, but I stand up and take my hat off in respect to the person who has built these missiles." He spoke about one of the tens of different types of missiles built here. Political masterminds worldwide express their respect for our country, our people, and their resistance and progress in such a way.

Second, our country benefits from many capacities found in few other countries. It has geographic, climatic, man-made, underground and above-ground capabilities. The capacities of Iran, which are extraordinarily important for the economy and progress of the country, are abundant. Of course, we have not used these capacities correctly. Once, I came across some statistics, and I mentioned them in a

Subjects in Need of Clarifications

meeting which was broadcasted. The statistical data revealed that we were the first in the world in terms of not using the capacities of our country! We have not used them. I have always advised officials to identify untapped capacities and to benefit from them for the country to generate national wealth. --This is the second point.

Third, you, the pious youth, are the country's capacity that has been actualized. This is the real image: our pious youth in the country have defensive and scientific capabilities, and they have capabilities in the area of cultural issues, social matters, and many other areas. --This is the real image of the country. The enemy who thinks in certain misleading ways about Islamic Iran does not see this vast number of pious youth in the country.

Fourth, after extensive research, the enemy has resorted to sanctions to confront the Islamic Republic. --This means that other paths are blocked to them. They have no option other than economic sanctions, and other paths are blocked. However, I will tell you that economic sanctions are more vulnerable than our national economy. Our national economy can defeat sanctions, and by Allah's favour and grace, we will defeat sanctions, and defeating sanctions means defeating the US. The US should receive yet another slap in the face from the Iranian nation with the defeat of sanctions!

Fifth, the fifth point, the Basij establishment in itself – Basij-e Mostazafeen[284] - accurately reflects the country's

---

284. Mobilization Forces to Assist the Underprivileged

condition. --This great organization, this foundation which exists throughout the country, and this great popular system has become a model for other countries. They, too, refer to their youth to solve their various problems.

Basij manifests this Holy Verse: "*Men said to them, 'A great army is gathering against you.' And frightened them.*" After the Battle of Uhud, word was being spread that Medina would be attacked, and they said that Muslims should be afraid of the enemy: "*But it only increased their faith.*" In the face of those threats and shouts, the faith of believers increased, and they said, "*For us, Allah suffices, and He is the best disposer of affairs.*"[285] This is representative of the Basij. Basij is the manifestation of this Holy Verse - not only does it not retreat in the face of the enemy's threats, but it also increases in faith: this is a strong point. Basij mobilization is one of the outstanding parts of the real image of our dear country, and the enemy is highly opposed to it. Their agents are incredibly opposed to Basij mobilization as well.

The sixth point concerns the outstanding and brilliant groups that one sees all over the country, throughout the year, including development-inspired groups. As I pointed out earlier, almost ten thousand development-inspired organizations are active in the country: Construction Based Basij, Rahian-e Noor, and those revolutionary rallies, i'tikaf ceremonies, and Hussaini and Ashura'i -- ceremonies which grow daily.--This reflects a realistic image of the country.

---
285. Surah Aal al-Imran – Verse 173.

Subjects in Need of Clarifications

These are phenomena with which one can get to know the Iranian nation. Of course, all organizations are responsible for helping the Basij and Rahian-e Noor.[286]

What I insist on, as usual, is that you elites and intellectuals, no matter where you are, should raise your hopes every day and should infuse the young generation with hopefulness. Instilling despair into people and painting a bleak picture of the future is poison. This fatal poison is administered to the nation through hostile propaganda. And this is what you should oppose.

The future looks promising in all sectors, and I hope such promising visions will be actualized in less than a generation. I hope our youth will see the day the Islamic Republic reaches its desired position. I hope our youth will see the day when other nations, scientists, and scholars worldwide feel they depend on our country to take further steps in scientific areas. Such a prospect could be actualized in the foreseeable future. I hope that just as humans need to learn certain languages to acquire some of the skills they need, other nations will one day feel that they need to learn your language and know about your culture. That day will come, and such hopes could be actualized.[287]

---

286. 04/10/2018 – In a ceremony of tens of thousands of Basij in Azadi stadium.
287. 06/05/2008 – In a meeting with the elite and highly educated students of the proivince of Fars.

The Most Fundamental Jihad for the Youth

However, before anything, my first advice concerns hopefulness and observing an optimistic outlook on the future. Without this fundamental key to any deadlock, not even one step can be taken forward. What I am referring to is authentic hope based on evident realities. I have always avoided false and deceiving hopefulness, but I have warned myself and others against unfounded pessimism and false fear. During these past 40 years, and today as ever, the enemy's propaganda and communication policy and its most active programs have revolved around making people and even our officials and statesmen lose hope in the future. False news, biased analysis, reversing facts, concealing the hopeful aspects, amplifying minor problems and berating or denying significant advantages have been constantly on the agenda of thousands of audio-visual and internet-based media by the enemies of the Iranians. And, of course, their followers inside the country can be seen using their freedoms to work in the service of the enemy. You, the young individuals, must be the forerunners of breaking the siege of such propaganda. Grow the plant of hope for the future in yourself and those around you. Drive fear and disappointment away from yourself and others. This is your first and most fundamental Jihad to make. Signs of hope—some of which were mentioned—are before your eyes. The growth of the admirers of the Revolution has been far more significant than that of outgoing fans, and loyal and helping hands and hearts are far more numerous

Subjects in Need of Clarifications

than the corrupted, the treacherous, and the greedy. The world has high regard and respect for the Iranian youth, Iranian's perseverance and ingenuity in many fields. Value yourself, and with the strength given by God, ascend towards the future and create epics.[288]

Progress

What I want to discuss now is wholly consistent with the nature of the youth and students of our country. It is about the future, and the future belongs to you. Your presence will be an effective and decisive factor in the future. I want to discuss the slogan of the fourth decade of the Revolution - "The Decade of Progress and Justice". This decade has already started. Of course, achieving progress or justice through talking or selecting a name is impossible. But both progress and justice can be achieved through clarification, reiteration, and making determined efforts. We should all try to turn the issue of progress and justice into a national discourse. If we do not make efforts, our plans will not be translated into action, and we will not achieve our goal.[289]

I want to discuss and clarify the issue I raised on the first day of my trip: the issue of progress. Progress is a crucial issue, and we should discuss it. Of course, discussing this issue should not give us a feeling that we have dealt with it completely: no, this is just the beginning. I pointed out

---
288. 11/02/2019 – Statement for the second stage of the revolution.
289. 17/05/2009 – In a meeting with teachers and students from Kurdistan.

that progress is a concept which - to a large extent - can potentially incorporate the goals of the Islamic Republic. I explained that progress is associated with change and movement: it is a path. How can progress be our goal? I explained that there is no limit to progress. Progress is a process. It is a path, but there is no end to it: it continues forever. This is because human beings change constantly, and human capacities are boundless. I pointed out that progress enjoys specific dimensions and that the Islamic conception of progress differs from the one- or two-dimensional conception of progress in Western culture. In Islamic thought, progress is multi-dimensional.[290]

Clarifying the Document of the Plan for Transformation to Managers, Workers and Teachers

There is another point about the transformation plan: its clarification. It was pointed out in the respected Ministers' report that this clarification is being done. Still, according to the reports that I have received – I am not present in the educational system, but I receive some reports – they are unaware of the transformation plan in many places. We speak about the transformation plan – I have placed great emphasis on the transformation plan for many years – but the managers in such and such organizations and divisions do not know what the plan is in the first place. Well, this cannot be done. When they do not know what it is and are

---

[290]. 20/10/2012 – In a meeting with youth from the provine of North Khorasan.

not familiar with it, they are not motivated to implement it. The plan should be clarified to them – not only to managers, the personnel, and even to teachers. Teachers should know what the transformation plan is. And you should prepare the plan so that it will be attractive to all of them so that they look at and understand it. My main discussion is about the transformation plan and the characteristics that it should enjoy, and I have mentioned them.[291]

Simple Islamic-Iranian Lifestyle

You should pursue the Islamic-Iranian lifestyle in theoretical and practical areas. You should sit and think about it. You should find its criteria, act on them, and publish them as guidelines. For example, you can print a pamphlet about the Islamic lifestyle on the roads. One of the examples that I gave two or three years ago about this matter was the issue of waiting at the traffic lights. This issue can be expanded and clarified. This is your job. It is the job of you, the youth, who have the patience, the talent, the intelligence and the capability to do so. So, you should carry out these tasks.[292]

Lifestyles are of different kinds. One of the most important goals of the enemies of the Iranian nation and the enemies of Islam is to change Muslims' lifestyle and to make it similar to theirs. The realities of life influence one's thoughts. Daily behaviour influences the hearts and souls of people – both

---
291. 01/09/2020 – In a televised speech with the heads and managers of the Department of Education.
292. 02/07/2016 - In a meeting with group of university students.

our souls and the souls of our audience and friends. They want to change this.

Islam has brought us a particular lifestyle. Take the case of one's manners. One of the essential tasks is to [promote] good manners. Westerners do not pay much attention to manners in regular contact with others. Since long ago, it has been well-known that we Iranians observe manners in our speeches and contact with others. We respect the other side. However, they want to change this, and unfortunately, they have succeeded in some instances.

Imagine that you disagree with someone on a particular issue and want to speak to others about him. There are two ways to do so: we can talk in a rude, disrespectful and vulgar manner or speak about that person by observing manners and tact. Notice that in the Holy Qur'an, when there is talk of the corrupt, disbelievers and evil people in the world, God says, *"But most of them understand not"*[293]. As you notice, He does not say, "all of them". After all, there is a minority among them who are reasonable. The Holy Qur'an observes their right by saying, "most of them".

One issue about lifestyle, good habits and life methods is reading books. Of course, this was pointed out in the report delivered in the meeting, but it is essential for us to encourage the people and youth to read books. You should introduce good books as well. I even think it is a good idea to turn Friday prayer places into centers of presenting good, up-to-date

---

293. Surah al-Yunus – Verse 55.

and ideal books so that the people come and see that such books exist and get them from the same venue or other such places. Of course, the gentlemen in charge should examine the different dimensions of this. We should encourage people to read books and encourage outstanding personalities to produce books. These are necessary measures.[294]

The Rights of Women[295]

Another issue among the essential responsibilities is the clarification of the rights of women and men from the viewpoint of Islam. Women themselves should work in this arena. However, those aware of Islamic teachings should put in more effort and clarify the view of Islam in places where the rights of men and women differ. This should be done so that everyone can see how it is in accordance with the nature and make-up of a man and a woman, and it is in accordance with what is beneficial for society. That being said, good work has been done. Today work needs to be done using the current language. Otherwise, good work has been done in the past in this arena, and they will also reach these conclusions if they were to study and be attentive to those works.[296]

---

294. 04/01/2016 – In a meeting with Friday Prayer leaders from across the country.
295. For futher reading refer to the collection of books published on the topics of Women and Family by the Islamic Revolution Publications.
296. 22/10/1997 – In a meeting with a group of women.

Family and Increasing Offspring

Now, I deem it necessary to express my respect for martyrs' mothers and wives in two different generations: one during the Sacred Defense Era and the other during the defence of the Holy Shrines. In those eras, martyrs' wives and mothers played a really determining and unique role, and one should bow down before them in respect. Unfortunately, there are few artistic productions about these dear and great personalities. This is an extraordinarily outstanding capacity for which there is more room for work.

Some say that the hijab hinders a woman's growth and advancement. No, it is the other way around because the hijab prevents those useless ostentations that prevent a woman from moving forward. Today, we have thousands of great and prominent women in various scientific, practical, social, political and technical fields, all living while in complete hijab. When we look at women in this way, their role in the family also becomes prominent: Their role as a mother, a wife, the lady of the house and the like. This is what is becoming less and less important in the West. The family is declining in the West. The family is a warm and blessed centre in which the most robust foundations of human education are laid. The first and most important foundations of human spiritual and intellectual education are established in the centre of the family. Home is the best place for the comfort of body and soul; it is the best centre for relieving the fatigue of body and soul; it is the most real environment for intimacy. No intimacy is imagined or exists in any environment as much as in a family.

Who is the pivot in this blessed centre? The mother. Who is the main element? The mother. Who is the centre of the circle? The mother. The mother is the pivot of the family. Western propaganda machines and, unfortunately, some Westernized figures inside our own country are trying to undermine this. They either try to make the people misunderstand this or avoid showing the mother's role entirely. Housewives and those without work outside the home have rendered the most essential services! It is necessary to appreciate the value of those women who have preferred to be housewives. Although women have had, do have and will have duties outside the home, and although there is nothing wrong with this, their most important service is attending to household duties.

Well, now that we are discussing the family issue, I wish to say something about marrying at an appropriate age and without delay. You, dear reciters, who are an important and valuable medium in our country – later on, I will expand on this matter – should promote these issues. Marrying on time and without any delay is a necessary task. Having children and increasing the population is an important and fundamental responsibility that should be carried out. Both of these issues – early and timely marriage and increasing the population – is one of the vital needs that the country has in the present time and also in the future. Well, these concepts should be given a due place in your recitations.[297]

Hijab

Hijab is a value in accordance with the nature of mankind. Nudity and moving towards more mingling of the two sexes and exposing them to one another is a move against human nature and volition. The holy Shariah of Islam has also set out certain restrictions and limits for it, and those who are believers and religious cannot disapprove of hijab. Of course, there might be people who are uninformed or ignorant. One should first familiarize them with the hijab. During the early years after the revolution, I realized that women who practice hijab, yet do not appreciate it well, do not have any information about the law, philosophy and benefits of hijab. That is to say; they have seldom been told about it.

In your university environment, in your publications, communicate with other publications that focus on women. Write things, spread them and spread thoughts in society. This should be done using reasoning and logic. The best way to acquire hijab is by confronting it with logic. Albeit, if something becomes law and someone acts against it, then it is possible that the law will engage them, and without doubt, it will. Despite this, what is fundamentally necessary and more important is that the minds of these young girls

---

297. 03/02/2021 – In a televised speech for eulogists.

and women, most of whom are young women, must be made aware of the hijab. This means it should be explained to them what hijab is according to the Shariah and logic. The correct reasoning should permeate their minds regarding hijab. I am hopeful that, God willing, it will get better daily. That being said, one factor that negatively affects this arena is some of the movies that place the Western lifestyle within grasp. These are pacifying the minds of the people regarding the issue of hijab. Some reminders must be given about the spread of some of these movies.[298]

Unity and Avoiding Division

If you look at their propagation, you will see that concerning our dear country and great and courageous nation, which at the same time is oppressed, they focus on a few points.

The first point is the differences, duality and schisms. The same story as before, divide and conquer. The same pain and catastrophe from old have befallen the heart of our nation. They are at the forefront of spreading discord and spreading sectarian rumours. You can observe that this conference, by the grace of Allah and divine honour, has become a source of honour for the Islamic Ummah and the dear nation of Iran. They saw that this gathering was a sign of unity, oneness, strong management and amicable cooperation between state officials and the people and that it had the potential to

---

298. 23/02/1999 – In a question and answer session with officials and heads of university publications.

carry out great and sophisticated work. So what will they do now? They started spreading rumours and creating divisions. From the first day of the conference till today, they have propagated the rumours of division. However, no one's ear is for sale, and they are not paying attention to them. This is because all that can be witnessed, all of the indicators and documented evidence, stand against all the rumours. However, they are busy doing their work.

It is evident they give a lot of importance to the issue of divisions. You must move in the complete opposite direction of this movement. Firstly, strive to ensure there are no divisions; secondly, strive to ensure there are no sectarian rumours that the enemy is trying to create and grow. Someone who strengthens the sectarian rumours internally is the same as someone who is the source of divisions. Lowly, weak and impure hands strive to create divisions. They strive to spread rumours suggesting a divide if they see that divisions are not being made. It is as if the enemy is trying to damage the front of Truth, and when they know that it is not possible, they start spreading rumours that the front of Truth has been defeated and is about to retreat! This is what the enemy does. You must work in the opposite direction. This is a service the enemy does for us. The enemy shows us that they are sensitive regarding this issue and, in reality, exposes what we should be focussed on. That being said, we do not act in a reactionary manner towards the enemy; it is just logical and intelligent analysis.[299]

Obstacles to Progress[300]

The Revolution aimed to prove to all the people in various corners of the Islamic world that this model was practical. And this [the Revolution] is a case in point. This was the goal of the Revolution. This goal existed since the beginning of the Revolution, and I should tell you that it is still our goal today and will be our future goal. This is a constant goal.

The second aspect of the issue is that the Islamic Republic had this goal, but we are not living in a vacuum. We are living with the realities. The issue is how much the surrounding realities contribute to or hinder our progress towards these goals. Indeed, it would not take long to reach this goal if the obstructions, which I will talk about, did not exist. A solid and unified group would have probably been able to actualize these goals in 5 to 10 years. But there are always barriers in the path of mankind. It is the existence of such obstacles that make one's efforts meaningful and morally proper. This is what we call jihad. If there were no barriers, jihad would be meaningless. Jihad means making efforts seriously together with overcoming obstacles.

---

299. 24/12/1997 – In a meeting with a group of scholars.
300. For further reading in understand the obstacles to the progress of the Islamic Revolution, refer to the book *Aramghaan* and *Rawshnaaye Aayende*.

What were the barriers? We faced two kinds of obstacles - internal and external. What were the internal barriers? The internal barriers are those things that exist among ourselves - decision makers, the people, and the supervisors who were not part of the Revolution and its challenges. This is what I mean by internal barriers. The internal barriers are the weaknesses - weakness of thought and wisdom, being laid-back and carefree, and not taking matters seriously. These sometimes present obstacles to the achievement of our goals. Our estimations and calculations about the problems and our actions should be realistic or at least close to the realities. Not taking matters seriously is the same as being laid-back and carefree. This is also one of the problems. Trying to escape challenges is also one of our internal weaknesses.

One of the other internal weaknesses is the social attitudes and the historical habits which existed among us [the Iranian nation] at the beginning of the Islamic Revolution. Today's youth might not have a correct picture of our psychological state or historical attitudes during the Islamic Revolution's victory. Today, we see that the idea of being capable [of making achievements] is prevalent among everyone. Even if they ask you whether you can outperform the pioneers of the world's most delicate and accurate industries, you will say you can. If we make efforts, we can. The young Muslim scientists of the Islamic Republic believe they are capable of doing anything. However, this was not the case at the beginning of the Islamic Revolution. Previous attitudes were

Subjects in Need of Clarifications

precisely the opposite of this. Whenever there was talk of a new challenge, they said they could not handle them. They were asked to make something but said they could not. We said we had to oppose the false mottos spread worldwide, but they said they did not have the power to do so. In those days, the belief that "we can" was replaced by "we cannot". This is the historical attitude that has been left from the previous era.

Being oppressed, bullied, and witnessing debauchery in those from whom society expected justice, decency, and purity had become a habit. Before the Islamic Revolution, people would not be surprised if they were informed that some high-ranking government official - the highest-ranked official was the Pahlavi Shah - or minister had been involved in debauchery and immoral behaviour. They would say this is something evident! They were used to the indecency and corruption of the officials who were supposed to have acted morally and ethically.

I was surprised to know that some intoxicated caliph had led the morning prayers of a group of people. Such stories exist about this caliph and a king appointed by one of the caliphs. This story exists in the history of Islam, and it is a famous and true story. The morning prayers consisted of two units, but since he was intoxicated, he had prayed six units. They had told the king that you prayed extra units, and he had said: "I am happy, and I can do even more if you want." This story exists in history. In those days, people saw that the caliph was involved in such immoral behaviour, but they just tolerated and acted indifferently towardssuch behaviour. This was the case during the Pahlavi era as well. Things were all the same during the Pahlavi era - which we went through prior to the victory of the Islamic Revolution. People would not be surprised to see that the ruler of an Islamic country was involved in debauchery, drinking, and libertinism.

I may have told you before that one of the great scholars of Tabriz, who was very knowledgeable and whom I had seen before - he was my father's teacher, was a very scholarly but naive person. I once travelled to Tabriz and heard his students and friends who were interested in him narrate a story about him. They said once Muhammad Reza Pahlavi had come to Tabriz during his youth and had gone to see this great scholar. He had gone to see him in the school where he taught as a sign of respect for him. This scholar, who was very knowledgeable and faithful but naïve, had been attracted to the Shah and started praising him. His friends had told him that the person he praised did immoral acts, which would be very obscene in his opinion. For instance, they told him that the Shah drinks alcohol. He had said: "Well, he is the king. Do you not expect him to drink? ". They had told him that he does gambling, and he had said: "He is the king. What other games do you expect him to play?" The common belief was that because someone was the king or because someone was a minister, he could get involved in debauchery and libertinism or exhibit immoral behaviour.

Subjects in Need of Clarifications

This was one of the habits that were common in our society. These are the internal barriers. These things place obstacles in the way of achieving a lofty goal. Wrath, untrained and uncontrolled desires, being attracted to superstitious habits and beliefs inherited from the past, and misunderstanding the principles of religion are among the internal barriers.

Some people did not understand many of the issues. We were leading a campaign, but some people were against such campaigns based on the belief that every flag raised before the flag of the Imam of the Age (a) is to be burnt. They said: "Do you want to start a campaign before that of Imam Mahdi (a)?" They said that the flag of such a campaign is to be lowered. They had not correctly understood the meaning of this hadith. A group of people who had heard at the beginning of Islam, at the time of the Imams (a), that Imam Mahdi (a) would come and fill the world with justice. There were even some people who were not sure about the issue themselves. You should note that such claims existed both at the time of the Umayyad Dynasty and at the time of the Abbasid Dynasty. Such beliefs were also common among other people present at the time of the Abbasid Dynasty and the following eras up to the present moment. If someone raises such a flag, it is to be burnt. This does not mean that people should not oppose tyranny or that people should not fight or rise to form a divine and Islamic community based on the principles set by Imam Ali (a). This represents a misunderstanding of religion. As you see, these were all the internal barriers that existed after the Islamic Revolution's victory. We wanted to direct the country towards these goals despite those barriers. Every one of those problems hindered our progress towards our goals.

Of course, the problems were solvable. Many of the problems were solved through clarification. Therefore, in Islamic campaigns, enlightenment plays an important role. Let me tell the youth who feel responsible in this regard that clarification plays a crucial role. In Islamic movements, enlightenment - the expression of facts, propagation, and the way the message is conveyed - is critical, and one should not ignore this fact. This is contrary to the Marxist ideology that was common at that time and opposed to propagation. They believed that campaigns were phenomena that occur naturally whether you want it or not or whether you propagate it or not.

This means that according to their dialectic, they believed our campaign had no need for enlightenment. In 1970, a youth from Mashhad who was familiar with me and connected to one of these newly formed groups met with me somewhere. They were a group of communists - the Jungle group and the like. He explained to me what they intended to do. I told him that what they wanted to do was not possible in that social context. I told him to talk to people a little, clarify their goals, and explain to the people what they wanted to do. But he said with total inattention, "That is the Islamic method". Yes, this is the Islamic method. The

Islamic approach is rooted in enlightenment, and it was due to such enlightenment that the Islamic Revolution overcame many false historical traditions and backgrounds. Of course, we have not been able to overcome some of those traditions yet - like consumerism, being extravagant, and the things which some of you talked about - and this has its reasons. This is among the things we inherited from the past, and we have unfortunately kept this inheritance. We - the Iranian nation - should quit this nasty, irritating habit. We are a very consumerist nation, and we should solve this problem. Everyone should cooperate to solve this problem. Of course, the national broadcasting service undoubtedly plays a role in this regard.

Then, there are the external factors which were many. All those disadvantaged in one way or another by the Revolution or its goals rose against the Revolution. Some people are disadvantaged by security. Some are disadvantaged by justice, and some by the rejection of non-divine governments. Others are disadvantaged because domination from external forces is rejected. Some people are also disadvantaged due to the rejection of despotism. These are clear facts and need not be explained. Who is disadvantaged by justice, independence, freedom or the like? All these people have risen against the Revolution, and their opposition continues.

You might not remember the beginning of the Revolution. During the first year of the Revolution, there were clashes and conflicts in all corners of the country due to ethnic reasons. In Baluchestan, in Kurdistan, in Turkmen Sahra, and different parts of the country, there were clashes due to ethnic reasons. When they investigated the matter, it was found that none of these ethnic groups had any problems with Islam or the Islamic Revolution. I had previously lived in Baluchestan. I had been banished there, and I knew the Balochi people. I knew that they did not have the slightest problem with the Revolution. But some people, under the name of Balochi, opposed the Revolution through a scheme. The same thing is true about Kurdistan and Turkmen Sahra as well. Later, their plots were foiled, and we discovered where they were being provoked from. These were the barriers which lay ahead of the Islamic Revolution. It was not the case that we were continuing our path without any obstacles.

After the issue of ethnicities, there was the issue of our internal battles. It has a bitter story, a very saddening one. Then there was the imposed war. The incredible power which our nation used against the enemies, and which brought the enemies to their knees would have helped us make a great deal of progress if it had been used for construction purposes in the Islamic Republic. Of course, we benefited from the imposed war. The Iranian nation turned all threats into a great opportunity and a great test in the real sense of the word. It was a great stage for gaining experience, and we gained many benefits from that.

But there was also the reality that imposing war on a country causes great problems for that country. The world's monopolistic powers, the internal rebels, the plots of the superpowers, and the tempting political and economic propaganda of the superpower that had been denied any rights to Iran by the Islamic Revolution - namely the U.S. whose policies continue - acted all as barriers to this great movement of the Iranian nation. Now you evaluate the movement of the Islamic Revolution and the Islamic Republic towards those goals despite these barriers. If I were to assess this movement, I would say the performance of the Islamic Republic has been good. Can anyone tolerate all these problems? At that time, such government changes had taken place in Africa, Asia, and many other places. None of the governments could tolerate the difficulties. Also, during the pre-Revolution era, many great revolutions worldwide - such as the French and Russian revolutions of 1917 - could not resist against these different forces. I mean, they deviated from their course from the first day.

Being democratic, Islamic, and moving towards the ideals - the fact that a youth comes here after thirty years and shouts that the ideals of the Revolution are his wishes and demands - is a great achievement for the Revolution. It was never the same in other revolutions.

Take a look at the literary works of the 19th century in France, which go back to the end of the 18th century when the French Revolution took place. Early in the 19th century, Napoleon started his rule. Then, look at the literary works of mid 18th century - 1830 to 1840 - which are many. Look at their poetry and novels, and you will see what a situation they were in 30 years after the victory of their revolution. There was total despotism, corruption, and a dreadful state of class discrimination at that time, despite their mottos of justice, equality and anti-despotism. This achievement of the Islamic Revolution is outstanding. Worse than that was the Russian Revolution of 1917. And such events in the contemporary era were mainly revolutions in name only. They were mainly coups or armed groups seizing power in a country like Cuba and other places. Most of these movements happened in the same way I mentioned. They could not overcome the difficulties or remove the barriers.

Consider the obstacles. All these barriers are among God's laws. The existence of these barriers is not accidental. Obstacles accompany all efforts and movements. Otherwise, jihad would be meaningless. *And thus did We make for every prophet an enemy, the devils from among men and jinn, some of them inspiring others with gilded speech to deceive (them).*[301] In all invitations made by the Prophets (s), enemies - hindrances - such as man and jinn were present. There is another Qur'anic verse: *And thus have We made in every town the leaders of its guilty ones, that they may make plans therein. And they plan not but against themselves, and they perceive not.*[302] There have always been groups of people in every community whose presence is the cause of evil and deception. These are all among God's

---

301. Surah al-An'aam – Verse 112.
302. Surah al-An'aam – Verse 123.

laws. The Prophets (s) never said they would only enter the scene without the presence of obstacles. They entered the arena while the atmosphere and the stage was challenging and full of battles, just like the Islamic Revolution and the Islamic Republic.

But it is also God's law that if the Prophets' (s) movements or divine movements, an instance of which is the Islamic Revolution, were persistent and continued, all obstacles would be removed. Two verses in the Chapter of Fath read: *And others which you have not yet been able to achieve -- Allah has surely encompassed them. And Allah is ever Powerful over all things. And if those who disbelieve fight with you, they will certainly turn (their) backs; then they will find no protector nor helper.*[303] This means that if you stand up and resist, do not lose track of your goal, and do not stop making efforts, you will undoubtedly emerge victorious out of all battles. This is the essence of what I was trying to tell you, dear youth.

Today, the obstacles from the first day of the Islamic Revolution still exist. Some exist in different forms, while some new barriers have been created too. Unfortunately, as these youth said, consumerism and competition in gaining wealth and making money have formed a new class in society. The Islamic system is not opposed to acquiring or producing wealth. Instead, it encourages such actions. If there is no production, and if wealth is not produced, the life and continuity of society will be in danger, and the required

---
303. Surah al-Fath – Verse 22 and 23.

power will not be gained. This is an Islamic principle. However, people craving an aristocratic life or wealth is very undesirable. This is what, unfortunately, exists among us. As I previously mentioned, consumerism and indecency are two undesirable traits.

And there are external obstacles as well. Today, the US has stood against the Iranian nation with all its power - propagandistic, political, economic, and international power. That is why they pay much attention to the Islamic Republic and speak of it as a great danger. Of course, this is true.[304]

The Enemy and Their Schemes[305]

Well, we are close to our fortieth year. The fortieth year of what? The fortieth year of a phenomenon that has managed to change and shake the world's power structure. You should not say that such and such a power in the world still holds its place. Well, our claim is not that we want to destroy all powers in the world. This is not our job. Of course, this will happen one day, but it will be done by a divine hand. Our job is to destroy the structure and system of power – the system of domination – in the world. And we have done so.

The system of domination means dividing the world into two groups of countries and nations: the first group is the dominator, and the second is the dominated. We have

---

304. 03/05/2008 – In a meeting with professors and university students from universities in Shiraz.
305. More comprehensive discussion can be found in the books *Dushman Shinaasi* and *ndeesheye Muqawamat*.

Subjects in Need of Clarifications

destroyed this wrong system and wrong formula in the world. We have shown that a nation that is neither a dominator nor dominated can exist. This nation neither wants to bully others nor does it want to accept others' bullying. The people of Iran have shown this in practice. It was the Revolution which created this reality. The Islamic Revolution changed structures in the world.

They are not sitting idle in the face of this change in structures. Their enmities began from the first day. It is around 40 years now that they have been showing enmity. Throughout the past 40 years, they have shown all sorts of hostilities. You know these enmities, but these things should be clarified for the new generation. Their hostilities include waging wars, imposing sanctions, hurling abuse, making accusations, infiltrating the country, hatching plots, doing intelligence and cultural work, and creating domestic rifts. They have done everything they could with their money but failed in all cases.

It is close to 40 years now that they have been doing these things. If their plots were supposed to work, the Islamic Republic should have been uprooted a hundred times over until now! As is commonly said in Farsi, the Islamic Republic should have rotted in its seventh death shroud until now. However, today, we have 40 years of power. The people of Iran have managed to resist and overcome 40 years of enmities, malevolence and pressure.[306]

Our responsibility as the people and as the members of the Islamic Republic is first to know the enemy. We should know the enemy and not err in recognizing them. You should not say that all of you know who the enemy is. Yes, you know who they are. The enemy is comprised of the Arrogant powers, Zionism and the US. You know this, but there is a tremendous effort to make you look the other way and to change people's opinions with complex propaganda apparatuses. Everyone should be vigilant. It is essential to know the enemy. This is one issue, and another is to understand their plan, what they are doing and what they want to do next. After that, we should know how to confront the enemy's plan.

Our people should know this because we are reliant on the people. The Islamic Republic is nothing and is utterly meaningless without the people's demands, assistance and votes of confidence and willpower. The people should know the enemy, their methods, and how to confront such practices. This is the duty of intellectuals. Fortunately, we are not lacking in brave and insightful people in the country. We have insightful, brave, intelligent and well-informed individuals in the military, scientific and political arenas. Therefore, we should listen to what they have to say. What they deem necessary should be correctly implemented

---

306. 27/12/2017 – In a meeting with members of the Cooperative Council for Islamic Propagation.

Subjects in Need of Clarifications

in the country and society. We do not have a shortage of these individuals.

Fortunately, the number of graduates of Imam Khomeini's school increases daily. Once, Imam Khomeini said during the war that training the youth and growing these promising saplings was the master key of the Revolution. Imam Khomeini said this once, and what he said was completely correct as he was a man of wisdom. All victories and all these crucial tasks are small compared to the task of building outstanding individuals. Today, we, fortunately, have many such individuals.

We should know the enemy. I want to say this firmly and definitively: the enemy comprises the US, the Zionist regime and the apparatus of the Arrogant Powers. The apparatus of the Arrogant Powers do not only consist of the US and such governments; it is comprised of a collection of companies and global looters and oppressors who are opposed to every centre which fights against oppression and looting. It is they who form the enemy. We do not consider an enemy such and such government inside or outside the region which might say something against us. We do not consider them an enemy as long as they do not make a move in the enemy's service and against the Islamic Republic. It is the former whom we consider as the enemy. Therefore, we should not make a mistake in identifying the enemy. We will succeed if we know who the enemy is and how we should confront them. The enemy plans to undermine the determination and willpower of our people in various areas. This is the enemy's basic plan. They want the people to doubt their faith and firm determination. I previously discussed these two elements and keywords: faith and religious zeal.

Arousing doubts in the people's faith and religious zeal is what the enemy is after. They know that should this happen, the offensive and even defensive power of the Islamic Republic will be influenced and eradicated. That is why they are hatching plots. Of course, this is not the only plot hatched by the US and other such powers, but it is the most important one. They hatch plots against the Islamic Republic in the arena of politics, the economy – you are witness to the sanctions – and security.

A few days before the incident of Aban – the incidents related to gasoline and other economic matters – an American agent and a few mercenary and treasonous Iranians gathered together in a small, malicious and evil European country to design schemes and plot against the Islamic Republic. And their plot was what we witnessed in the subsequent days on the issue of gasoline. In those days, people were upset about the gasoline price, and some took to the street to protest. However, as soon as the people – part of the people, they were not very large in number – entered the arena, those deceived individuals and those agents and mercenaries embarked on implementing the enemy's plot. In other words, their mission was to destroy governmental and public centres, set buildings on fire, kill people, sabotage, and start a war.

This was their plot beforehand. Of course, when I say a few days before the incident, it was just an effort to update their plans- they had already hatched the plot, had already trained some agents, and had given money to those mercenaries. So, they do such things as well and do them as much as possible.

On that day, I said in a meeting with the people [Supreme Leader's meeting with several nurses] that American elements rejoiced in Washington when that incident occurred in our country. They said to a politician [who was in Washington D.C. at that time] that Iran was done and over with, but it became clear after two days that they themselves were done and over with. They were very sad and upset, and they were feeling down. The enemy's plan should be understood. And we should consider our fundamental tenets in the face of this plan. The fundamental tenets are ideological principles – whether Islamic or revolutionary – and national unity. The unity which was fortunately witnessed under the pure coffin of Martyr Soleimani and the martyrs that accompanied him should be preserved. The people should adopt this orientation: the orientation of the Revolution, commemorating revolutionary men and respecting martyrs and whatever reminds one of the revolutionary values.

All of us should know that the enmity of this front I spoke about is not seasonal and temporary; rather, this enmity is intrinsic and perpetual. They strike whenever they can. The cure for this is to strengthen ourselves in the areas of the military, security, politics and the economy. We should strengthen ourselves in different arenas so that the enemy fails to deliver their blows; otherwise, their enmity is intrinsic. Some people think if we take a step back and show a bit of compromise, the Americans will stop showing hatred. This way of thinking is a big and grave mistake. Some people nurture the thought that we should not do something to enrage the US – some people say this: they write it in newspapers – this is the exact opposite of what God says, "And their similitude in the Gospel is: like a seed which sends forth its blade, then makes it strong. It then becomes thick and stands on its own stem, filling the sowers with wonder and delight. As a result, it fills the unbelievers with rage at them"[307].

As it happens, the growth of pious personalities, strong saplings, and religious youth is to fill "The unbelievers with rage at them". The aim is to enrage the enemy. And that is why they are even angrier! They are angry at the youth active in the arena of science, jihad, public services and the military. They are angry at them.[308]

Infiltration[309]

Infiltration is a critical issue. When we speak about infiltration, some people react. They say, "The issue of infiltration has become a point of partisan contention. They

---

307. Surah al-Fath – Verse 29.
308. 08/01/2020 – In a meeting with he people of Qum.
309. For futher reading, refer to the book *Andeeshey Muqawamat*.

Subjects in Need of Clarifications

are making partisan use of it." I have nothing to do with such statements. Well, they should not make partisan use of it, and they should not say nonsensical things about the issue of infiltration. They should not speak about infiltration without having serious content. We have nothing to do with such issues, but no matter what statement is made and what serious course of action is adopted, we should not show negligence about the reality of infiltration. We should not forget that the enemy is after infiltration.

Later on, I will expand on the infiltration issue and say what it is and how it is exerted. We should not show negligence about the essence of infiltration. Parties should not accuse one another. Some parties might say, "When you spoke about infiltration, you meant such and such a thing", and others say, "No, you meant another thing." That is not important; instead, what is essential is that the reality should not be forgotten. The enemy is formulating plans to infiltrate.

There are two kinds of infiltration: one is individual infiltration, and another is systematic and network infiltration. There are many examples of individual infiltration. This is what it means: imagine that you have established an organization in which you have a responsibility. Now, they send someone to your organization who has disguised themselves and is wearing a mask. You think that they are your friend, while they are not. They appear as friends so they can do what they are supposed to do. Sometimes, their goal is to spy, which is the least important form. The least important form is spying and gathering intelligence. But sometimes, they do something more important than spying. They change your decisions. You are a manager and official, and you make crucial decisions. You can make a significant and efficient move, but if you make it in a particular way, this will be to the advantage of the enemy. They show up and deceive you into making it that way. This is decision-building, and it has been witnessed in all organizations.

This is not particular to political organizations. Seminarian, religious and other such organizations have witnessed this. The late Sayyid Hassan Tahami – a great religious scholar in our country who resided in Birjand – had gone to Birjand to live there. He was a great mullah; if he had stayed in Qom or Najaf, he would definitely have become a Grand Jurist because he was very wise. He himself narrated a story for me. He said, "When the Iraqis were fighting against the English – in the year 1918, which is approximately one hundred years ago – one of the Grand Jurists of the time had a servant who was a very good man. He used to speak to the clergy in an affectionate and friendly manner, and he had a friendly relationship with everyone." The late Tahami used to mention his name, but I had forgotten it. He continued, "Later on, when the English achieved victory and occupied Iraq, Najaf was the last city they occupied. Then the clergy were informed that that servant was an English officer!"

The late Tahami added: "I did not believe it. I said, 'Is such a thing possible?'"

After that, he said, "We were walking in the Hovish Market – a well-known market in Najaf – and I saw seven, eight, ten English officers approaching us on horses. At that time, they used to come and go on horses. I saw that an officer was leading them. I moved aside so that they would pass. When they reached me, I saw that the officer leading them on his horse said, 'Sayyid Hassan, how are you?' I saw that he was the fellow who worked as a servant for such and such Grand Jurist. We used to see him for many years!" Sometimes, infiltration is like this. It is an individual. They penetrate someone's house or organization. And there have been many such cases in political organizations as well. Today too, such a thing may exist, which is, of course, dangerous.

However, the more dangerous form [of infiltration] is systematic infiltration. Systematic infiltration means creating networks inside the people utilizing money. It is here that the role of money and economic matters becomes clear. The most important means are two: one is money, and another is sexual attraction. They attract and gather individuals and fabricate fake and false goals to draw those personalities who can influence society towards their ideal direction. What is that ideal direction? It is changing beliefs, ideals, outlooks and lifestyles. They want to do something to make the targeted individual and the influenced personality think in the same way that the Americans do. In other words, they want to do something to make you look at things like an American does. Of course, American politicians have nothing to do with the people of America. They want to make you make decisions like a high-ranking CIA agent would like you to and consequently want the same things they want.

If they exert systematic infiltration on those personalities who play an essential role in the country's fate, politics and future, notice what will happen. Ideals, values, goals and beliefs will change.

This way, they feel relieved and at ease as you work for them without needing them to take risks and enter the arena. This is the goal. This is the goal of infiltration: they want to exert systematic, network and comprehensive infiltration, not individual infiltration.

In the present time, when you take a look, you come to believe that on the issue of Palestine, a people are clearly being oppressed. You are seeing this. This is how you look at it. He – an Arab Palestinian, whether a Muslim or a Christian – who is being oppressed in his own house is condemned from an American perspective. From your viewpoint, he is the oppressed party, but when they change your outlook, you will look at the issue the way they do and then say that Israel is defending its own identity. Did Obama not say this? At the same time that they were shooting, day and night, at the people of Gaza and at the same time that they were attacking defenceless people and their houses, their lives, their farms, their children, their schools and their hospitals, the U.S. President said that Israel is defending its own identity. This is how they look at things. Creating networks and orientations makes individuals adopt such an outlook regardless of whether they live in Iran or another country. Notice how dangerous this is.

Who are the targets of this infiltration? Primarily outstanding and influential personalities, decision-makers and decision-builders are targetted. It is such individuals who are infiltrated. Therefore, infiltration is a danger, a grave one. Now, when someone says, "Such and such a person wants to make partisan use of the word 'infiltration'," this does not diminish the issue's importance!

Infiltration is fulfilled by actions taking place on the outskirts. One of the things that completes infiltration is criticism of those individuals who insist on honourable principles, correct outlooks and values. I do not want to say that those who criticize Basij and accuse it of extremism, harsh measures and the like are intentionally cooperating with the infiltration agents. I do not make such a claim and am not aware of such a thing, but the truth is that this is a kind of help. Those accusing – in different areas and ways – the Basij of extremism, fanaticism and the like are completing the act of infiltration. The projects of infiltration are being completed through such individuals. This is because the Basij are a solid fortification. The Basij are a solid fortification that should not be weakened and undermined.[310]

---

310. 25/11/2015 – In a meeting with officers of the voluntary Basij battalions.

The Stage We Are In[311]

There are specific goals, and at each stage, the Islamic government pursues one of these goals to make progress, achieve transcendence and create the great Islamic civilization. The Islamic government should try to achieve this goal at this stage. Of course, there are certain stages and phases to reach these goals. Experts, intellectuals and officials in charge of this are identifying these phases and objectives, and, as a result, our collective movement will begin. Everyone should try to make any movement they make, at any stage, one that helps reach its respective goal. This is a proper system which is based on logical and rational measures. All activists in the arena of politics and the macro management of the country should always keep this in mind. All the people and you, the dear Basij too – those who are active in the arena of the Basij - should always keep this in mind.[312]

We should maintain the support of the people, and you intellectuals, authors, poets and religious scholars can do this. The most significant people are religious scholars who have a heavy responsibility. They should clarify for people what they want and where they are going. They should enlighten them about the problems and the enemy. They

---

311. The Supreme Leader of the Revolution has spoken about the stages of the Islamic Revolution in various speeches. An example of this would be the speech given in a meeting government officials on 02/12/2000.
312. 20/11/2013 – In a meeting with 50,000 officers of the Basij from all over the country in *Musllaaye Imam Khomeini,* Tehran.

should help the people remain vigilant. In this way, no harm will be inflicted on the Islamic Ummah.[313]

A logical chain exists; we have said this before, and it has been discussed. The first link [in this chain] is the Islamic revolution, then the formation of the Islamic system, then the formation of the Islamic government, then the formation of the Islamic society and then the formation of the Islamic Ummah. This is a continuous chain that is linked together. What is meant by the Islamic Revolution? The first link is a revolutionary movement. From one aspect, the concept of revolution is included in all of these stages. Over here, what we mean by the Islamic revolution is a revolutionary movement that overthrows the oppressive, old, puppet and evil system and creates the grounds for the establishment of a new system. The following link in the chain is the Islamic system. What I mean here by the Islamic system is that general identity with a specific definition that the nation and the owners of this revolution, the people, choose. In our case, our people chose the Islamic Republic. Islamic republic means a system in which democracy is ascertained from Islam and exists alongside Islamic values. We have also moved past this link in the chain. The Islamic government means that a constitution is created based on whatever was decided in the stage of choosing the Islamic System. The institutions and organizations managing the nation's affairs

---

313. 11/12/2012 – In a meeting with participants of a conference for teachers from across the Islamic world and the Islamic Awakening conference.

are specified—this collective of management institutions is the Islamic government. Over here, what is meant by the government is not just the Executive branch. It refers to the collective of various management institutions responsible for managing a nation's affairs. The next part of the chain is Islamic society. This is an essential and fundamental part. After the Islamic government has been established, the responsibility of this Islamic government is to actualise the Islamic society. What is the Islamic society? A society in which the Islamic goals, objectives and great aspirations Islam has presented for humanity are actualised. We are in pursuit of a society that is just and free. A society in which the people have a role and an effect on its management, future and their progress, a society that has national pride and sovereignty. A society that is prosperous and far from poverty and hunger and has multifaceted advancements such as academic, economic and political progress. Ultimately pursuing a society that is without stagnation and pausing and continuously progressing. This is the society of which we are in the pursuit of. However, this society has not been realized yet, but this is what we are after. This is our real and main middle objective.

Why do we say middle objective? Once the Islamic society has been formed, the most important responsibility of such a society, government, and environment is that under its' shade, mankind can reach divine and spiritual perfection. "I did not create the jinn and the humans except that they may worship Me."[314]. So that mankind can reach servitude. They have defined the phrase "To worship" as "To know". This does not mean to worship is to know or worship and knowledge are the same. Instead, it means that worship has no meaning and is impossible without knowledge and, therefore, would not be worship. Thus, a society that can reach the servitude of Allah has reached the perfection of knowing Allah. They become a creation in accordance with the ethics of Allah. This is the perfection of mankind. That is the ultimate objective. The objective before that is the creation of an Islamic society, which is very lofty and grand. The grounds for forming an Islamic Ummah can also be created when such a society has been made. This would mean the spread of the Islamic society, which is a different discussion. What has been presented here as an objective is a very lofty deed.[315]

Prayer[316]

This responsibility, on the individual level, is to increase the quality of the prayer. At the level of society, this responsibility is to promote it and make it widespread.

---

314. Surah al-Dhuriyyaat – Verse 56.
315. 16/10/2011 – In a meeting with university students from Kermanshah.
316. For futher reading please refer to the book *Khalwat e Uns* by the Islamic Revolution Publications.

Increasing the quality of prayer means executing it in a good manner and with the presence of the heart. The one who prays should see prayer as the meeting with God on the Day of Judgement, speak to their God, and see themselves in His presence. As much as possible, they should pray in a mosque and congregation.

Promoting prayers is any move or effort to make them widespread, clarifying their importance and making them more accessible.

Through their speech or words, the thinkers and the eloquent speakers, those with media or pulpits, using the arts and attractive means, or the officials in organisations related to this institution can attend to this great responsibility.[317]

In my opinion, one of the essential tasks that the honourable public prayer leaders should do in mosques is to explain the issue of daily prayers to the people so that they appreciate their value. If this is done, then the quality of daily prayers will improve. The truth is that in many cases, our daily prayers are of poor quality, or they do not have the necessary quality. We should get to the depth of the religious utterances in daily prayers. Our daily prayers should be immune from indecent illnesses. They should be immune from the sickness of negligence while praying, from the disease of inattention to the concept of daily prayers and from the negligence of the addressee of our daily prayers, the Divine Being. This is one of the illnesses of daily prayers.

---

317. 04/09/2013 – In a message to the 22nd Nationwide Prayer Convention.

The late Agha Meshkini said in this Hussainiyah, "If a device is invented which we can connect to our brains and which can record our memories from the beginning to the end of daily prayers, the result would be strange and bizarre." From the moment we begin to say our daily prayers, which places our minds wander, which paths they take, which issues they solve and which matters they show interest in! This is one of those illnesses which I referred to as indecent disease. If we can protect ourselves from this sickness and also if we can save ourselves from another illness which is hypocrisy – there is a narration which says, "And free my heart from hypocrisy, love of fame and doubts about Your religion"[318] – then our daily prayers would have only reached the status of being ordinary and regular prayers. However, they would still suffer from a lack of depth.[319]

Selected and meaningful sayings from the Infallible Aa'ima (a), thinkers and religious experts have enlightened the hearts looking for guidance and raised awareness about the reality and wisdom behind this great divine obligation. Despite this, it must be said that the lofty status of prayers has not been correctly understood yet by the people, even those who accept it as an obligation and carry it out. Without a doubt, those who are aware in the Islamic society have a heavy and great responsibility in this regard. All methods

---

318. Al-Kaafi – Vol 2 P 586 Kitaab al-Dua.
319. 21/08/2016 – In meeting with congregational prayer leaders from the province of Tehran.

of clarification and enlightening should be used to spread the true understanding of prayers.

It must be said that prayers are the fundamental bridge for the journey of mankind which has been set by the divine religions in front of man so that they can use it to get to the ultimate objective of life. [The ultimate objective] is attaining success and victory in this world and the afterlife. Prayers are the first step in the journey towards Allah. However, this divine factor has the capacity to give wings even to those who are at the peak of perfection for mankind. The best person in all history, the Holy Messenger of Islam (s), has stated, "Prayers are the light of my eyes.". When the time of prayers would arrive, he would ask his reciter of the call to prayer to bring peace and ease his heart by the call of prayer. There may be no other act of worship that can help everyone at every stage of their journey towards perfection, resolve their entaglements, give them energy, and develop them.

Prayers should be recognized as one of the most critical factors for the organisation and discipline of society. Firstly, it gives health and loftiness to the ethics and spirituality of the individual in society. Secondly, due to its structure and content, it takes the one who prays towards discipline and rescues them from fruitless and futile endeavours. If prayers become common among people with the presence of the heart and passion and recited at their time of virtue, they will attain those characteristics. It is evident that prayers born out of laziness, which lack the presence of the heart and is carried out to show off, will not lead to any of the benefits mentioned being attained.[320]

Accountable and far-reaching efforts need to clarify the capacity of prayer and the understanding of its secrets and beauty. Small and easy-to-understand leaflets full of meaningful and fresh content should be added to the university books on the teachings of religion and the school books of courses before university.[321]

The Days of Allah

One point is that we should not let the memory of great days be consigned to oblivion. The great days of every country and every nation are days during which a divine event has occurred through and by the people: "Teach them to remember the days of God"[322]. In the Holy Qur'an, Allah the Exalted orders His Messenger to remind the people of the days of God. We should not allow these events to be consigned to oblivion. The Holy Qur'an teaches us valuable lessons. It has been mentioned in the Holy Qur'an: "Also mention in the Book the story of Ibrahim"[323], "Also mention in the Book the story of Musa"[324], "Also mention in the Book

---

320. 09/09/1999 – In a message to the Prayer Convention.
321. 21/09/1996 – In a message to the annual sitting for prayers.
322. Surah al-Ibrahim – Verse 5.
323. Surah al-Maryam – Verse 41.
324. Surah al-Maryam – Verse 51.

the story of Idris"³²⁵, and "Also mention in the Book the story of Maryam"³²⁶.

We should not allow these events to be forgotten. The Holy Qur'an teaches us to remember and to repeat these events. Notice how often the stories of Hazrat Musa (as), Hazrat Ibrahim (as) and others have been repeated. These things should be remembered, and we should not allow them to be consigned to oblivion.³²⁷

The 29th of Bahman is an unforgettable day. Of course, the people of Azerbaijan and Tabriz have many unforgettable days which are not particular to the 29th of Bahman. In our contemporary and recent history and our history during, before and after the Constitutional Movement, there are certain days, each of which is a source of pride for a people if they are described and delineated. These days belong to you. They belong to Azerbaijan, and they belong to Tabriz.

Of course, we have shown negligence in this regard. Such great popular movements should be highlighted and repeated in different artistic, explanatory and promotional fields and areas. To be honest, we have not worked enough on these areas.³²⁸

---

325. Surah al-Maryam – Verse 56.
326. Surah al-Maryam – Verse 16.
327. 06/03/2017 – In a meeting with officials, workers and a group of volunteers serving the *Rahyaan e Nur* alongside a group of Officers from the Holy Defence.
328. 16/02/2016 – In a meeting with the people of Western Azerbaijan.

The Lives of the Martyrs

One is that in preparing the biographies of martyrs, we should try to explain the characteristics of their life, their simple lifestyles and their way of life. This is important. Well, the excitement of going to war and to the arena of battle is one issue – of course, it is valuable to risk one's life by going to war – but individuals' spirit, characteristics and intellectual and ideological background is quite another issue. The latter is essential. How did a martyr - from whose memory, sacrifices and martyrdom you become enthused in the arena of war - live within his own family? How did he act in his ordinary environment of life? These are essential points. Another question is this: how did they act in the case of issues vital to us in the present time?

For example, in the present time, we show sensitivity towards extravagance, transgression against public funds, and adoption of an aristocratic lifestyle. These are fundamental today for sympathetic groups of people in our society. What was the outlook of our dear martyrs towards these matters when they were alive and when they used to live in their cities and their own families?

Yesterday or the day before, a program was being broadcast on TV. It was about some of our martyrs, and I watched for a few minutes by chance. What was said about those martyrs in their biography, or what has been stated in their wills, would astonish one because of the greatness of their spirits. One of the martyrs said, "I am an educated person and I am afraid that my education – that has cost the country some money – has been an imposition on public funds and that this falls on me. When I am martyred, you should sell my moped, take the money I have in my bank account and put it in public funds instead of the money that was spent on my education." These are lessons. These are lessons!

How did martyrs live their ordinary life? For example, how was their marriage? In the memoirs of some martyrs, which are, in fact, their biographies – of course, I have seen, read and looked at part of these biographies – the issue of their marriage comes up. The discussion is about how they married, their way of choosing a spouse – the kind of spouse they were looking for – their marriage ceremony, and their behaviour towards their family. All of these are peaks of Islamic ethics.

Today, we have severe problems in this regard. Today, we need these things. How do our youth think, and how should they think about choosing their spouse in the present time? Those role models should be kept within their sight. They are role models. Our martyrs are role models. Sometimes, some people come to us and complain that we do not introduce role models to our youth. Well, these are thousands of role models! There are 3,000 role models in North Khorasan province and 1,800 role models in Kohgiluyeh Boyer-Ahmad province. And there are thousands of role models in various other provinces.

You should highlight these role models. You should keep their enlightened faces within sight of our youth. I do not have any objections about preparing albums and the like, but this is not the primary task you should carry out. Speaking about what they used to do in their lives, how they acted, behaved, spent money and looked at their responsibilities is one of those critical issues that can create role models.

Our artists should step into the arena. They should benefit from the art of writing and textual illustration. These are very important things. They should not only benefit from movies. Movies are good and very necessary. I have emphasized their role and recommended them many times. At present, I recommend them as well. However, this emphasis on movies should not make us ignore books.

If some people are skilled at drawing and are talented in these areas, they should sit and prepare illustrations. They should write short books so that the youth have the patience to read them. They should produce books. And they don't need to exaggerate. It is not necessary to say untrue things. They should write about the things that really existed in a correct, beautiful and eloquent manner. This will attract hearts. This will influence individuals.

So, one point is that we should portray and present our martyrs' lives and simple lifestyles for our youth and future generations. We should show them this so they see what existed and what happened. This is because the imposed war – which was, in fact, a Sacred Defense – was not a small event. After many years, we have not yet explained to our audiences the important dimensions of this war correctly.

That war was an international war. It was a global war against Islam, against the authority of Islam, and our magnanimous Imam Khomeini. It was such a war. Of course, they made that lowly and foolish Baathist element – Saddam – the spearhead of the battle. But there was a front, made of other forces, behind him. They were people who used to help and show the path to him. They were people who used to provide him with the necessary tools and who used to strengthen him whenever he became vulnerable. They used to do this so that he would not become weak. We were faced with such a war.

Who were the people who managed to save the country from such a disaster? This is important for our youth in the present time. Who were the people who managed to save the country and who stepped into the midst of the battlefield? These are essential points. Therefore, one issue is that it should be clear to today's audiences how those youths behaved.

Another issue is about their ideals. Well, what were the ideals of those youths? What lofty goals did those youth who went there and fought have? Was the issue confined to a land and border dispute and the like? Was it only about an enemy who had transgressed against our borders and whom we wanted to force into retreat? Was it only about this? What were the ideals of parents? Those parents – who had raised their youth, were not prepared to see their youth come to any harm and did not want their youth to have the slightest disease – sent them to the front lines without being sure they would return.

With what ideals did those parents send their youth to war? These points are important. You should pay attention to these points. Many people are trying to keep these points hidden. Their ideal was Islam. Their ideal was God. Their ideal was a religious and Islamic government. It was this that drew youth towards the front lines.

Those who do not believe this should take a look at their wills. Our magnanimous Imam Khomeini used to say, "May God accept it if you have worshipped Him for 50 years. But you should also go and read these testaments once." He said this because such testaments show why those youth went to the front lines and what attraction and magnetic force moved them. These testaments show how they forgot about youthful desires, their lessons, their university, and the comfortable environment of living with their parents, and how they tolerated the cold in the western part of the country or the heat in Khuzestan to fight against the enemy and lay down their lives.

Fighting against the enemy looks easy from a long distance away. As long as you do not go there and you do not hear the sound of artillery, guns, explosions and the like, you do not understand correctly what is happening. Those youths went there, risked their lives and went through many dangers.

What was the reason? This has been reflected in those wills. They did so for God, Imam Khomeini and the hijab. You have seen the great emphasis on hijab in the martyrs' wills. Well, the hijab is a religious rule. These ideals that the martyrs had should not be forgotten.

It should not be the case that we think it was only a war like the others fought worldwide. We should not presume, "Every country has an enemy. Sometimes a war breaks out, and certain youth fight on the front lines. And eventually, they are killed, injured or return home alive. This war was like the other wars." The reasons why these youth went to war were not the same as why others have gone to war. It was for religion, divine ideals, the authority of Islam, the Revolution and revolutionary Islam. An Islam that drew the youth to the war effort.

The same is true of their parents. If it were not for God and not for the hope of divine kindness and blessings, how would parents allow their youth to go to the arena of war and wait for their return afterwards? I have told families of martyrs and parents many times that their patience prevented this movement and this flame of resistance and fighting in the way of the truth from being extinguished. It was because of the parents' patience; otherwise, if parents cried, wept, complained and fought here and there when their youth went to the front lines and were martyred, the next family would not send their child. It was the families of martyrs and these spirits that preserved the Revolution. This is a spirit of self-sacrifice and altruism.

Perhaps, I have narrated this memory many times. Of course, there are many such memories in hundreds of places and possibly many more. This memory relates to one of the cities I visited during my presidency. When I delivered a speech and wanted to return, the people gathered around us and showed their kindness. I was going towards the car and wanted to get in. Suddenly, I heard a lady continuously shouting my name from the middle of the crowd. I found out that she had important business. I stopped and said, "Let that woman step forward so that we see what her business is and why she is shouting in the middle of the crowd." She stepped forward and said, "Sir, my son became captive a while ago." I think that she said, "My only son". Most probably, she said, "My only son".

She continued, "A few days ago, I discovered he was martyred in prison. Say to Imam Khomeini, "He has been sacrificed for you!". She continued, "Even if I had another son, I would send him too." This was the message that the mother of a martyr wanted to deliver.

Notice what extraordinary spirit this is! I returned and delivered that message to Imam Khomeini, and he cried when he heard those sentiments. He shed tears. Whom and what were those feelings for? When the mother of two martyrs puts her sons inside the grave, holds back her tears and asks others around her to stop crying because she has offered her sons in the way of God and is happy, one cannot find any non-divine reason. These are ideals.

Therefore, we should not forget the ideals of martyrs – God, Islam, revolutionary Islam, Islamic government and the authority of religion. We should not normalize the event by saying it was a war like the other wars that broke out worldwide. Some people are killed, and some are injured or become captives. In all wars, some youths are killed. This was not the issue, and we should not forget this. This is another issue.

Another point is that you should use the remaining time to speak to parents. Fortunately, I witnessed this in the speeches that the gentlemen in the meeting delivered and that they paid attention to it. Many parents have passed away, and we have missed the opportunity to find the reasons behind the movement of those youth. When parents speak, they clarify in what environment their child has been raised. This is very important. It should become clear in what environment they were raised in regarding their social position, social class and their different orientations.

Besides, speaking to parents can clarify the details of the martyrs' lives for us. This is another benefit of talking to the parents; therefore, you should not miss this opportunity. You should meet with the parents. About 30 years have passed since the end of the war. Many parents have passed away, and some others are on the verge of their demise. You only have a short time left. You should consider this as one of your priorities. Primarily, you should meet with the parents that exist, with martyrs' spouses – those who had a spouse – and with their brothers and sisters, for those who had brothers and sisters. You should ask them about their martyrs, their behaviour, and their spirit, and then provide that information to the younger generation.

Good tasks are being carried out in these commemoration gatherings. Some of these tasks are impressive. This is good. Outstanding tasks are necessary. The auspicious names of martyrs, their photos, pictures, and their quotations on some of the streets and passageways are eye-catching and necessary. However, creating content-based output is more important. There should be an effort to strengthen the informational, educational and instructional aspects of these commemoration gatherings.

Every commemoration that you organize exerts a profound influence on a large number of people. I am not saying that they influence everyone, but individuals are different from one another, and they are influenced in different ways. However, such commemoration gatherings exert some influence on a group of people. The condition of the war and front lines should be portrayed using the martyrs' words. Today's youth and teenagers should know what the Sacred Defense was when we speak about it. This should be explained through martyrs' language.

Some books have been written on the martyrs, and I have written some notes in some of them. Some of these writings are good because of the details that have existed in the war, those innovations, those self-sacrificing acts, those lonely times, those selfless and courageous acts that individuals did during and before military operations and the things that they did during those difficult times have been portrayed and illustrated in a good way. These things should be clarified for youth as well.[329]

One's presentation should be imbued with clarification, understanding, truth and outstanding and positive points about the Sacred Defense era and its values. Presentations should be like this.

Of course, I am not saying that you should exaggerate. I do not advocate exaggeration, embellishment and other such methods in any way. On the contrary, we had both successful and unsuccessful attacks in those eight years. For example, we launched an unsuccessful attack in Operation Ramadan or Karbala-4. We launched successful attacks as well. For instance, during Operation Val Fajr-8, our youth managed to go to the other side of Arvand Rud. However, even those successful attacks were accompanied by hundreds of problems. Not all individuals are the same. There were many difficulties. Some individuals would turn back, some would change their minds, some would not advance, and

---

329. 26/09/2016 – In a meeting with members of the orgnisations facilitating the commemoration of the martyrs of the provinces of Kehgiluyeh and Buyerahmed.

some would think about what was being said about them more than thinking about carrying out their duties.

We had such individuals as well. We can mention these facts as well. There is nothing wrong with this. These factors were only part of those extraordinary exhibits – those peerless individuals and those dear and lofty martyrs who showed their value and excellence. Therefore, it is not necessary for us to exaggerate and speak as if they were alien individuals because this was not the case. They were like us but knew the path better than we did. They understood life better than us. They were more blessed and relied on God more than we did. That was why Allah the Exalted paid more attention to them by quenching their thirst from the spring of His blessing and grace.[330]

War veterans share legacies from times of arduous struggle, and they are teachers of sincere effort. The explanations they give in their own words of the events in those noble days should be valued. Their truthful accounts and narrations must be conveyed to eager ears and hearts.

I hereby thank the community of war veterans who narrate their war experiences and ask God, the Highest, for their success.[331]

The Value of Work and the Worker

---

330. 06/03/2017 – In a meeting with workers from *Rahyan e Nur*.
331. 26/09/2021 – In a message to the Narrators of the Holy Defence conference.

One of the great responsibilities of the Islamic society and the officials is to clarify the value of labour in the sphere of public understanding. Labour should turn into a value, not a mere need. Of course, labour is needed: society, individuals, and life need labour. There is a psychological and mental need for labour. However, it is not merely a need. Labour is a lofty value in society. This should be made common in the public's minds and understood as a fact. If this idea is clarified in the true sense of the word, then the value of labourers will also increase. Labourers should be described as being valuable in society. And it does not make a difference in which fields: labourers are valuable in all fields – including the areas that were mentioned in the meeting, fields which you, friends, represent. Wherever labour, dynamism and production exist, it is appreciated.[332]

Labour and the position of labourers are critical issues from the Islamic and rational perspectives. If we consider the matter rationally, labour is an essential link in the chain of our vital needs. That is to say, if a society had all the money in the world but lacked the element of labour, it would not be possible to address the needs of the people of that society. The element of labour is what addresses the needs of mankind. And labour depends on labourers. Therefore, the capable hands and creative minds of labourers play an obviously important role in the life of human beings - both

---

332. 24/4/2019 – In a meeting with labourers and workers on the occasion of Labour Day.

their individual life and their social life. Those who ignore the working class and labour communities ignore this essential role. And the same is true about the people who think of labourers as an instrument, just like other instruments. This is the rational perspective, and the logic is entirely sound.

But the logic of Islam is superior to this rational perspective. According to Islam, the labourers' work to feed themselves and their family is a kind of worship and good deed. That is to say, the work that labourers do is not limited to this world; rather, Allah, the Exalted, has attached great importance to the issue of labour in His comprehensive plan for the life of humanity in this world and in the hereafter. The Holy Prophet (s) said, "This hand will not feel hell fire." Everybody was surprised when the Holy Prophet (s) kissed a labourer's hand. Then the Holy Prophet said, "This hand will not feel hell fire." That is to say, when we engage in midnight prayers, recite the Holy Qur'an and rely on Allah the Exalted, we are, in fact, building walls between ourselves and hellfire. And when we work, we do the same thing. This is a significant point. This is the Islamic view.[333]

Work and Societal Discipline

The two slogans: Efforts for creating a conscience for work and efforts to develop societal discipline must continue

---

333. 27/04/2011 – In a meeting with a group of workers and labourers.

within the people, the society, the officials and workers of this nation, and all those busy working.

Whoever is a protector and inviter to the cultural field must promote those two matters. They must open up those matters to the people and clarify them. Those who are strategists must plan how to breathe in the spirit of work and societal discipline among the people. Those who are working should create these two spirits within themselves. Everyone must work on this for themselves. Those who give the people reminders and propagate to them, they should speak about this. Do something so that for those working, their work becomes a divine act, whether in the field of culture, economics, society or politics. All must feel what they are doing is an act linked to the divine, whether a simple labourer, a simple admin worker, a high-ranking official, or one heading a vital industry. Whether it be a high-ranking government officer or a teacher, student, preacher or religious scholar, everyone must feel they are carrying out a divine act and an act that is good and pure. Everyone must tend to their work with seriousness and goodness. It has been narrated from the Noble Prophet (s): "The mercy of Allah is upon any person that carries out an act in a manner that is pure, robust, established and correct."[334] Leaving work to its own state and not attending to it, and being negligent towards carrying it out robustly should be avoided.

---

334. Masaa'il Ali ibn Ja'far Wa Mustadrakaatiha – P 93.

The same is to be said about societal discipline. Everyone must adhere to the societal boundaries set by law, agreements and divine legislation. This will lead to a healthy and correct lifestyle. Protect both of these slogans this year. Those who can talk, speak about it, those who can write, write about it, officials must strategise regarding it, and every individual of the society must use these as yardsticks to hold themselves accountable and recognise whether they are progressing.[335]

The Value of a Teacher

No institution is more important than the educational system. This means there will always be room for more material and spiritual investments in the educational system. The educational system is our society's heart: now and in the future.

I want to speak about your role as teachers. Teachers are responsible for training people who will run the country in the not-so-distant future. Your young students will soon be responsible for the affairs of our society, no matter what level they are at. Prominent figures of the future are among your students. Sincere mujahids of the future are among your students. The competent people who will manage the economy and culture of this country are among the children who come to your classes. You are responsible for training them to do their future duties well and bring about progress,

---

335. 21/03/1995 – New Years Message.

not regression and corruption. Take note of how important your job is.

As I said, your influence as a teacher is sometimes even more vital than genetic factors. Humans are born with certain genetic tendencies, but it is possible to change them through practice. Teachers can play a role in this and help their students change their tendencies through practice. That is to say, you can train individuals who are true to the level of Islam. You can prepare a workforce that is to the level of the Islamic Republic. This is the role that teachers should play. These are not compliments: they are facts.

One of the necessary things is that our people and government officials, young and old, should appreciate the importance of teachers. They should understand the value of teachers. These things are essential. The media and government officials should play a role in this regard. This should not be reduced to ceremonial gestures. It is necessary to help people realize the importance of a teacher's role in class - the gentleman or lady who spends his life educating our youth and children. Of course, teachers should also understand their role appropriately and appreciate the importance of their role. This is essential.

Everybody should pay attention to this: the people, government officials and the Ministry of Education. Everybody has specific responsibilities towards teachers.

Everybody should be committed to these spiritual and material responsibilities and try to fulfil them.[336]

Modern History and Constitutional Revolution

This is a country that has been under pressure from various sides for the last two hundred years, so its outstanding characteristics are damaged, it is weakened and yields. If you observe the history of these two hundred years, you will better understand the greatness of what Imam Khomeini did. I emphasise that our youth must read this chapter of history. The propagation institutions must also clarify the realities that befell the people during this period. In my opinion, very little work has been done in this regard.[337]

I want to stress the issue of the historiography of the Constitution Revolution. Many years ago, I discussed this matter with different friends. We really need a rich, clear and well-documented history of the Constitutional Movement. We should illustrate it correctly and adequately. When this history is written and prepared at different levels - whether at a school, academic, or research level - it can be published and promoted. The truth is that we do not have a complete and comprehensive history of the Constitutional Movement. This is while writings about the Constitutional Movement - such as Nazim al-Islam's work or others written at that time

---

336. 04/05/2011 – In a meeting with a group of teachers from across the country.
337. 01/10/1999 – Friday Prayer Sermon.

- are available to the people. They are reading such works and making some interpretations about the Constitutional Movement, which are mostly wrong.[338]

Internal Capabilities For Resolving Problems

The issue of paying attention to reliance on domestic hands for the sake of solving the country's problems should turn into a well-established idea in people's minds. This should be repeated, explained and clarified until it becomes a definite discourse.

We have motivated youth and skilled individuals. We have good producers, promising entrepreneurs, labourers, farmers, teachers and professors. Such individuals should improve their work. It is these individuals who should eliminate the problems of the country. It is also they who should solve the economic issues and various other problems related to business.

I am not saying you should break off your relations with the world. This is not my opinion in any way. From the beginning of the Revolution, I have been among those individuals who insist on establishing – relations with the world. In the present time, I have the same belief, but the point I want to raise is this: we should not exchange our powerful natural legs for a foreigner's cane. This is wrong

---

338. 29/04/2006 – In a meeting with the central council and academic committees set up for the 100th anniversary of the Constitutional revolution.

if we rest on a foreigner's cane instead of standing on our own feet and relying on ourselves.

Of course, there is nothing wrong with negotiations in international relations. The problem that I had and continue to have with the nuclear talks – I have discussed this matter in private and public with officials – is this: I am saying that it was okay to negotiate, and there was nothing wrong with negotiating. Still, those negotiations should have been conducted with care and precision, so much so that even a tiny move by us would not be considered a violation of the JCPOA, while the same would not apply to every wrong move that the other side makes! This is wrong! This should not happen. This happens due to a lack of trust and attention to domestic power. This state of affairs happens due to reliance on the other side and foreign elements.

I will tell you that we should not pin our hopes on foreigners. We should work with the world; I am not opposed to this. Working with the world naturally has certain requirements. We accept these requirements, and we shoulder them. However, we are not relying on foreigners. This is because our enemies are too many outside the environment of our society and the country. There is a front of enemies against us. Well, thankfully, we have delivered blows to this front until today. We have defeated it and pushed it back, and this will be the case from now on, but we should know that we are not faced with a single enemy; instead, we are faced with a front of enemies.[339]

The Dangers of Distortions and Innovations

Recently another weird and unfamiliar innovation has been added to the topic of Ziarah! Whilst entering the Shrines from one of the doors with the intention of Ziarah of the graves of the Purified Aa'ima (a), they lie down on the floor and make their way to the shrine in such a manner! You are aware that the shrines of the Holy Messenger (s), Imam Hussain (a), Imam Al-Sadiq (a), Imam Al-Kadhim (a), Imam al-Ridha (a) and others have been visited by many people, scholars and great jurists in Medina, Iraq and Iran. Have you ever heard that any of the Aa'ima (a) or the scholars conducted themselves in such a manner from the shrine's doors to the shrine itself? If this act was desired, rewarded, accepted and good, our respected personalities would not have hesitated to do it, but they did not. It has even been reported that the Late Grand Ayatullah Burujerdi, the great scholar and robust jurist who was a heavyweight and a thinker, had obstructed the kissing of the shrines, even though it may have been a rewardable act. The reward for kissing the shrine is most probably present in our narrations; we know it is undoubtedly present in our books of supplications. What comes to mind is that there must also be a narration for the

---

339. 21/09/2017 – In a meeting with the head and members of the Assembly of Experts.

kissing of the shrine too. Even though this act is *Mustahab*, he stated, "Do not do this so that the enemies do not think the Shia prostrate to the shrine.". However, today you have individuals who enter the doors of the shrine of Imam al-Ridha (a), lie down on the floor and go across the floor for two hundred metres in that state to get themselves to the shrine! Is this act correct? No, it is wrong. In fact, it is an insult to the religion and Ziarah. Who is it that promotes such innovations among the people? Could it be that this is also an act of the enemy? State this to the people and make them aware of such things.

Religion is logical, Islam is logical and the most logical form of Islam is the explanation for Islam that the Shia have. It is a strong explanation. Shia theologians, each one in their own times, shone like a bright sun and no one could have said that their logic was weak. These theologians [with strong logic] were many, whether they be at the time of the Aa'ima (a), such as Mo'min Taaq and Hisham ibn Hakam, or those that came after the Aa'ima (a) such as Bani Nobakht and Shaikh Mufeed, or even those after them, such as the Late Allamah Hilli. We are the people of logic and reasoning.[340]

Incidents of Events

Sometimes, certain events in the country need immediate clarification. At the time of the movement and after the

---
340. 07/06/1994 – In a meeting with a group of scholars from Kehgiluyeh and Buyerahmed.

victory of the Islamic Revolution, there was a need for immediate clarification. In those times, it is necessary for every individual in society, especially the influencers, to come out into the arena of clarification. The following are some of these examples in the history of the Islamic revolution: The crimes committed by the Pahlavi regime in the spring of 1963, the clarification of which was ordered by Imam Khomeini to the scholars and propagators for the month of Muharram. The event of the insults against Imam Khomeini by The Information Newspaper in 1977. The clarification of the presence of the people on the streets in 1979. The clarification of the concept of the Islamic Republic during the days of the referendum. The clarification for the obligation of helping the front lines during the Holy Defence. The clarification of the crimes and steps taken by Israel and those conspiring against Palestine. The clarification for maximising participation in the elections and demonstrations. The clarification of the actions of Ayatullah Muntazeri and other examples.

Ayatullah Khamenei: "The responsibility of the guidance of the people is a divine duty. The speakers and writers must create awareness."[341]

---

341. 26/11/1997 – In a meeting with a group of Basij on the occasion of the Week of the Basij.

Chapter 5
Other Important Passages

Those in Place of Responsibility – The Officials

Speak to the people. Speak to the people face to face and tell them about the issues. Tell them that the enemy wishes to make use of the economic crisis. State this frankly to the people. Tell them we have an economic problem, and the enemy desires to use it. We will not let them do this; however, we require you [the people]. We must say to the people that we will not allow the enemy to use this crisis and attack us or cause harm to us; however, we require your help. Tell them that we will remain steadfast with all of our strength. If you just go and open up a factory, that is not enough. It is not enough that you go to a part of the country and cut the ribbons for the opening of a factory. If you can see good work has been done and this factory is working well, then go among them, let the people see, and this should be shown. Go and establish contact with a labourer or a worker and see what is being produced and where it is stored.

Go with the workers, speak to the unions, and enter the workplace. If this happens, the people will say, yes, work is being done. When we go, and they escort us to where we have to cut the ribbon for an opening, this does not make the people's hearts happy. The people had seen many openings;

many of you will remember when you were ministers and how much was opened. Sometimes an opening ceremony for an operation would take place despite it not being ready. Whatever is being mentioned here are things we are informed about; they are not rumours. This used to happen during our time too. If work is being done, and there is good work in the country, genuinely good work is being done; this must be shown to the people and clarified.[342]

Of course, you can adopt two approaches to the criticisms levelled against the administration in the media, newspapers and certain official centres. One approach is to justify and explain your measures, which is good. The other approach is to adopt a hostile attitude, which is not good. You should not think that simply because the administration is faced with hostile and spiteful criticisms, you should respond similarly. No, you should explain and clarify. Clarification is necessary, and the right way is to explain things in your meetings with the people. You should let them ask questions, and then you should present answers and explanations. And your responses should be reported in the media. If you clarify well, the ulterior motives of spiteful people will not get anywhere.[343]

Another challenge occurs when some individuals think that people can not endure problems. This is not true.

---

342. 15/07/2018 – In a meeting with the President and members of his cabinet.
343. 28/08/2011 – In a meeting with the President and members of his cabinet.

The people have actually endured hardships. If issues are explained to the people in the true sense of the word and with complete honesty, our people are loyal. They are people who stand firm and resist.[344]

Talking to the people and discussing problems and solutions with them is another aspect of popularity. You should discuss your issues with the people. Sometimes, there is a problem for which a solution exists. Of course, you should not let your words create despair in the people. Some individuals ignore this point, saying improper and untrue things which make the people lose hope. There is a solution to every problem. You should open up to the people, talk to them and ask for their help on various matters – help in terms of thoughts and practical solutions.

Sometimes, a mistake is committed. Well, we all make mistakes and are not short of errors. You should apologise to the people, acknowledging explicitly that a mistake has been made, and you should apologise for it. All these factors affect popularity. You should also present a report about the services rendered: a sincere report without exaggerations. You should genuinely say what has been accomplished.

In his important governmental decree to Malik al-Ashtar, the Commander of the Faithful (a), mentions the above factors. I advise all you friends to take a look at it. He says, "Then, do not keep yourself secluded from the people for a long time." Of course, scholars have put forward other

---

344. 23/06/2015 – In a meeting with government officials.

variations and suggestions for this part: do not be secluded. It means a ruler should not be absent from the people for long. Officials cannot be constantly present among the people, but in some periods, they should certainly be present. Do not be secluded means: do not lengthen your absence from among the people.

After expanding on this, the Commander of the Faithful (a) says, "If the subjects suspect you of high-handedness, explain to them your position openly."[345] If there is doubt in people's minds about you, you should present your explanations to them and speak to them openly. Notice that the relationship between the ruler and the people should be like this. This relationship is a brotherly and friendly one. "And remove their suspicion with your explanation". You should dispel doubt with your words and explanations if they have a doubt. These were explanations about factors affecting popularity. Therefore, you should really try to observe these aspects of being with the people. Officials in all sectors should have these qualities.[346]

The next point is about presence among the people, which I just mentioned. One of Agha Raisi's strong points in the judiciary branch was his presence among the people. You should not stop doing this. The honourable officials in the judiciary branch should not stop doing this after his

---

345. Nahj al-Balagha – Letter 53.
346. 28/08/2021 – In the first sitting with the President and his cabinet from the 13th round of Presidential elections.

departure. This is an excellent and vital course of action, and as I mentioned earlier, it will yield many blessings. It is being among the people and being in contact with active groups in society – such as academic, seminary and economic activists and activists working on matters related to women and the ones working on tribal issues that is important. It is imperative that judiciary officials, especially the head of the judiciary, be in contact with the groups that work in these fields.

There is so much information in the production field that one cannot understand it until one has contacted and heard from the people active in production – such as officials in charge of labour issues and labourers themselves. Communication with these active groups is part of the popular presence and public communication; therefore, we must pay attention to it. The first benefit of it is that you can hear from them what the main problems are and secondly, you can explain things to them. It is often the case that organisations have specific policies, some of which are protested against from the outside. They have no bad intentions but oppose them because they do not have enough information. In other words, they do not know the reasoning for this decision. So, because they do not know, they protest. All right, you could explain it to them. Some things need to be explained and clarified.[347]

---

347. 28/06/2021 – In a meeting with the head and officials of the Judiciary.

Friday Prayers - Headquarters for Clarification

We are engaged in such a battle. We are engaged in such a jihad. They are attacking the faith of our people. They are attacking the insight of our people. They are attacking our piety. They are attacking our morality and spreading various dangerous viruses among us. Well, what should we do now? We should defend. This requires a base, just like the bases in the arena of war. Friday prayers are one of the most important bases. They are the base of faith and piety. We should look at Friday prayers like this and you are the commanders of this base. The bases in the arena of war each have a commander. The commanders of the Friday prayer base are Friday prayer leaders.

Well, the main goal of this base is to clarify and explain. The issue of clarification is the primary goal. The main purpose of divine prophets was to clarify and explain the truth. This is because the thing that makes people deviate from the straight path is a lack of knowledge about the truth. Their main goal was this. Some people know the truth, but deny it. However, the main source of deviation is a lack of knowledge about the truth. Divine prophets appeared to explain and clarify the truth for the people so they would not have any excuses. The issue of clarification is this: "Ulama are the inheritors of prophets"[348]. You are the inheritors of prophets, including on this issue of clarification.

---

348. Al-Kaafi – V 1 P 32.

Friday prayers – as the name suggests – are a place of gathering and congregation. This is a great opportunity for clarification. Sometimes, you have to knock on this and that door or benefit from some indirect means. Although the means of mass communication that exist today are shared among everyone – the internet, social networks and other such means are very common – looking directly into someone's eyes, the feeling of direct presence, and the very essence of listening and speaking among a group of people is something else. Gathering together is better. Several hundred thousand people may receive a message through the internet and text messages, but this is entirely different from gathering together in one place so that someone can speak to you.

Looking directly at someone exerts extraordinary influence because they are available to you and they can respond. This is very important. Those who do not know much about religion – foreigners and some poor individuals inside our own country who are deprived of this blessing – regret that they cannot do so and that they do not have any means with which they can gather the people together so that they can speak to them and exchange opinions. This is why they want to do this with different other means. However, they do not succeed as much.

Now that this is the case, Friday prayers are the cultural heart of every city. Of course, there are certain requirements and conditions, some of which I will mention later. Friday prayers are a place where guidance is provided. I want to stress that such guidance is not merely political guidance. It is both political and cultural. We should not think that if we let out a loud cry on such and such a political issue which is our point of concern, and if we express our viewpoints articulately, the issue will be over. This is not the case. We consider cultural guidance as more fundamental than political guidance. Political guidance is essential and we should not forget about it, but cultural guidance and the culture and morality of the people are more important.[349]

If there is a question or critique about something you have stated or about clarifying a narration, the explanation of a verse or a jurisprudential matter, get the people in the habit of writing to the office of the Friday prayer leader regarding it. The office should organise them and hand them over to you. You should study those matters well and present them if needed. If, in any case, any matter requires clarification, clarify it.

The people's questions must be attended to. From these questions, it must be understood what the people are after. What is ruling over the people's thoughts currently? You may realise that in the city where you have been assigned the great responsibility of being the Friday prayer leader, there is a doubt about Islam, the Quran, the fundamentals of Prophethood, or foundational and ideological matters

---

349. 04/01/2016 – In a meeting with Friday Prayer leaders from across the country.

about the system. But then you go to the Friday prayers and speak about a subject which has no relation to that doubt. It is evident that youth struggling with that doubt would not come to prayers and listen to such a sermon. This is because their question is not discussed here. However, if their question is discussed, you will see that they will come.

Regarding their propensity towards religion, the youth are the best generation—those who say that they are further away from religion are mistaken. The youth are closer to religion. Internal forces within them that would push them away from religion are weaker. Unfortunately, even the animalistic desires are stronger and more active in some who have left their youth. The youth have some astonishing and beyond-belief days, which leave a person astounded. Have you not seen the battlefield?

If the youth knew their religious problems would be solved here, they would passionately come to Friday prayers. For example, if they are at university, their professor comes and says something or someone else comes and presents a question or creates a doubt. This leaves that youth restless. It is not as if just by hearing something, they will believe. They are waiting for you, waiting to see what you will say. They're waiting for a scholar and those claiming to be religious propagators. They are waiting to see what they say. They come to a Friday prayer and realise that we speak about irrelevant stuff, regardless of how deep the discussion is.

Therefore, the content should be strong, sourced, logical, persuasive, and relevant to the youth's spiritual and intellectual questions. This means they should be in accordance to the need that exists.[350]

The Heavy Responsibility of Prayer Leaders

I believe that one of the major tasks is managing and leading the mosque. This is an important task. We should not look at it as a peripheral task. If we attend to our daily tasks and jobs and then rush towards the mosque in a great hurry because there is heavy traffic and other such problems, and if we go there to lead public prayers while we are late half an hour, forty-five minutes, this is failing to do our duty towards the mosque. This should be considered an essential and fundamental occupation. I am not saying we should abandon all other tasks when becoming a public prayer leader. This is not what I am saying. We can attend to further scholarly and non-scholarly tasks within the scope of our capacity, but our duty towards the mosque should be fulfilled. Before it is time for daily prayers, we should go to the mosque with peace and tranquillity. Then, we should prepare ourselves for saying daily prayers and lead the prayers with good quality.

After that, if we plan to deliver a speech, we should turn to the people and speak to them to clarify the issues. Thankfully, you now have different programs in mosques. In our own

---

350. 19/09/1993

time –when I used to lead public prayers in Mashhad and go to the mosque – many undertakings were uncommon. We and other public prayer leaders did not know these things. Whatever we did was considered novel and new. Thankfully today, these tasks are common. Standing up or taking a minbar to speak to the people between or after the two prayers, using a board to write narrations on it and clarify the issue for the people, and forming an ideological chain with the youth of the mosque to explain different matters and answer their questions – these are tasks that are common these days based on the feeling that we get from reading reports and from others' opinions – were not common in those days.

At that time, public prayer leaders were satisfied with saying daily prayers and then leaving the mosque. Meanwhile, they could answer one or two religious questions if there were any. But there was nothing more than that. Thankfully today, these things are prevalent. Therefore, the quality of such tasks should be enhanced daily.[351]

Scholars and Preachers

Dear people, honourable scholars, esteemed luminaries and young seminarians, you should know that today the responsibility of the clergy is heavier. The clergy have always had to shoulder a specific responsibility: the duty of clarifying

---

351. 21/08/2016 – In a meeting with Friday Prayer leders from the province of Tehran.

and delivering the messages of God. "Those who deliver the messages of Allah."[352]. This responsibility has become heavier today. Why? There are two reasons. One reason is that there is currently an opportunity to promote Islam in both the Muslim and non-Islamic worlds. I will explain this briefly later on. The other reason is that because of Islamophobia, the attacks on Islam have increased in number. Therefore, this responsibility has become heavier. A new opportunity brings a new responsibility with it.

Your responsibilities become heavier when you face increased attacks, hostility and aggression because of a new opportunity. Today you are in such a situation. But you must not be afraid. "Fear Him, and do not fear anyone but Allah."[353] Do not be scared of anything. Do not fear the hardships you will face on your path. This is not to say that you should pretend your responsibility is easy. No, your responsibility is demanding, but you should not fear it. Try to welcome difficult tasks. Try to do things that are considered impossible. After all, this is what happened in Iran. The achievement made in Iran - all analysts of the world would sit down together for hours and days and nights to discuss it, and all of them would reach a unanimous conclusion: that it was impossible.

What was it that they thought was impossible? Our country was culturally dependent on the West. It was

---

352. Surah al-Ahzab – Verse 39.
353. Surah al-Ahzab – Verse 39.

under the political hegemony of the West. Its economy was a plaything for the West. The officials and leaders of the country believed that they had no choice but to carry out America's orders without question. Of course, the government of Mohammadreza Shah did not like that it had to obey America, but government officials of the country were like unhappy slaves who still had to listen to their master. Yes, they were unhappy about this, but they had no choice. It was a country whose culture, politics, economy and officials were like that, where everybody was moving away from Islam and towards dependence on the West. Suddenly everything made a U-turn in our country. The government that came to power did not trust the West and considered it an enemy in certain cases. It changed the orientation towards Islam and the implementation of Islamic rules. Thus, the Islamic Republic was established. All analysts said this was impossible, but it happened in Iran.

Even some of the revolutionaries said that it was impossible. The late Agha Taleghani told me, "Imam Khomeini says that the Shah must go, but obviously, it is impossible for the Shah to go." He could not believe that the Shah could go. He told me that Imam Khomeini was saying strange things. Certain things were considered impossible, yet Imam Khomeini made them possible. One of those things was the downfall of the Shah. Imam Khomeini said that the Shah would have to go. Nobody could believe him, but the Shah was forced to go. Not only the Shah but also America, the West, the colonial powers and the arrogant powers had to leave. Nobody could believe this, but it happened.

Nobody could believe that the most significant revolution would happen in Egypt among the Islamic countries: the Egypt of Camp David Accords and the Egypt of Hosni Mubarak. There might have been certain people who considered such a revolution possible, but nobody thought it would happen in Egypt. Yet it happened. This is what we must keep in mind.

Go after things that are considered impossible and try to make them happen. In order to do heavy tasks, tackle them in a determined way. "And fear Him, and do not fear anyone but Allah.". What are the problems? What are the difficulties? The answer is, "Allah is sufficient to take account." Do not forget God: He will consider what you do. God will never ignore your sufferings, work, patience, and stoicism. "Allah is sufficient to take account."[354]

This is our path. In one part of the Holy Quran, we religious scholars are advised to fear God; in another, we are advised to "deliver the messages of Allah". Allah's messages are the same ones that His Prophets (s) delivered. Allah the Exalted says, "And thus did We make for every prophet an enemy, the devils from among men and jinn, some of them suggesting to others varnished falsehood to deceive (them) and had your Lord pleased, they would not have done it, therefore leave them and that which they forge." Divine prophets are

---

354. Surah al-hzab – Verse 39.

Other Important Passages

surrounded by devils "from among men and jinn"[355]. They are attacked by devils from among mankind and jinn. If we are supposed to promote the messages of God, we should expect to be attacked by devils from among mankind and jinn. They will attack us, so we should prepare ourselves for their attacks. We must build a spiritual wall against the enemies within ourselves - a wall of piety and reliance on God - so that we do not collapse from within. Physical retreat and defeat are the results of inner retreat and defeat. The inner self of human beings imposes a physical defeat on them. If you are not defeated in your heart, nobody can defeat you. The wall that must be built in your heart is the wall of piety and reliance on God. "And in Allah should the believers put their trust."[356] "In Allah let the trusting put their trust."[357] "And whoever trusts Allah, He is sufficient for him."[358] "Is not Allah sufficient for His servant?"[359] These are lessons for us. We must carefully recite the Holy Quran. We should learn these lessons: they are guidelines for life. This is one aspect of preparing ourselves.

Preparation in the external world is another aspect. The devils that are supposed to attack us will not always attack in the same way. The modern devils who attack you through the internet, satellite channels and highly advanced

---

355. Surah al-Aan'aam – Verse 112.
356. Surah Aal al-Imran – Verse 122.
357. Surah al-Ibrahim – Verse 12.
358. Surah al-Talaaq – Verse 3.
359. Surah al-Zumur – Verse 36.

communication tools speak about current things. Their hardware and software have been modernised. They create fallacies. They create ideological problems. They give rise to intellectual confusion. They promote despair. They foment discord. I have received reports that currently, petro-dollars are being spent on certain projects. Often these reports are not made publicly available.

On the one hand, they spend vast amounts of money establishing anti-Shia groups among Sunni Muslims in certain Islamic countries. On the other hand, they pay certain so-called Shia preachers to insult and level allegations against the Mother of the Faithful, Aisha, in the name of Shia Islam. These are their methods. What do you do as Shia or Sunni Muslims when faced with these methods? We must not be deceived by what they do. Discord among us is the biggest blessing for them.[360]

In summary, if you consider a scholar, they have three fundamental duties. Firstly, religious, ideological and spiritual guidance. Secondly, political guidance and increasing political insight; thirdly, guiding social services, sympathising with the people and providing services for the main body of the society. These three tasks are the duty of a scholar. No matter which work you are busy in, in the field of scholarship, you will be forced to carry out these three tasks, at least partially. When we say religious guidance, a part of it

---

360. 12/10/2011 – In a meeting with a group of Shia and Sunni scholars from Kermanshah.

is clarifying religious ideology. The market of doubts is fully open! The online space can help with this. Our opposition has political motivations to inject ideas into the minds of our youth. This needs to be countered. It is a battlefield; we must be armed and readied to enter the arena. This is an arena of jihad. You are preparing yourself for this, and this is not something small; the objective is not something small; it is the clarification of the pure and Islamic ideology.

Pure Islam is an Islam that relies upon the Book, the Sunnah, and it makes use of the human capacity to think. We wish to spread this. We want to attain this and then transfer it. This was the work of the Prophets (s). Like the Prophets (s) faced difficulties and enemies, yet they strove, you and I must also go on the same path. We must be in the pursuit of fulfilling this message and this mission. It requires effort and has headaches, but this was the path of the Prophets (s).

However, if a person wants, they could shrug off their responsibilities and say they do not want to do it. Fine, they can go and live their everyday lives; however, they will be prevented from gaining that divine bliss, favour and attention and fall from the lofty heights God Almighty has established for them. They will end up with empty hands.

One part of religious guidance is guiding the people regarding Islamic ideology. This is the duty of seminarians. One part is the practical guidance for the people towards worship, to the apparent of religion. This is also something essential. Obliging the people towards prayers, maintaining the sanctity of the Holy Month of Ramadhan, upholding their trust in their societal connections and fighting against injustice and the oppressors are all concepts that need to be explained to the people. We may know many narrations, verses, religious teachings, and knowledge; however, the layperson does not, even those who have studied to a high standard. We must get this information to them. Understandably, they do not know as they may be specialising in a specific field. It is our duty to get this to them—this is one part of religious guidance. From the point of view of being scholars of religion, it is our responsibility to make people understand honesty, trustworthiness, healthy social relations, piety, purity, promotion of virtues, detachment from vices and a simple Islamic lifestyle. This is our task. This could be through the pulpit, the management of a mosque, the management of an institution, being present in universities, being present in governmental bodies or other means. This needs to be clarified and explained.

Another matter is the matter of giving depth to inherited beliefs. The people are religious and believers; however, this belief of theirs is inherited and can decline. This belief needs to be given depth through correct reasoning. If this deep Islamic understanding and reason do not exist, it opens the door for flooding in incorrect, imported, and materialistic ideas. When they suppressed and persecuted the scholars using various means, naturally, Marxist thoughts began to spread in the country. At another time, Liberalism was gaining traction in society. If the correct ideology does not enter, the wrong doctrine will find land to ground on and flood in. Therefore the presence of the right ideology is necessary. We must consider the sources of Islamic teachings, the Quran, trustworthy narrations and logical understandings. These are the responsibilities of scholars in religious guidance.

Political guidance also requires an in-depth study. This humble servant says, be revolutionary, and the seminaries need to be revolutionary so that if the scholars of religion need to enter the political field and fight [they can]. This grand event [the revolution] in Iran would never have occurred if they had not entered. In previous efforts, the religious scholars also entered the arena and had an effect; however, ultimately, that stagnated. The issue of the edict against tobacco was a passing event; however, in the constitutional revolution, the scholars entered the arena, leading to other sectors of society joining in too. This is why the constitutional movement was victorious. The intellectuals will say they had gatherings, circles, and secret meetings, which is true. These existed; however, these gatherings alone could not have transformed tyranny into being constitutional. If the scholars did not exist, if the people did not exist, and if those gatherings did not exist, they would not have been able to carry this out. The presence of the scholars caused it. In the end, differences were created between them and the scholars and one by one, they were removed, and the constitutional movement turned against itself. Firstly, they did not allow a sound constitution to be created; secondly, it slowly turned into the dictatorship of Raza Khan. However, the progress made in that era would not have been possible without the help of the scholars.

The Nationalisation movement was the same. I experienced the Nationalisation movement myself, even though I was young; however, I saw and was present in it. The previous era I had only heard about. If the Late Agha Kashani was not there, if other representatives from the clergy were not present and if some scholars did not exist in some of the cities, the Nationalisation movement and the nationalisation of oil would not have occurred and would not have been possible. The enemy would have cut their hands short from the beginning, created the grounds for ruining the work that had been done, and they would have been able to overwhelm them.

Imam Khomeini's key skill was the ability to create an environment that did not let the enemy prohibit the presence of the clergy. In the movement he created, his character, capability and readiness that Allah had placed in him all had an effect. The grounds had been prepared for this too. The clergy entered the arena; if they had not, then the people would not have entered either. If the people had not entered the arena, this revolution and transformation would not have happened, and this thousand-year-old worn-out castle would have remained and not been destroyed. Imam Khomeini was able to carry this out, supported by the clergy as they entered the arena. If the clergy did not have a presence in the war, in various events after the war, in creating peace among the people and in creating contentment and hope for the future in the people, this system and revolution would not have continued. For certain, it would not have continued. This is precisely what the Americans wish to do today. They are applying pressure and force but have not and will not be able to. They would have been in those first few days if they could have been successful. With the blessings of the clergy and religious scholars, they have been unable to.

The process is also evident. The process is the clergy being connected to the people, to be influential among the people, and to focus the people's hearts in a particular direction. So the presence of the clergy means the presence of the general public. Once the general public start walking behind their leaders, nothing can get in their way, and nothing can defeat them. This is how it was in other places. In this Islamic Awakening, it was the presence of religion that was able to cause the general public to move and create the earthquakes we witnessed in some of the countries. Ultimately the problem there was that their religious institutions were scattered. They have numerous founders and claimants [to the religion], and each pulled the people in their direction; therefore, they could not continue. It existed for less than two years and was finished. This is not the case in the Islamic Republic. The presence of the clergy and scholars in showing the correct path was decisive. This political role is vital. They were creating insight and giving political guidance.[361]

Students and Youth

Today our youth have to shoulder a heavy duty in this regard. Not only should you identify the truth, but you should also promote insight in the environments in which you live and clarify things to the people around you. One essential point is that falsity does not always appear in an apparent form in front of your eyes and is not easy to identify. Falsities often enter the arena disguised as truths or half-truths. The Commander of the Faithful (a) said there would be no disagreements if the truth and falsity entered the arena in their apparent forms.[362]

Once, I said that our youth are the officers of the soft war. The youth should not let this happen[363]. They should nurture hope and advise others to resist and avoid laziness and tiredness. As I said earlier, these are the tasks that fall on our youth – who are the officers of the soft war.[364]

Dear youth and students, the apple of the eye of the nation and the hope for the country's future, must attach importance to the issue of clarification. Many truths need

---

361. 14/05/2016 – In a meeting with heads, teachers and seminary students from the province of Tehran.
362. 26/10/2010 – In a meeting with university students and youth from the province of Qum.
363. A reference to the creation of hopelessness mentioned previously in this speech.
364. 11/03/2021 – In a televised speech on the occasion of Eid al-Mab'ath.

to be explained. Clarification neutralises the enemy's misleading plot, pouring toward the Iranian nation from hundreds of directions. The enemy's scheme and moves are aimed at influencing public opinion, and this is one of the significant goals of the enemies of Iran, Islam and the Islamic Revolution, and they wish to put the minds of the people, particularly the youth, in doubt.

As a duty, each of you should shed light on your surroundings like a lamp. Fortunately, today, the field is open for the dissemination of ideas. In addition to the problems it may create, the internet also has great blessings. You can promote right, correct thoughts and answer questions. You can provide answers to ambiguities in this public space by making use of this opportunity. And you can struggle on God's path in the true sense of the word. Of course, the main principle is that one must follow an ethical approach. What some people do on the internet, in the press, in journals and in other places - confronting the public with abusive language, slander, deception and lies - should be strongly avoided. Truths should be promoted with strong logic, solid speech, complete rationality, and with consideration of human emotions and morality. Today we all have to move in this arena. Each of us is responsible in a different way.

I hope that God, the Exalted, will make all of you successful. Our youth today, praise God, are equipped with ideas, rationality and abundant awareness, and they can make great endeavours in these areas. You should prepare yourselves, increase this preparedness and then enter the field of clarification and disclosure. This is the path that Lady Zainab al-Kubra (s) took during those 40 days. The greatness of those 40 days is due to what that honourable Lady, Imam al-Sajjad (a), and the others around them did as they endured many hardships. If we speak in the language of eulogies, Lady Zainab al-Kubra (s) came and delivered a report to Imam Hussain (a) on the day of Arbaeen saying that they did such and such things, we did such and such, we went like this, we endured such and such hardships, and we gave such and such explanations and clarifications.

Imam Hussain's (a) path is sacred; it is a sweet and successful path. It is a path that definitely gives results. God willing, you will be able to be inspired by Hussain's (a) movement and Hussain's (a) teachings and bring this country to the peak of spiritual and material felicity in the true sense of the word. This is the way. This is the path. The right way is to move in the light of the guidance of Hussain (a), the Imams (a), the Qur'an and the Holy Prophet's (s) Household (a).[365]

Artists and Poets

For fifty to sixty years, we were ruled by those who were not in control themselves. It is not as if we were not there, but a people's government in Iran in this manner has not existed. How we wish they would have been dictators such as Nadir

---

365. 02/06/1999 – At the commencement of the Arbaeen commemorations.

Shah or Agha Muhammad Khan, who came into power using their strength and scheming; however, this was not the case. Others came and imposed these rulers and pillaged all the spiritual and material wealth of the nation. Through many tribulations and efforts, a great movement stood against this evil phenomenon. It was able to get somewhere through sacrificing their lives and bearing their chests in opposition to the hostility of the disloyal enemy. Is this not beautiful? How can the arts pass by this and remain apathetic? This is not the expectation from the revolution. Revolutionary arts, which we have said from the first day of the revolution, should not remain impartial. Is this too much to ask? Music, movies, theatre, paintings and other art fields must heed this. These are necessary things. The revolution's expectation of the arts and the artists is not an expectation that is forced or beyond reason. It is based on identifying beauty, which is fundamental to the arts—being artistic means being able to detect beauty. This beauty does not necessarily mean flowers and birds; sometimes, throwing a person in fire and their tolerance of it is more beautiful than flowers and birds. A person of the arts must recognise, feel, and clarify it through the language of the arts.[366]

The most important responsibility is propagation and clarification as is stated in the Qur'an: "deliver the messages of Allah and fear Him, and fear no one except Allah, and

---

366. 23/07/2001 – In a meeting with a group of experts in the culture and arts fields.

Allah suffices as reckoner."[367]. This is one yardstick. Clarify the reality that has been understood. No one expects you to speak against what you have understood. No, whatever you have understood, state it. However, you must put in the effort and strive for those things you have understood to be correct and sound. At times of sedition, it is difficult to understand the arena, the two sides of the conflict: the attackers and defenders, the oppressors and the oppressed, and the enemy and the friend. If it is such that a poet will also be fooled like others and lack of insight troubles them, then this goes against the status of a person of the arts and working in the cultural field. Therefore the reality must be understood, and then that reality must be propagated. It is impossible to work in the manner of politicians in the artistic world—this is against the status of the cultural field. In the world of cultural work, knots need to be opened, reality needs to be opened, and intellectual problems need to be solved. This clarification is necessary; this is the same work of the Prophets (s).[368]

We have unique and exclusive resources against this effort of the enemy. We can respond through the internet and through the methods they employ - of course, their work is much broader in scope - but we have certain means exclusive to us.

---

367. Surah al-Ahzab – Verse 39.
368. 05/09/2009 – In a meeting with a group of poets.

One of these means is you, the society of eulogists. Your face-to-face communication and your utilisation of art for conveying concepts to the audience in a comprehensive and wide-ranging way - that is to say, the issue is not about two, three, ten eulogists, rather thousands of eulogists are doing this throughout the country - is an exclusive means that we enjoy. It is a means that they do not have.

Pulpits are one of these unique means. The same is true of mourning ceremonies. The same is true of religious hayats. If the content of our minbars, eulogies, hayats and recited poetry is appropriate, then no means can confront and oppose them.

What is worse than missing this opportunity is using it badly. If our religious ceremonies and eulogies make the people lose their belief in the future, we have wasted this opportunity and not appreciated the value of this blessing. If the people leave our pulpits and our eulogies while they have not understood their conditions and responsibilities, we have wasted this opportunity. If God forbid, our meetings shatter unity, we have missed this opportunity. Suppose the way we speak or the content of our speech helps the enemies succeed in their goals. In that case, we have turned this divine blessing into blasphemy and ungratefulness: "They have changed Allah's favor for ungratefulness"[369].

We should be careful about this. We have often said that today's sectarian discord among Muslims is a weapon and a

---

369. Surah al-Ibrahim – Verse 28.

trump card in the hands of our enemies. This is completely clear to those people who are well-informed about global developments. Such denominational discord is a sword in the hands of our enemies. Publicising differences, expressing them outspokenly and speaking about issues which fuel fitna is one of the means our enemy makes maximum use of.

If we act in a way that the enemy's goal is achieved, this is changing Allah's favour for ungratefulness. In religious ceremonies, sectarian discourse should not be highlighted. How many times should this be repeated? We have said this often, but some people do not want to listen.

What do you do if you want to guide those people who do not believe in your denomination and your true beliefs? Do you begin to curse and speak ill of their sacred beliefs? This will make them drift entirely away from you and destroy all hopes of guiding them. The way to guide them is not this. As you can see today, the world of Shia Islam is under attack. Those who had not heard the name of Shia and Sunni Islam - the leaders of arrogance - are constantly highlighting the name of Shia Islam in their propaganda. They continually speak about Shia Iran, Shia groups in Iraq and other Shia countries. They continuously highlight the issue of Shia and Sunni.

Why do they do this? They have found a good tool for provoking a grudge among Muslims. Well, we are proud that we are Shias. We are proud that we have gained an understanding about the position of Wilayah. Our magnanimous Imam Khomeini carried the flag of the Commander of the Faithful's (a) Wilayah, and this became a means for the world of Islam - whether Shia or non-Shia - to feel proud of Islam.

Now, should we do something to turn this feeling of pride and interest in Islam into enmity, hostility and a grudge? This is precisely what the enemy wants. We should not allow him to achieve his goal. This is a critical point. You should be careful about this. You should be more cautious than other people. We should not do something to help the enemy achieve his goal and sharpen his sword. Our great personalities, our ulama, our grand jurists and the great personalities of the world of Islam have always advised us to be careful about this issue.[370]

Well, poetry is an influential element, and it is more effective than all other verbal arts. That is to say, no word and statement can exert the same influence that poetry does, no matter how eloquent, beautiful and meaningful it is. Poetry is such a means and element. Poetry plays a motivating role where the environment is ripe for motivation. It plays the role of a guide, leader and director for the audience and for those who read poems for themselves. When you have a fortune and a gift with which you can accomplish incredible feats, you have neglected your responsibilities and duties if you do not benefit from them. This makes one responsible. Allah the Exalted has given you this blessing, but like all other

---

370. 20/04/2014 – In a meeting with a group of eulogists.

blessings, one will be questioned about it. You will be asked, "What did you do with this blessing?" With the tool of poetry, you can guide your audience towards both the straight path and the deviant path - one that ruins your audience.

A brilliant task carried out in the country is the quick response our young poets make in the face of different events. Thankfully, this was witnessed in our meeting, as was seen in the past. I am really satisfied with this because it is precious and good. No one should think that this is a negative phenomenon. On the contrary, it is a very positive one. Throughout history and in the contemporary century - close to our time - we have had certain poets whose quick responses produced the best effects.

When the Israeli aeroplane was hijacked by that girl [Shadiyya Abu Ghazala], the late Amiri Firuzkuhi composed a qasida. Those who know Amiri Firuzkuhi know he was not a revolutionary youth, but he composed a beautiful and brilliant qasida in the 1960s because of his feeling. This composition was in line with the requirements of the time, and it began with: "There stood a gazelle..." Now, I do not remember many of its couplets, but at that time, I knew them by heart. I had heard it from Agha Amiri himself.[371]

---

371. 01/07/2015 – In a meeting with poets.

Eulogists

What is before our nation today is clarification on the concepts of the Islamic Revolution. This is a responsibility which you can undertake perfectly. I have repeated this many times in this meeting: sometimes, an ode, sonnet, masnavi and couplet composed by you can be as influential as a pulpit. You should not miss out on this.

Poems should contain Quranic and Islamic content. As you often say, it should be Hussaini and Fatimi. You should include revolutionary goals with broad-mindedness and intellectuality in your poems and convey them in your meetings with good recitation and artistic methods. This will exert a profound influence on the great movement of the Iranian nation and also on the Islamic movement and Islamic Ummah. Sometimes, I hear that neither the poems nor the themes that certain skilled eulogists use are in the direction of raising awareness. This is a sin. This is an act of oppression. You have artistic talent, you have capabilities, and you have opportunities society. This opportunity did not always exist. If you manage to obtain this opportunity at every hour and every moment of your precious life, it is valuable, and it should not be missed.

Today, we can promote Islam. There was a day, this was possible only with books, pulpits and speeches. Today, as well as these, you can do so with recitations and eulogies. In the past, during the non-divine regime, there were not so many good reciters and eulogists at the Ahlul Bayt's (s) service. Today, there are, thankfully, many. Both quality and quantity are outstanding in this regard. You should improve on this quality daily. Today, the enemies are carefully looking at every angle of our lives and our revolutionary nation to find a weak spot from which they can infiltrate. You should identify these areas of the enemy's infiltration and deploy your forces there. We should not waste time.

Today, all of us are responsible. All of us have duties in this regard. The Society of Eulogists is one of the responsible societies in the country as well. You should promote Islamic teachings. Of course, the language of exaltations and eulogy differs from the language one uses when delivering speeches. You benefit from poetry, imagination and artistic activities; nothing is wrong with this. Still, the direction and content should be the same direction we expect in a good speech, book or film. The direction should be the same. The enemies of Islam were not born yesterday. The enemies of the truth and the enemies of God have been gathering their troops since the emergence of God's religion. Today, the same forces exist. "The sweet and salty waters in the world flow in different veins, and they will be the same for humanity until Israphil [the angel who blows his horn on Judgement Day] blows his horn." [from a poem by Moulavi].

From now on, too, this will be the same. This deployment is the same one that Ibrahim (a), Musa (a) and the Last Prophet (s) stressed. Today, you are in the same line that Musa (a), Ibrahim (a), the Holy Prophet (s), Ammar and the

Commander of the Faithful (a) stood upon. We will make a mistake if we do not identify our line correctly. We will make a mistake if we do not identify the enemy line. In the Battle of Siffin, Ammar witnessed that part of the army was worried and confused and did not know the goal or direction. He felt he had a responsibility. Ammar was the Commander of the Faithful's (a) spokesperson. He faced the crowd and said, "Do you see the other side's banner? The banner belonging to Bani Umayya? We had the same banner against us in the Battle of Badr and Uhud. It is the same banner."

I will tell you that the banner standing against the Revolution in Asia, Europe, America and in every part of the world is the same: the banner hoisted against Ibrahim(a), Musa (a) and Isa (a). They were destroyed, but Musa (a), Isa (a) and Ibrahim (a) are alive. They are alive because Allah the Exalted said to Musa (a), "Fear not: for I am with you: I hear and see everything". He said they should not fear, panic and make an error in calculation because He is with them. He said, "I am with you." Two unarmed individuals seem nothing in the face of the large army of the Pharaoh, but in reality, power belongs to them. This is because power belongs to God, and He says He is with them: "For I am with you: I hear and see everything."[372] He says He sees, hears and knows everything.

Those who do not believe this should look at the past 40 years during which our enemies, the centre of material

---
372. Surah Taha – Verse 46.

power in the world, came with all their might and stood against this Revolution and this movement. They struck and made all their efforts in the true sense of the word. They did whatever they could, but after the passage of 40 years, they were weaker than the first day, and we are more robust than the first day. This shows that "I am with you." Allah the Exalted is with us: "I hear and see everything." However, there is one condition. You should be with God, too: "If you help the cause of Allah, He will help you, and make firm your feet".[373]

It was our magnanimous Imam Khomeini who taught us this lesson. We, too, did not understand this correctly before that. We did not understand the depth of the issue either. However, that great personality understood this perfectly. He would say to us that we should be with God, and he himself was with God. Being with God means what I said initially: you should carry out your duties. You are eulogists. This in itself is a great honour.[374]

---

373. Surah Muhammad – Verse 7.
374. 26/02/2019 – In a meeting with eulogists.

www.ingramcontent.com/pod-product-compliance
Lightning Source LLC
Chambersburg PA
CBHW020015300426
44177CB00012B/321